With every good
wish —

Sincerely —

Marguerite Carter

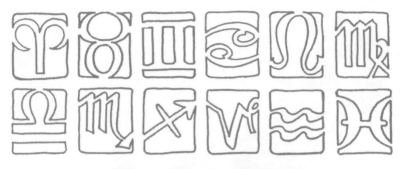

The Time When
Your Luck Will Change

according to your birthdate

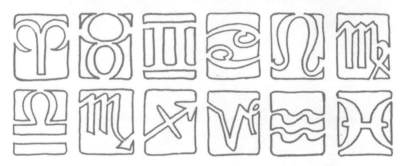

by MARGUERITE CARTER

Published by

ALAN McCONNELL AND SON, INC.
546 S. Meridian St., Rm. 602, Indianapolis, Ind.

first printing January 1971
second printing April 1971

Library of Congress Catalog Card Number: 77-143497

TABLE OF CONTENTS

Page No.

TABLE OF CONTENTS *(Continued)*

MY DEEPEST GRATITUDE

Many, many people have aided my efforts to gather material for this book and enabled me to get it written. Among those cherished associates whose very special contributions, each in his or her own way, made it possible for me to walk through doorways to new and exciting revelations, I wish to thank, with grateful love: ALAN C. McCONNELL, ALAN R. McCONNELL, JUANITA McCONNELL and MARGOT MASON.

Travel guides who have led me through the experiences mentioned in this book have frequently touched my life only briefly, but each has left in my heart a warm remembrance which I feel I shall never forget:

The wonderful woman in Turkey who gave the hospitality of her home with such GREAT generosity . . . Although I was not aware of it at the time, the reason for this was to protect me and keep me safe from political unrest in her country.

There was the comic guide in Germany, typical of his birthsign, who gave me assurance that any obstacle on earth would evaporate in his hands, for a fee. Thus, I would confidently take even severe risks, only to discover that he had done all the wrong things (which, by the way, always required another fee). "Ve do it", he would say, staunchly leading me forward with such conviction that I never questioned, even for a moment, his ability to carry out my wishes. For example, I would tell him that I wanted to order a certain item on the menu in a restaurant; he would glow with approval, reminding me that my tastes were more expensive than most. When I paid him accordingly, he would faithfully say, "Ve do it!", taking me to my chosen destination . . . and then he would order exactly what HE wanted!

At one point in my travels, it was impossible to get a guide in Paris. A bell boy at my hotel suggested a telephone operator, who was "off duty", might take me around. She got me into places even the most distinguished guide could never have reached. I have pictures of her beautiful wedding, and precious little daughter, which remind me constantly of the enriching experiences I enjoyed with this lovely person. Thus, I extend my deep appreciation to MICHELLE LeLOWN.

As it turned out, most of my guides were born under the sign of Aries. I certainly had ample opportunities for proving the observation that these people were "enterprising"! If they couldn't find "a trail" they would MAKE A NEW ONE, every time! Among these were:

BRIAN T. GROSVENOR, who had SUCH energy! He left no stone unturned in taking me about England — and he sang all the way!

JURGEN WOLF, a young "singer" who had made one fine recording and was in the process, then, of making another. He was a splendid young man and an excellent guide — the one who took me to Kepler's home site, even though everyone had tried to discourage such efforts!

ALFONSO PALOMINO was another who very admirably displayed the true Aries courage. He acquired a professional hunter — and thereby brought me into the heart of the jungle in Palenque, where an archaelogical discovery there, considered to be as great as King Tut's tomb, was completely closed to all newsmen and others. It was here that a very important astrological discovery was made and I thank Alfonso sincerely for the invincible use of his Aries "drive" and resourcefulness which resulted in my observation of it.

CARLO MARINI in Rome, honored me by taking me to historical spots difficult to reach and of interest astrologically. He guided many of the most wealthy, distinguished people of the United States, so he knew which steps to take for special favors.

I am extremely grateful to ALL of these "Arians" for the favors they extended.

I shall not soon forget the grand little guide who showed me around Poland;

And I am especially beholden to PROFESSOR AHMET UYSAL in Turkey, for the abundant courtesies which proved so very helpful to my endeavor.

INTRODUCTION

LIFE IS NOT MEANINGLESS, BUT EVERY LIVING THING HAS PURPOSE! These writings are a tiny segment in the vast, endless seas encompassing astrology's dramatic, historical role where Destiny's hand reached out and touched the world's great nations who left behind their imprint upon the pages of time! This is not an attempt to defend astrology for it needs no defense — no scientist has ever been able to disprove it! Great minds who displayed surpassing excellence so that we speak of them today with reverence, bowed to this ageless, noble belief. Astrology holds to the concept that this universe was designed by a Master Intelligence and is mathematically perfect, so "cause and effect" must be one of its first Laws. It is impossible to attempt to follow in the footsteps of such men as Johannes Kepler, one of the world's renowned master mathematicians, who made his living by writing horoscopes, or Carl Jung, honored scientist, who maintained that astrology has its rightful place without sensing an "inner knowing" that it does conform to truth and reality! I would not attempt to cover the magnitude of its history in a complete sense for this ancient wisdom is beyond any one individual's lifetime — it is so vast in scope.

It is my wish to present here little-known facts because they are dismissed or overlooked in our universities where they should be taught, for they are a part of the history that formed the pattern of our modern day concepts. The majesty of this study requires "a willingness" to search with an open mind and to believe in a Creator of Supreme Intelligence in place of the materialistic viewpoint held now that this entire universe is accidental and we are pawns where conditions beyond our control can or will destroy us! The doctrine taught today in our schools and universities that nothing exists except matter by certain exponents does not answer "a deep hunger" felt by thousands. Astrology can lead us through that gap which is a dark chasm of fear, for it teaches an outlook on life that promises fulfillment and not an endless void without meaning. This study, scholars old in wisdom followed, has survived all hatreds, skepticism and attempts to destroy it, and it still shines like a lighted torch pointing "the way" toward understanding and knowledge, for it is "THE PATH" that can lead mankind to a more peaceful world! There is a way!

A Queen Whose Every Success
Hung on Her Astrologer's Advice

"I am come amongst you . . ."

"You will become Queen and will succeed in overcoming all your enemies" — these are the words in general of Lord Burghley by historians, a promise that Elizabeth would be victorious and would reach the throne before she had any hope of attaining England's highest dominant position as ruler, or Burghley any promise of becoming a Lord when he calculated her horoscope!

No more startling prediction and its fulfillment exists which still plays its role upon your life today, even as to the language you speak, as well as our country's powerful influence upon world affairs can be shown, in my opinion! At that time, Queen Elizabeth I of England was not only held prisoner but the likelihood of her survival was exceedingly grim. In her time the beheading of one's enemy was almost a certainty. Elizabeth's mother, Ann Boleyn, was beheaded, leaving her, Elizabeth, a small child of two and a-half years, in "the Tower" of London, a cold, friendless world where those awaiting execution passed lonely hours, and even years, without hope of any future. Fate has strange ways — for some unexplainable reason, Queen Mary, after moving Eliza-

Tower of London

beth I from one place to another, but always as a prisoner, had her brought to Hatfield House, although still to be imprisoned!

The small tower at Hatfield House with its dark, narrow, foreboding, winding stairway, although now closed off by a small iron gate inside, is still standing as a reminder of Lord Burghley's prophecy. The rooms where this young girl, a prisoner, spent long hours are easily seen from the outside. Surprisingly, it was here that Elizabeth I experienced a turn in "the wheel of fortune" that was to reshape England's history!

Hatfield House, where Elizabeth was prisoner with no hope of fulfilling the prediction that she would succeed in overcoming her enemies! Then, as is true in all life, a climaxing point "exploded" into the midst of the monotonous pattern that had previously shaped her life.

Seated under what was then a sturdy oak one morning, the young princess was greeted by a man on a snow-white horse who had ridden with all speed eighteen miles from London to be the first to bring her the news: "The (old) Queen is dead — God save the (new) Queen, Elizabeth of England!" So Elizabeth I — became queen against overwhelming odds!

This once mighty Oak, now a skeleton of its former self, still marks the spot where "the destiny of the world" was being shaped.

Just 18 miles from London lies one of the most famous spots in all England historically. Here is mute evidence to the fulfillment of astrology's promise that Elizabeth I, against bitter enmities, would enjoy a successful forty-four year reign! No more seeming impossible turn of events could have been foretold. She chose William Cecil who later became Lord Burghley to be her chief counselor, as he had been so accurate when casting her horoscope. Today, Hatfield House is owned by one of his descendants! Queen Elizabeth I from her rise to the throne of England to the end of a dramatic, long reign, always had an astrologer by her side to whom she turned for important advice, according to authoritative sources!

Her country's affairs demanded a shrewd mind. No greater need for guidance ever faced a sovereign than the one posed by the Spanish Armada, the mightiest force ever assembled up to that time which held the possibility of complete destruction for England and might well have changed your way of life today. Elizabeth I had a gift for choosing the right men and moment to act. One of her astrologers whose name found its place on the pages of history was Doctor Dee who selected "the day" most auspicious for Queen Elizabeth's coronation, and who taught her astrology! Riding on a white horse to Tilbury — this valiant woman rallied her small army so that should Sir Francis Drake fail to stop the Spanish Armada at Plymouth, a last stand would be made at this point, which I photographed.

An echo today of those brave men who were outnumbered and out-gunned, stood on this spot as defenders of England against Spain's overwhelming force!

Ships with 2,431 guns, manned by more than 27,000 men, set sail with high hopes of invading England and overthrowing the throne on a July morning according to today's Gregorian calendar.

Writings by accepted historians describe Sir Francies Drake as finishing "a game" he was playing of "bowls" before moving with deadly accuracy against "the invincible" Armada. One hundred and twenty-five vessels from Spain entered the English Channel on that fateful day and ONLY HALF RETURNED TO THEIR HOMELAND IN SPAIN!

"I am come amongst you — resolved in the midst and heat of the battle to live or die amongst you . . .". Her courageous words when her small army awaited destruction at the ruthless hands of the Spanish — still echo on. Fortified by her astrologer's advice, she stood as a monument of courage at one of England's critical periods — and won!

This is a small outline of the part astrology played historically in the life of one of England's majestic Queens who left her country a great legacy and in so doing, struck a dominant note upon our lives today!

Sir Walter Raleigh, that gallant English gentleman who spread his cloak before his queen that she might not soil her shoes, lived a very colorful life as he too was a prisoner in that foreboding "waiting room" for death known as the Tower of London. Like the educated of his day, he too believed in the influence of the stars upon all life. In his History of the World, a volume the pages of which are yellowed with age, Sir Walter Raleigh states: " . . . and if we cannot deny, but that God hath given virtues to springs and fountains, to cold earth, to plants and stones, minerals, and to the excremental parts of the basest living creatures, why should we rob the beautiful stars of their working powers? For seeing they are many in number, and of eminent beauty and magnitude, we may not think, that in the treasury of His wisdom, who is Infinite, there can be wanting (even for every star) a peculiar beauty and operation: as every herb plant, fruit and flower adorning the face of the earth, hath the like. For as these were not created to beautify the earth alone, and to cover and shadow her dusty face, but otherwise for the use of man and beast, to feed them and cure them: so were not those uncountable glorious bodies set in the firmament, to no other end than to adorn it: but for instruments and organs of His Divine Providence, so far as it hath pleased His just will to Determine." This leaves no doubt as to his convictions.

Are you cognizant that the world's top Universities taught Astrology and of one where the King of Poland in 1460 granted Astrology a permanent chair?

Halls of Learning Where Astrology Was Taught

The leading universities of the world taught astrology as well as astronomy! Following are listed just a few of those that are categorized as being most notable in today's Halls of Learning — where astrology was taught.

This is the famous Oxford University in England. The first chancellor of Oxford, Robert Grosseteste, accepted astrology/astronomy as "the supreme science" which he had studied in Paris. A seal was struck with his likeness on it!

King Charles the first, learned astrology from the founder of the Library at Oxford! He also consulted Wm. Lilly, England's astrologer!

This photograph shows the entrance to the rooms where Sir Isaac Newton, the famous astronomer, lived while a student at Trinity in Cambridge. According to "Early Science in Cambridge", HE HAD NO TRAINING IN MATHEMATICS before he became a student but became interested because of reading a book on Astrology he had purchased at Stourbridge Fair, which fascinated him. He decided to pursue the study further, thereby purchasing a Euclid as a beginning. His reply to Halley of Comet fame when chided about astrology, rings down through astrological writings — "I have studied it — You have not"!

Vine-covered Cracow University lies behind the iron curtain — in a remote part of Poland. It has the look of a well-loved book where thousands of hands have turned the yellowed pages in quest of knowledge to be found inscribed within its breast. It was necessary to leave from East Berlin in the dark of night, acquiesce to being thoroughly searched as we crossed the border while surly communist guards watched as even the small coins in our purses were counted, thus we left "the free world" behind in order to visit this classical Hall of Learning! The rickety plane scheduled to leave after loading us aboard, sputtered and gasped but refused to budge, fortunately. (A few months later, ON THE SAME FLIGHT, it rose in the air only to plunge to earth killing everyone aboard.) Hours passed while we waited among people who spoke no English and were finally transferred to "a train" some distance away where we found seats in a compartment shared with three Polish ladies and one gentleman. By taking Polaroid pictures of our strange companions as "gifts", something they thought was magic, we made friends of them and their friendship became invaluable although they

couldn't understand one word we spoke. A few hours had passed, as the train rattled and jerked through the night, when three communist guards suddenly appeared, demanding our papers in an arrogant manner. Even our passports were taken from us. Silently, we remembered we'd been warned in West Berlin that we couldn't make the trip and return in safety. Then just when the guards appeared about to take drastic measures, these Polish women rose as our defenders in a demanding chorus of words that even the communists understood.

Hours went by and finally they returned and brusquely handed us our passports. A CLOSE CALL! These kind people had saved us — two American women, seeking only to visit one of the universities ranking among the top in the world where astrology had played such an important role!

Cracow University

Johannes Kepler and Copernicus were both students in Cracow, Poland and according to authoritative sources, became fast friends while at this famous University. A KING OF POLAND HAD A PERMANENT SEAT OF ASTROLOGY ESTABLISHED AT THIS WONDERFUL OLD SHELTER OF HIGHER LEARNING! If the King had not taken such a step, we might not have our outer space explorations today.

A monument stands in the center of Warsaw, Poland, to-day of Copernicus, who is considered one of the world's foremost scientists. He used, as well as believed astrology! It is well known that he cast horoscopes as did Kepler and others who are spoken of today with reverence as being among the foremost great minds of all time. One of our as-tronauts just returning from "landing on the Moon" gave FULL CREDIT for today's space program to the part played by this brilliant man, who charted the way! Signs of the zo-diac can be seen on the monument's celestial globe.

This photograph shows the front of the building through whose doors students walked, who later became leading, re- nowned world scholars and scientists, as well as philos- ophers. It was the only place where information could be obtained as to the location of "the zodiac" in the floor of St. Gereon in Cologne, Germany. Even the Bishop in that city denied its existence. However, I interviewed a professor at Heidelberg University who assured me these zodiacal symbols were there — and they were!

NOTE: Many more universities could be included, par- ticularly in Italy, Paris, as well as others, but I do not wish to dwell at too great length in this area, as there are so many unknown other historical highlights of importance astrol- ogically.

Frankfurt, Germany — Monument in heart of this city with the zodiacal sign, Libra, commemorating its birthsign, prominently displayed.

Cairo, Egypt

One-thousand years ago, the astrologers of that day were assembled to choose the birthdate of this colorful, romantic city, that it might have a long life and honor the name of its builder! According to tradition, the workmen stood ready with their tools and supplies to begin when "a bell" was to signal the propitious time· for the birth of this great city. However, a crow alighted on the rope ringing the bells, thereby starting the laborers at their task — and strangely, its history has been one of accidental or unexpected turbulence in surviving for centuries with shocking contrasts between her people. When Egypt was at its height, astrologers were advisors to the pharaohs. Jeweled barges floated on the Nile and the air was heavy laden with the sweet scent of orange blossoms.

Great Pyramid of Gizeh

It is generally conceded that the purpose of this massive structure so mathematically perfect it has confounded all our historians, was astrological. It is written in Isaiah Chapter XIX — Verse 19: "In that day there shall be an altar to the border thereof to the Lord."

The great pyramid of Gizeh is the most perfect of the pyramids both mathematically and in form. The proportion of the height to the base = 7 high to 11 base and the modulus 40 measured in royal cubits of 20.61 inches multiplied by 7 = the height and 11 = the base. All of these numbers are very symbolical but the number 40 especially so. It is used many times in the Bible, always in association with a period of withdrawal. Today, obstetricians regard 40 weeks as equivalent to the pre-natal epoch, that is, the time from the onset of menstruation prior to conception until the birth of the child.

The proportion of 7/11 when applied to a circle, if the 7 represents the radius and 11 a quarter circle, will, when applied to the full circle equal 3 1/7 or pi.

The pyramid was oriented so perfectly that the Pole Star was visible through a shaft, the lower end of which is located in the lower chamber and may still be seen today, for I was there and saw it.

The ancient architects had a profound knowledge of their subject for not only did they demonstrate this in the mathematics of the pyramid but in its structure, they described their vision of the form of creation since the four compass points linked to the sun at its zenith would form a pyramid.

Sir Isaac Newton said: "The Egyptians determined the length of the solar year and fixed the solstice — by the assistance of a priest of Egypt created the science of Astrology grounding it on the aspects of the Planets."

Do You Know of the Numberless Churches and Cathedrals Where Astrological Symbols Are To Be Found Within Those Hallowed Edifices; The Part It Played At The Vatican and In Relation To Certain Popes?

Genesis I - 16 — "And God made two great lights; the greater light to rule the day, and the lesser light to rule the night: he made the stars also."

St. Luke XXI - 25, 26 — "And there shall be signs in the sun, and in the moon, and in the stars; and upon the earth distress of nations, with perplexity; the sea and the waves roaring;

"Men's hearts failing them for fear, and for looking after those things which are coming on the earth: for the powers of heaven shall be shaken."

Revelation XII - 1 — "And there appeared a great wonder in heaven; a woman clothed with the sun, and the moon under her feet, and upon her head a crown of twelve stars:

Revelation XXII - 2 — "In the midst of the street of it, and on either side of the river, was there the tree of life, which bare twelve manner of fruits, and yielded her fruit every month: and the leaves of the tree were for the healing of the nations.

Revelation XXI - 14 — "And the wall of the city had twelve foundations, and in them the names of the twelve apostles of the Lamb.

Revelation IV - 7, 8 — "And the first beast was like a lion, and the second beast like a calf, and the third beast had a face as a man, and the fourth beast was like a flying eagle. (Beasts as Aquarius, Taurus, Leo and Scorpio)

"And the four beasts had each of them six wings about him; and they were full of eyes within: and they rest not day and night, saying, Holy, holy, holy, Lord God Almighty, which was, and is, and is to come." (6 wings refer to 600 year Naronic cycle).

Ezekiel II - 10 — "As for the likeness of their faces, they four had the face of a man, and the face of a lion, on the right side: and they four had the face of an ox on the left side; they four also had the face of an eagle." (Aquarius, Taurus, Leo, Scorpio — the constellation Aquila is identified with Scorpio)

I Kings VII - 25 — "It stood upon twelve oxen, three looking toward the north, and three looking toward the west, and three looking toward the south, and three looking toward the east: and the sea was set above upon them, and all their hinder parts were inward."

St. Margret's with zodiac carvings over entrance of church in York, England.

Astrological symbols are to be found from the very humble houses of worship to the loveliest stately cathedrals. The Vatican in Rome has one of the largest libraries in the world devoted entirely to astrology. Among the oldest churches in Rome is one containing THE ASTROLOGICAL SIGN PISCES (fish swimming in opposite directions) in bronze, in its marble floor.

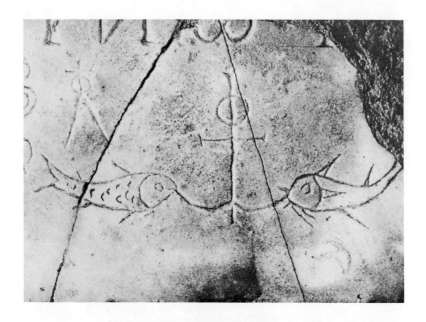

This zodiacal sign was used extensively by the early Christians and can still be seen today in the catacombs in Rome where hundreds hid in fear while seeking a better life! It has been said that Christ wore the sign Pisces as a symbol. Whether this is factual or not, certainly the symbols of the zodiac decorate edifices on every hand.

"Signs of the zodiac" in the museum at Bonn, Germany — where the heads of nations meeting in this city are attempting to settle or find a common meeting ground on important issues of today. These symbols are from the renowned Braunmeiler Abbey — 15 km. West of Cologne. This museum was given six carvings and the old Abbey retained six, as they are extremely valuable dating before 1143! The director is seen as he explained their history.

St. Gereon Church in Cologne, Germany showing the high altar where zodiacal signs were found in the floor, after discouraging reports that they did not exist from what should have been reliable sources. My extensive research led me to the unshakeable conviction that these ancient mosaical signs of the zodiac were still there — so, when the Professor at Heidelberg University stated I would find them if I went to Gereon, we were on our way!

At St. Gereon my guide points to his own birthsign. This "closeup" of astrological signs laid in the floor by hands long stilled — in almost perfect state of preservation. Strangely, there is a startling similarity in their placement to those found in world renown Canterbury Cathedral, except there they are of impressive bronze and here they are lovely mosaics.

Voices, long stilled, echo through these hallowed walls, while the dramatic scenes that once molded history with its intrigue and even murder, as well as the travails of "the faithful", although unseen, seems suspended in the very air as though awaiting a "returning".

At the high altar Kings and Queens have appeared for centuries. Large zodiacal symbols in "bronze" embellish the surrounding floor where the footsteps of the mighty have "not" erased this silent testimony to their timeless significance, part of which is now lost in man's memory. Even those who were supposedly familiar with "the history" of this world-renowned Cathedral, expressed no knowledge of these designs gracing this highly reverenced placement.

Photograph Showing the Sign "Aquarius"

On a column beside the High Altar (Canterbury Cathedral) hangs an explanation of the signs of the zodiac. IT WAS AN ARCHBISHOP OF CANTERBURY WHO LICENSED LIL-LY – ENGLAND'S MOST RENOWNED ASTROLOGER, TO PRACTICE MEDICINE, ANOTHER PHASE OF AS-TROLOGY'S HISTORY WHICH IS BEING PUSHED INTO THE BACKGROUND AND THEREBY LOST TO STU-DENTS OF TODAY.

The Catholic Encyclopedia, Vol. 2, P. 22 — "Astrology" contains the following: "Emperors and Popes became votaries of astrology, the Emperors Chas. IV and V, Popes Sixtus IV, Julius II, Leo X and Paul III". When these rulers lived, astrology was the regulator of official life; it is a well-known fact, characteristic of the age, that at the papal and imperial courts, ambassadors were NOT received in audience UNTIL A COURT ASTROLOGER HAD BEEN CONSULTED!

It would be possible to fill pages with religious background, but there are other paths to explore, so I will close with Leonardo da Vinci's famous painting of the "Last Supper" which I saw in Italy. The sign "Pisces" is represented prominently on the platter before Christ. Few other artists have given to the world such an expressive work that is so taut with emotion or the sadness felt when gazing at this "life-like" portrayal, with the meaningful word "Last" indelibly fixed upon one's inner thoughts.

Do You Know That Government Buildings, Even Our
Halls of Justice Still Bear Astrological Symbols?

Picture, at left, of ceiling in Doges Palace in Venice, Italy. The sign Libra is prominent over the door representing "Justice" which is still used by all our high courts in this modern day. Originally, twelve jurors were chosen, one from each sign of the zodiac so there would be impartial judgment. Today, we still have twelve jurors, but without consideration as to each one's capabilities according to "the inner" processes which may influence that individual's judgment of another person.

The beauty of this room is almost beyond description as symbols of the twelve signs embellished in gold on the ceiling turn back the pages, to a time when each city had an astrologer very similar to our health official of today!

The exquisite panel below is an astrological motif.

This photograph shows the Parliament building where money was last voted expressly for (England's final sovereign) Queen Ann, enabling her to fulfill her desire to send to Holland for Van Galgebrok, an astrologer of considerable reputation whom she maintained at her court as an advisor. HE IS CREDITED BY AUTHORITATIVE SOURCES AS FORE-TELLING HER DEATH TO THE MONTH AND YEAR WITH AMAZING ACCURACY!

Highlights of Interest
Famous Men, Strange Predictions

In the heart of London stands the "Fire Tower" commemorating a terrible holocaust predicted by Wm. Lilly, an eminent astrologer, so accurately that he was forced to defend himself in court — which he did. He later became one of England's most noted exponents of this subject and today, his books are preserved in Oxford University's Ashmolean Library! Not only did he become a famous man, he became fast friends with England's most distinguished thinkers, among them, Sir Elias Ashmole. So deep was this friendship that at WM. LILLY'S death, Sir Ashmole had his friend buried IN FRONT of the HIGH ALTAR IN ST. MARY'S CHURCH at Walton on Thames! Photograph of Lilly's Memorial inside St. Mary's Church

Above illustration shows the gates to the city of York where part of the old wall is still to be seen!

One of the prophecies that has found its way down to us through history's pages is that of Septimius Severus – noted Roman ruler who foretold by astrology he WOULD LEAVE ROME, WOULD QUELL THE REBELLION IN NORTHERN ENGLAND, on the Scottish borderline, BUT WOULD NEVER RETURN TO ITALY, HIS HOMELAND! He fell ill in England after putting down the uprising and strangely died there, as predicted, in York, England!

In Rome, Severus Arch stands in silent memory to the courage and loyalty he displayed to his country, for Rome is still remembered as one of the most powerful empires the world has known!   The doorway in the building to the right of the arch is the spot where Caesar is said to have been murdered after ignoring a warning against taking any action during the "Ides of March".

During Julius Caesar's reign, "four" men of patrician background were elected to choose "the auspicious time" for state undertakings.

"If the Duke of Wellington and Napoleon ever meet in battle, Napoleon will be vanquished and will never lead another army to the field" — so stated Warsdale, distinguished astrologer in general context ELEVEN YEARS before the battle of Waterloo! History of course, verified this tragic prediction, which could have served as a warning had it been heeded — then your course of life and mine would once again have been completely altered from what we know today, for France at that period in history was fired with the ambition to conquer or subjugate every adversary. To understand Napoleon's loss, it is only necessary to visit Versailles, a palace of grandeur beyond description and this fabulous estate was only one of many!

Napoleon

"How the mighty have fallen" — descriptive words which come to mind as your footsteps resound in this silent courtyard where Napoleon tragically spoke "a last farewell" to his loyal troops. There is a story which bears repeating because of its seeming authoritative source, that Napoleon used to climb the stairs to seek astrological advice from an old monk named LaClerc. The night of Napoleon's fateful move against the Duke of Wellington, a terrible storm was brewing but the old monk set out on foot to stop him. He was found dead the next day with the horoscope clutched in his hand — a small remnant of it is said to exist today!

Catherine de Medici

An 18th century engraving is said to exist of her consulting an astrologer. She is known to have been a firm believer in planetary influences according to reliable, historical sources, following the advice of her astrologer, Cosmo Ruggieri. His prophecies are startling in their accuracy — covering her MARRIAGE, HER HUSBAND'S SURPRISING RISE TO THE THRONE, THAT SHE WOULD HAVE DAUGHTERS WHO WOULD BECOME QUEENS AND EACH ONE WOULD "FAIL" TO BEAR CHILDREN! She had an observatory constructed not far from Paris because of her interest in advancing study of the stars!

Guide explaining the surprising influence astrology had on one of the most celebrated observatories in the world! Greenwich Observatory, showing the spot where Flamsteed, founder of the world renowned observatory is said to have worked. He not only practiced astrology and made some astounding predictions as revealed in historical writings but chose the most fortunate date, astrologically, for the laying of the cornerstone of this famous observatory which has traditionally been used as the standard reference point for the correction of time all around the world!

Flamsteed also became the first Royal astronomer. His effects are still to be seen and a wide white line is drawn in the floor which the guides there graciously point to as being the original spot from which Flamsteed made his calculations with antiquated instruments that they proudly point to because of their accuracy today.

Goethe's House – Frankfurt, Germany

One of the brilliant men who drew the intellectuals of Europe to his home was Johann Wolfgang Goethe! His lovely home as it originally was, at least on the ground floor, is one of the most delightful experiences to be found in all of Europe, for it still breathes the atmosphere of sparkling conversation by the elite of Europe who gathered from far and near to take part in important discussions within these gracious walls. HE WAS A FIRM FOLLOWER OF ASTROLOGY – so his home reflected this belief as he commissioned German painters to do exquisite paintings covering all the signs of the zodiac in unusual colorings depicting scenes from the lives of children. These cover the walls of an entire room! He was knighted and today is referred to as one of our world's great!

Notice the symbol of the goat can be seen, representing Capricorn, over our German guide's head, and the bull over Juanita McConnell's shoulder, who accompanied me on one of my sojourns to seek out unknown astrological influences which were historically important. Both my guide and Juanita were of incalculable aid in uncovering authentic material that has been hidden or lost to the world.

Goethe wrote in his autobiography: "On the 28th of August 1749, at mid-day, as the clock struck twelve, I came into the world, at Frankfurt-on-the-Main. The aspect of the stars was propitious: the sun stood in the sign of the Virgin, and had culminated for the day; Jupiter and Venus looked on with a friendly eye, and Mercury not adversely; the attitude of Saturn and Mars was neutral; the moon alone, just full, exerted all the more as she her power of opposition had just reached her planetary hour. She, therefore, resisted my birth which could not be accomplished until this hour was passed. These auspicious aspects which the astrologers subsequently interpreted very favorably for me may have been the causes of my preservation." I believe this is unmistakable evidence of his belief in astrology.

A Great Scientist Who Wrote Horoscopes For a Living

Building in heart of "Linz", honoring Johannes Kepler's memory with a stone cutting — the master mathematician whose "Laws of Planetary Motion" are a major contribution to our space age!

Johannes Kepler, the celebrated mathematician, gave so much to the world and received so little! Poverty always dogged his footsteps. Unappreciated for his tremendous concept of "the unseen" which makes up this Universe, he shuttled from place to place and only survived by casting horoscopes — an important part of his life story that is completely overlooked or ignored by our universities, so that our students are unaware of the imposing part astrology played in his life!

The first requirement of a man of science is to approach any subject, or theory with an open mind until it has been disproven — and up to this time, no one has disproved the ancient science of astrology. Kepler's exact words on Astrology were: "For nothing exists nor happens in the visible sky that is not sensed in some hidden manner by the faculties of Earth and Nature: so that these faculties of the spirit here on earth are as much affected as the sky itself" — "That the sky does something to man is obvious enough; but what it does specifically remains hidden" — "The belief in the effect of the constellations derives in the first place from experience, which is so convincing that it can be denied only by people who have not examined it" — "In what manner does the countenance of the sky at the moment of a man's birth determine his character? It acts on the person during his life in the manner of the loops which a peasant ties at random around the pumpkins in his field: they do not cause the pumpkin to grow, but they determine its shape. The same applies to the sky: it does not endow man with his habits, history, happiness, children, riches or a wife, but it moulds his condition . . "

Illness in addition to lack of money and "an aloneness" were his constant bedfellows.

Wallenstein, according to historians had little regard for Kepler's welfare, but he desired his astrological judgment regarding both political and military moves. Yet, Johannes Kepler not only became a court astrologer as did Tycho Brahe but his voice was the most authoritative as Europe's first astronomer! Our advancement in space science has been accomplished through standing on the shoulders of this mental giant!

- 51 -

Gateway to the old castle in Linz which is a museum today. This is the city Johannes Kepler returned to as his home many times and suffered perhaps his greatest sorrows.

Carl G. Jung

Carl G. Jung

Another distinguished man whose name will filter down through the shafts of time when the records of those who have striven for "answers" to hidden knowledge is that of the Swiss scientist, Carl G. Jung, 7/26/1875—6/6/1961.

Known as the father of psychiatry and being foremost in his field, the memory of him will never grow dim nor will his place be filled by another. He employed an astrologer and made hundreds of tests of birthdates.

When I arrived at his institute, which bears his name, in Zurich, Switzerland, I found myself in the midst of several hundred scientists from all over the world who had come to attend a series of lectures. Here his son, secretary and staff still carry on his work. In spite of their very busy schedule, they very graciously granted me time. I am deeply grateful to Dr. Jung's son who gave me a copy of his last book and the photograph that appears on the reverse of this page.

These are his words from the book, "The Interpretation of Nature and The Psyche", by C. G. Jung and W. Pauli: "I must call the reader's attention to the WELL-KNOWN CORRESPONDENCE BETWEEN THE SUN-SPOT PERIODS AND THE MORTALITY CURVE. The connecting link appears to be the disturbances of the earth's magnetic field, which in their turn are due to fluctuations in the proton radiation from the run. These fluctuations also have an influence on 'radio weather' by disturbing the ionosphere that reflects the radio waves. INVESTIGATION OF THESE DISTURBANCES SEEMS TO INDICATE THAT THE CONJUNCTIONS, OPPOSITIONS, AND QUADRATIC ASPECTS OF THE PLANETS PLAY A CONSIDERABLE PART IN INCREASING THE PROTON RADIATION AND THUS CAUSING ELECTRO-MAGNETIC STORMS. ON THE OTHER HAND, THE ASTROLOGICALLY FAVORABLE TRIGONAL AND SEXTILE ASPECTS HAVE BEEN REPORTED TO PRODUCE UNIFORM RADIO WEATHER."

There is no doubt that Dr. Jung was led to believe through his research that the existence of mathematical order as discovered by modern science proved the existence of Divine Intelligence.

Although the fact of discontinuity in cause and effect has been established, nevertheless the existence of mathematical series in atomic structures as well as other orderly mathematical relationships in nature convinced him that these inter-relationships existed not as a result of a random series of accidental events but must have been the creation of Supreme Intelligence. His astrological experiments fell short of expectation due to the limitation of statistical variety, the basis of his studies being limited to the astrological coincidence of the Sun and Moon in married couples' charts. At this point, I would like to stress that I do not intend my remarks to be critical of Dr. Jung for I feel great admiration for his insight and would not presume to judge the validity of the statistical part of his research.

However, I consider the reasons for marriage to be very complex. Rather than to assume that a greater number of married couples would necessarily have the Moon of one in the same position as the Sun of the other, that it would be more revealing to learn whether of those couples in whose charts there exists such an affirmative relationship, the marriage is more successful than for those couples in whose charts there is revealed a lack of affirmative aspects.

The evidence I have seen in examining thousands of charts from this very standpoint has convinced me of this fact and as Dr. Jung concluded from his studies, I believe further scientific research in astrology would be very valuable.

- 56 -

Astounding Evidence of
Superior Knowledge In
Ancient Western Societies

Experiences in Yucatan on Visits
During Past Years to Mayan Ruins

*The search for metaphysical truth
among the priests of these ancient civilizations led them to become highly
versed in Astronomy and Astrology.
Their observational accuracy is a marvel
to modern scientists.*

The National Geographic Magazine, one of my favorite
monthlies, printed an article to my surprise announcing the
uncovering of a Mayan Temple only a few miles from the
heart of the bustling small city of Merida, Yucatan. How it
could have escaped notice earlier is a mystery, although
ancient temples are scattered all over this general area and are
being unearthed by Smithsonian explorers and other men
and women of the same scientific bent in great numbers. Today so many people have visited here that what I tell you
may seem different — but you must remember, I went there
when it was undeveloped.

My office was understaffed because of ailments and other
afflictions which arise with trained employees in specialized
fields so the "work-pile" on my desk had grown increasingly
larger although I carried work home at night and on week-
ends in an effort to keep delays for those who awaited the
mailman's knock at a minimum. I reread the article and noticed the mention of a road that would accommodate eight
modern day automobiles driven abreast, being found which
astounded everyone as it led straight to this temple — a master

accomplishment for people generally thought to be exceedingly primitive. Then the idea seared its way into my mind that here might lie unnoticed additional astrological artifacts of value, particularly to me in spite of the numerous visits I had made to that part of the world solely for study. There is something about all-consuming desire which burns so deeply "within" that nothing can diminish its flame, which will shape events so that fulfillment of this passion reaps realization!

Suffice to say, I compromised by pledging I would fly there, take only my smaller camera, remain two days, three at the most, then would return to my work which I knew would be overburdening by that time. The aid of a guide whom I knew well from my many other trips would speed my efforts, so off I went, my conscience appeased because of the intrinsic worth which would follow.

My trip was uneventful — having travelled alone all over the United States, Canada and other points when writing a horoscope feature for leading metropolitan newspapers and magazines — I never thought of danger. I arrived at the familiar hotel in the heart of Merida, Yucatan, went up to my room, not unlike the numerous ones there where I had in the past awakened to the call of church bells many times that are so different from any other bells I have ever heard in distant parts of the world, for these have a harsh demanding tone calling to the faithful and those who are not so faithful. As I looked out the window, I was reminded that Merida was known as the city of windmills. I felt thirsty, so without changing from the high heels and tailored suit I wore on the plane, I strolled down to the dining area for refreshments. As I turned in the direction where I planned to renew my natural energy as the climate change is exceedingly debilitating, I saw the familiar face of the guide, Jose Novelo, across the street, whose help was essential in order for me to accomplish the mission I had begun and then return as planned on schedule. His friendly greeting was one that warms the heart of all who emerge from that cold, aloof exterior we of northern heritage present by a stiff handshake while those from warm southern climes are imbued with affectionate expressions of hospitality we might feel but never show. He knew immediately what I wanted to photograph and by his enthusiasm, overcame my suggestions of delaying our visit to view the newly discovered Mayan ruin. It was of such antiquity the scientific world was filled with excitement. Dressed in high heels, street attire, and with my camera over my shoulder, I took off without a moment's thought concerning the suitability of my dress.

On the way, I felt completely parched, I was so thirsty, then as we drove on I noticed a small shabby cold drink stand along side the road — but long ago I had the "common tropical tourist complaint" with which all who are not wary of particular foods and drink are certain to become entrapped, so we passed it by. I was sorry later because of what happened, and later I decided this oversight had caused me to become dehydrated. Our conversation turned to pleasantries. We halted shortly at what looked like an overgrown pineapple field but actually was sisal with a miniature railroad blocking the only path to the temple. My guide suggested we walk. As it was a short distance, I eagerly agreed — so we set off. We had only walked a short way when I suddenly became keenly aware of the intense heat and breathlessness, as the plant life in the field in rows cut off all flow of air. I am not one to give way easily, so I made no mention to Jose but struggled on down the narrow gauge freight tracks where the loaded cars held sisal "cuttings" to be taken to distant parts of the world later. My face must have shown what I refused to give voice to as Jose said he thought I'd better sit down while he returned to his car and endeavored to find a way back through some "round-about" road, to which I agreed. I kept moving slowly on, after he left, and suddenly there it stood just as the article in National Geographic had described it, with the wide highway clearly as I have previously mentioned, that would enable eight cars abreast to drive side by side on this amazing thoroughfare when the large boulders that "time" alone had flung there, were cleared away. What made it so "impressive" was that there was no evidence that the Mayans had vehicles that would require such a broad avenue — for the wheel, according to some authorities, was unknown to that civilization! I am sure they knew of it for I actually saw a wheel carved on a temple at Chichen Itza. It could have been possible that they had a tradition similar to the one in Tibet — which prophesied that the coming of the wheel there would mark "the end" of their civilization. In a sense, this prophecy has been fulfilled for shortly after the royal ruler of Tibet imported an automobile, the Communist Chinese overran the country bringing to "an end" one of the most stable and long-lasting governments of modern times!

I stood in utter enchantment and awe as I tried to turn back in my mind to the voices, long stilled and the colorful garments worn by those whose hearts beat with longings and desires just as ours do today even though so remote we find few written words to unveil the fabric of one of the most remarkable peoples to grace civilization. I lifted my camera and as it clicked away, I suddenly felt faint. I was aware that it seemed a very long time since my guide left. Then, as I turned to try to walk back to where I thought I might meet him, I knew the moments were growing increasingly short for my being able to inch my way, however small my steps, to any spot. I looked for a shaded tree. There wasn't even a small scrubby one for this area was completely barren. Black spots began to "come and go" as I tried to focus my eyes. I struggled to find a rock on which to sit so that I might conserve my strength as the tropical heat bore down without mercy. I thought of the movies I had seen and the books I had read, each one admonishing the traveler to conserve his, or her, strength. Then without warning, my head whirled and I had no control over my legs or arms as I flung myself down on the nearest boulder.

Time dragged on — I wondered how long I would remain conscious and when I lapsed into unconsciousness what then? — strange voices at first in the distance then coming closer, faintly reached me. It was two men in dirty, tattered clothes that once had been white, with worn sandals and calloused feet, returning from their labors. One had a water bottle strapped over his shoulder. I thought they were going to pass me by, as they were a short distance away. I struggled to get their attention and as they came toward me I motioned to their water bottle. They looked at me in a startled fashion and shook their heads — it was empty: But there is a common meeting ground among all peoples of the earth when disaster is about to strike. These men who couldn't utter one word to make me understand gently lifted me between them and guided me a few feet to an ancient Mayan well that had been there for centuries. They bathed my face by dipping their water canteen down a small, round, very deep hole beneath the crusty hard surface. Looking down I saw water filled with insects so thick on the top, it showed only blackened scum, and believe it or not, I drank that bug-infested water gratefully! I learned at that moment one of the most significant lessons of my life which has always been foremost in my mind and will always remain with me. When any one member of the human race actually faces "that destination point" where their earthly journey hangs in the balance and an alien hand can tip the scales in either direction, not one, will stop to question if that hand is black or white or if it belongs to a member of a particular religious sect!

When each one of us makes that final exit, I'm sure the only regret we will, at that last moment, feel deeply ingrained and will carry "on" with us will be that of not having lived up to "the very best" that lies within each and every one. A part of that sense of having not risen to our highest potential will be our one regret because of a lack of deeper understanding of one another even those with whom we have rubbed shoulders in daily contact — and through what might have been deep understanding knelt to help one another without question or some troubled wayfarer whose path crossed yours for a fleeting second as he ventured on his earthly quest. For whether we realize it or not, we are all relatives of human kind even though distance separates us in many ways. The words of a familiar play comes to mind — From the farewell of Death (as Prince Sirki) to his mortal friends: "Goodbye my friends. Remember, there is only a brief shadow between your world and mine. When I call you come bravely through that shadow, and you will find me only your very familiar friend" —

I believe wholeheartedly that we have nothing to fear but only the need to live up to the charge which all the great religions of the world exhort — "Do unto others as you would have others do unto you" — or THE GOLDEN RULE.

One to ten centuries before the birth of Christ this same thought was expressed in the great world religions and philosophies: Confucianism; Buddhism; Zoroastrianism; Hinduism: Judaism and by Plato. Despite the tremendous difference in time and locale, all are strikingly similar.

Plato: "May I do to others as I would that they should do unto me."

No ill effects came from the most distasteful drink I have ever swallowed. I have watched foreign people relish fried worms, eat monkey which looked to me like a child, leaving me without any desire for food and an inability to explore into their strange eating habits yet, somehow the lesson that had tapped me on the shoulder to be reminded of, all the days of my life, was one of priceless worth to follow the Golden Rule, no matter how it was written.

Then, too, maybe those insects were something my diet lacked? Today, I have come to the conclusion that when you are thirsty enough, if bugs are present, any bad effects are nullified — que sera, sera!

One of the mysteries, which lies unsolved, is the similarities found between the ancient Mayan civilization and that of the Egyptians who, when they were at their height, left behind them one of the "Seven Wonders of the World"! The early Mayans had "King-Priests" the same as the Egyptians — both wore similar hats — both had calendars, the Mayan Venus calendar, the equal in accuracy to ours today! They counted in tens — and had THE SAME FIRST LETTER OF THE ALPHABET — yet we are taught in our schools that there was NO COMMUNICATION between Yucatan and Egypt!

My thoughts jogged in tempo with the monotonous pace of the boney mule I was riding, behind a professional hunter, our guide, a native hunter who was familiar with the area and his retinue who ran along on foot while we rode in single file under a threatening, tropical sky. No other part of the world, in my experience, has such literally "tar black" heavens during a storm as though some ominous cataclysm was about to descend upon the earth from which there was no escape. Being unused to such primitive surroundings, I was saddle sore as I had ridden many kilometers that day, dripping wet with perspiration and in the mood to accept

whatever the elements showered upon me. I had started out early that morning, eating my breakfast while wild parrots flew "in and out" of the only native place where food was sold and where these birds occasionally found it to their liking to stroll across the table pecking at crumbs or whatever they thought was a delicacy, while the dirt floor had much to offer strolling hungry dogs — for this was Palenque where the body of a King-Priest buried in the days of Christ, 2,000 years ago, had been discovered by Senor

Alberto Ruz, one of the world's now renowned archeologists because of this recent, startling find after five years of searching. It is considered equal in significance to the discovery of King Tut's tomb so as soon as the London Illustrated News and the metropolitan newspapers in the states carried blazing headlines of Senor Ruz and his uncovering the majestic remains of a man whose stature was that of a King-Priest but who also was an astrologer, I was on my way —

Painfully, I lifted myself to ease the sore areas where the unpadded wooden saddle was making riding almost unbearable — "Put your poncho on — Here comes the rain" someone called to me from one of the lead horses. It did, in torrents! I've never seen such large drops — nothing like the tear drops with which we are familiar in the United States, or Europe.

I didn't move to cover myself — why should I? I wouldn't be any wetter than I was from what can only be termed "body sweat". Soon I hoped we would find our way back to our original starting place that morning. This had been a trip of wondrous adventure for me. We carried heavy camera equipment which had to be ferried across a river after leaving

Mexico City as the bridge was washed out. The train went only so far — then our baggage was shifted to a different conveyance, then again transferred to a makeshift boat which took us across to a train that had backed up on the far bank of the river for the few passengers who found it necessary to use its simple accommodations. Our guide and professional hunter who accompanied us from Mexico City and with whom we had established a warm friendship because of earlier visits to the ruins in Yucatan took charge because of his knowledge just of the jungle.

Landing at "a speck" called a "way station", in the darkest night I have ever seen, we found our way a few miles distant to the small village of Palenque and the only shelter there. Newsmen had made a path to this unheard of spot from the world's leading magazines and newspapers heralding the importance in their writings — but they were the only ones who had attempted such a hazardous journey. Soon after we arrived, it was closed to everyone, so I was fortunate to be one of the early arrivers.

My room was a small cubicle, with a tin roof overhead, a tiny cot without the luxury of sheets, bearing the body odors of many tired fellow human beings who had rested there and most important of all, a hole in the corrugated metal directly overhead in perfect position so that raindrops hit me squarely no matter how I turned my head — but I slept.

And now this torrential rain poured upon a very tired, saddle-worn, soft body — one that was not inured to strain or physical hardship but had spent hours in a padded office chair and consequently became shaped to a pen and a desk. I wondered as my mind strayed over the recent events, if my overpowering urge to seek out "the truth" about astrology and the dominant role it played in world history and now lies moldering in hidden abodes — and whether it would be as meaningful to others as it was to me. Then as the rain splashed on and on with full force, my thoughts turned to what my eyes had beheld that day and I decided that no price was too great — for few people would ever be so favored

as I had been. Only a few short hours ago I rested my hand
on the holy receptacle where this once venerated, majestic
personage had resposed in silence for 2,000 years and had directed my mind's eye through the many centuries which had
ensued while this ancient king had awaited "the touch" a
hand that would someday come, exposing to the world the
timeless faith, that down through the ages had marked civilization, a belief in an Intelligence responsible for an orderly
world! Had you or I walked in that far away time under the
self-same sky this august ruler saw and turned our eyes
heavenward, as he must have, we would have been able to
calculate to the exact degree where each star is stationed
today, like silent sentinels appointed to "a duty" of muni-
ment authority in this world scheme by a Universal Intelligence. I had crawled on my hands and knees that afternoon
through a passage-like tunnel just large enough to permit

room for a human body with our guide Alfonso and professional hunter, Raoul ahead, who was experienced as a jungle
guide. I have never relished a small enclosure without light
or air where it would be possible to smother so that death
might embrace me as its final last act. As we crawled what

seemed an endless distance without light or air, doubts and hope alternated through my mind. When we came to the end of this small tunnel I heard two thumps and as I reached that spot I saw the flicker of "a lighted match" only — which seemed very small and then the two men who guided us, urging me to jump a distance of approximately five to six feet into black nothingness, saying they would catch me! I seemingly had no choice, so I did — and today I wonder at the strength of those men standing on a small ledge with no support, catching an object in utter darkness who never was a lightweight. We managed to inch our way forward to what became one of the most resplendent sights imaginable for stalactites as well as stalagmites glistened around an enormous, exquisitely carved, rose colored stone covering the encasement of the remains of this once revered astrologer-priest! The rich color of the stone slab still brilliant just as it was the day his mortal existence ended and he was sealed in this tomb! All entrances were closed after his burial and a temple constructed over the entire site, with dirt and rock being thrown down what once was a stairway, closing in finality the last opening. This sacred leader whose guidance was inscribed on the columns of the building showing mothers bringing their children to this kindly man to have their horoscopes cast was for all time to have his memory commemorated!

Strangely, the entire setting was so very akin to burial sites I have seen in Egypt and other parts of the world, separated by thousands of miles! A common belief in the influence of the planets upon life here on earth carved in stone stands as mute testimony to a knowledge of the heavenly bodies surprisingly accurate held by the ancient Mayans whose calendar is the equal of the one we use today!

As I mulled over the splendor of by-gone days and the veneration once held for "guide lines" left to all mankind if only in their restless search for "answers" to problems during their earthly journey, mankind would stretch forth their hands and in faith open closed pages to knowledge which is available to all who earnestly seek.

The mule I was riding came to a halt before the weather-beaten shell I welcomed as a shelter. This had been one of the resplendent moments that would touch my life. I have been very reluctant in the past to discuss my personal experiences only writing and speaking in lectures of astrological significance and always omitting my role as an individual, but under pressure now from others, I am relating the roads that had to be traveled in order to bring to you knowledge that is factual and cannot be disputed by the most skeptical. What I have written is not with a desire to speak of myself, but to present the thorny paths which must be traversed so that the gathered dust can be wiped from "great truths" which lie silently awaiting!

One of the impressive carvings I actually saw on my first visit to the Mayan ruins contained gods said to be representative of natural forces. One symbolized agriculture or growing things, another rain and so on. In the center was a completely blank square. I asked why this one space was left without a figure and the answer was that it represented God and no one had ever seen His face. This is a point of great confusion among current scientific articles — where the idea is frequently expressed that the Egyptians worshiped animals because many of their symbols, which were representative of these same natural forces, were expressed in animal form. It is equally obvious that modern day authorities who specialize in the ancient languages understand the fact that the gods represented "the forces of nature". Current articles by these authorities make this distinction. There is evidence in the Bible that the people of Moses' day understood this. Exodus 22 - Verse 28 — "thou shalt not revile the gods", indicating that the forces of nature although not to be worshipped should never-the-less be respected.

It is my belief that these lesser gods who were "symbols" actually were channels to whom they offered their prayers in the belief that they in turn would intercede with the Supreme Being.

This is one of the hidden paths to knowledge which lies awaiting still today.

This is the burial site of a Mayan King-Priest in Yucatan. I visited the site when it was first discovered. The columns across the front of this ancient structure are heavily carved with astrological inscriptions showing the mothers bringing their children to the priest for him to give advice according to their horoscope. This temple was found in the heart of the jungle at Palenque!

On the other side of the world
a people shared the knowledge
of the stars influence on mankind.

Denderah, Egypt

One of the enlightening manifestations as to the extraordinary high standards of those who lived in early times, and who paced their lives by "the stars" is the discovery of the zodiac at Denderah in Lower Egypt, a short distance from the city of Luxor.

This amazing evidence of the superior knowledge of these people now rests in the Louvre in Paris. The construction of this zodiac stands as mute evidence on not only "THE MATHEMATICAL SKILL" but reveals a profound scientific knowledge (at the time of Denderah) of the movement of the planets THOUSANDS OF YEARS AGO – some authorities say as far back in time as 75,000 years! Their attempt to leave a record of their way of life and knowledge which nothing could erase is invaluable and cannot be lightly dismissed as the handwork of a primitive people. Their way of life was merely different from ours today.

Babylon

The splendor that once was Babylon's stands silently in East Germany's museum today (following photograph). The voices that once were a dominant note and the hands which toiled to create this stately magnificent structure seem not to have lost their identity – although unheard and unseen now, their creation speaks of the grandeur of another day found only in the pages of history. It was with devout reverence "the sun" was worshiped in that by-gone time as "the giver of life" here on earth, since mankind cannot exist without its beneficence. The stars were regarded with the utmost respect and devotion as representative of an ageless "Divine Wisdom". Astrologers, therefore, were considered to be a source of knowledge. It has been stated that the horoscopes of a new-born baby were of first consideration. I recall reading somewhere that "the age" of recent excavations, being uncovered, was doubtful until they discovered a clay tablet which had the horoscope of a child inscribed on it. From this they could tell THE EXACT DATE because of its MATHEMATICAL ACCURACY and to the positions of the stars at that time! A civilization of ageless wisdom! Notice: Many references are made now to the ancient peoples and their gods rather than One God. The concept was that of many gods who were representative of the One Supreme God and through whom all blessings must be channeled. A religious belief similar somewhat to ours in this present day!

The anything but friendly gaze of armed soldiers made the visit to East Berlin a nerve-wracking experience. When one is allowed to pass beyond "the wall", you are struck by the almost unbelievable difference between East and West Berlin; a general drabness, streets virtually empty of vehicles or

pedestrians and buildings closed as if the city had been evac-
uated.   The great museum was in a poor state of repair and
was obviously no longer visited by the throngs of years gone
by.   Although the eerie atmosphere was depressing, viewing
the wonderful archeological treasures made it all worthwhile.

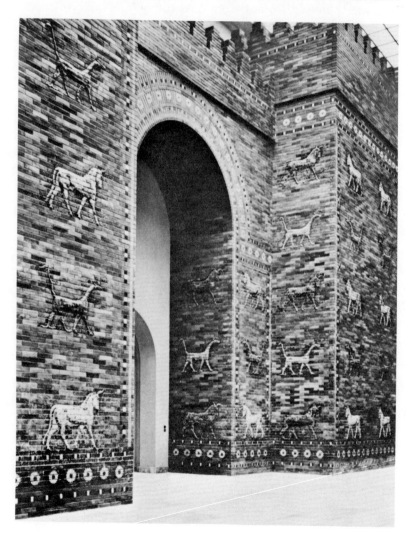

ROME – TURKEY

I love Rome. There is something about the air you breathe, the music, even the flowers lining the steep Spanish steps in its heart that fills your very soul with faith in Infinity, for here lies "Timelessness" – the threads that have woven the colorful tapestry of the lives of fellow beings, their joys and sorrows, as well as the courage shown at crucial moments when their very existence was held in balance.

I have wandered alone there many times, exploring niches and corners where astrology played a leading role on the stage of life. Few travelers whom I have met seem to connect Christ's short, few years here on earth with the period in which Augustus Caesar reigned. It was he, who when a youth with little promise, had his horoscope cast by a famous astrologer of that day, named Theogenes, who after looking at Augustus' birth chart is said to have fallen on his knees before the youth declaring he would hold the most powerful seat in all Rome some day. When this prophecy was fulfilled, Augustus Caesar was so impressed, he had a silver coin struck with the sign Capricorn on one side and his own likeness on the other commemorating his rise to supreme ruler as emperor under that sign of the zodiac. I have one of the coins I obtained after much research and overcoming many obstacles.

I am not going to describe at this time the various paths my feet have trod through shrines and noble edifices that mark the ending of an era and the turning to a new way of life still standing silently although surrounded by the froth of today's bustling masses in this well-named "Eternal city" – for my feet, on my last visit, were subsequently turned in another direction.

Traveling alone once again, I had completed my mission, gathering historical data and photographs of important events in England, Germany, Paris, Switzerland and Italy. On earlier trips I covered Egypt, taking my own caravan out into the desert near the great Pyramid where the camel train and a Gala Gala man (one who performs tricks of magic) camped for several days, and I had the joyous experience of riding on camel back at night under the desert stars. Greece too was one of the highlights of my research. Then on that same quest, to procure little-known but true astrological findings, I ventured behind the iron curtain to Vienna, that famed city in Austria. A small map was given to each stranger who successfully made the journey down a lonely 90 mile stretch of highway from which even our U. S. military officers, as well as others, disappeared every few days, I was told. This map had a fine black outline of a main street from which you were warned to never stray with only foreign names designating the one street to be followed because of the danger of being kidnapped and held for ransom. I still have the small map, grey permit card and curt instructions I was given.

But that was all behind me and this last effort concluded, so I was ready to bolt for home.

Rome was in the throes of a mail strike, so all letters were put on trucks that were being shuttled all over the countryside. After reaching their destination, they were not allowed to unload but were forced to continue on to some other destination where the process was again repeated. No mail was being received at the hotel, so I finished buying small gifts for my office staff and stood looking out my hotel window at the Spanish steps as my thoughts flew back in time to Shelley, Elizabeth Browning, and all the other notables who had loved this spot just as I did — all prepared mentally to bid au revoir — not goodbye — when a knock came on my door and a telegram was handed to me changing all my plans — making Ankara, Turkey my next point for research. A professor of modern English Poetry in the University there had a short time previously told me of the major role astrology had held in the lives of all Turkish people — until a short fifty years ago when Kemal Ataturk became ruler. Professor Uysal wired me to come, so what better time than now? Being typically American, I had wired ahead for hotel reservations, so I wouldn't inconvenience him, as I was keenly aware of the duties to which others are committed today. I was introduced at the airport to a strange young lady at whose home Prof. Uysal insisted I stay. An intuitive feeling of something I didn't understand being amiss, I followed "a small voice within" and accepted his decision — thereby experiencing one of the most exciting occasions I shall always recall vividly. This young Turkish lady spoke English quite well. I walked down a darkened hallway to what was to be my room for these few days, with my shoes on before I remembered to my embarrassment that I was in a Moslem home. I had noticed a huge row of shoes at the door as we entered her very nice apartment, but for the moment I had forgotten that this was "a clue" to a particular custom in Moslem countries. My hostess was one of the lovely young persons I shall always regard warmly in my heart. She insisted on preparing my breakfast each morning which really intrigued me. The black Turkish coffee wasn't bad, but I chose tea, then she offered me some special cheese her father had brought from Southern Turkey, a great delicacy, and salty, black olives — an unusual breakfast for me. The hard bread and very sweet preserved fruit I really liked at that early hour, but I was curious about the coarse black hairs I found in the cheese. Then I remembered reading how cheese was made in Tibet and I reasoned that they had followed the same method. I didn't mention it to her because of being fearful of causing embarrassment. In eastern areas I have seen it stated many times they make cheese by turning an animal inside out allowing the hair of the animal to tickle the curds into cheese. The dinners each night at Prof. Uysal's exquisite apartment were simply delicious. He is a most unusual man, a graduate of Edinburgh University in Scotland, as well as the University of Cologne, Germany. The university system is entirely different in Europe from what we have. Almost any university in the United States has many professors for a particular branch of learning, while over there only one full professorship is granted for each chair. Many men or women eligible for full professorship may have to wait 30 or 40 years in Europe for a vacancy. That is what made Prof. Uysal so unusual for by European standards, he is very young to hold this title. He, in addition to being a specialist in modern English poetry, has published in collaboration with an American professor the only book on Turkish folklore. He made it possible for me to visit the university and talk with general professors there on astrology and its prominent role in Turkey. Here once again I gathered information of considerable value to me. The history of astrology in this region of Asia Minor is older by thousands of years than Turkish civilization — in fact, it dates back here to the dawn of civilization and formed a central part of the traditions of one great culture after another which took root, flourished and passed away on this soil. Among these civilizations were the Hittites and the Assyrians, and I am showing you here the Moon Gates at Alaca-Hoyuk where in recent years artifacts were found designating solar and lunar cycles.

And next are the Lion Gates of Hattushash which was the capital of ancient Assyrian peoples. Recent studies by scholars of the early history of this area presents overwhelming evidence that the zodiacal symbols of Taurus and Leo were directly related to planting and harvesting periods used by these people for over 3,000 years.

Ankara is very modern in appearance as no minarets or mosque-like buildings are to be seen except in the old section. Teeming pedestrians threaded their way through automobile drivers who seemed to be playing the well-known game of our youth which is known as "chicken". This is the capital of Turkey where the head of government resides and all foreign emissaries come, yet it had no stoplights to aid those on foot. The streets were torn up and as Prof. Uysal explained, for the first time they were going to have that great modern invention known as "stop and go" signals. Void of brakes, lights, barely able to start the motors, these autos when they grasp that spark of life, become a force without direction of course — yet they are excessively expensive. A six-year old Chevrolet may cost as much as $7,000. My newly-found friend took me in her car that coughed, belched, stopped, then gathered its breath — tried again — and took off on the wildest of all rides as people somehow separated before us just at the last second, while the convertible top flapped violently, threatening to come loose and fly off into the "wild blue yonder". Did I say come loose? It was loose, one small fastening held it at a point so weakly, a mere jolt could easily break that final tie to the rickety body that creaked like a wild thing in pain because of having outlived its time. Yet, we rattled and banged safely to each place and to this day I think of her (the car I nicknamed) with warm affection.

Moslems disapprove of alcohol and it is said that they don't drink, but the way they drive, this point seems somewhat irrelevant.

There is an ancient city, the original remains having been as accurately dated 7,000 years before Christ! Ephesus, in Turkey, where the Virgin Mary is said to have once lived and walked even as you and I, is a breathtaking experience and is only "one" of the long-forgotten spots that seems to be hallowed ground — in Turkey. (Photo opposite page)

The afternoon was sunny, I was seated in the living room of my friend's apartment, while she was studying — when loud voices and a wild knocking came at the door. My friend opened it to three very attractive ladies who spoke excitedly and then would stop and look at me. I tried to hear one strange sentence or word that would give me a clue, but to my ears it was so much gibberish. I had seen newspapers on the streets with glaring headlines and a photograph of a man whom I didn't recognize, so I assumed it was like some of our wild news media with their sole purpose bent on selling newspapers rather than presenting the rather monotonous true facts — so I dismissed the glaring headlines and asked no questions.

These ladies whose entrance brought something hidden I could not fathom, had me in a quandary, for I sensed that I was involved. Their voices grew louder and more excited and as my hostess was trying to calm them, I reached the point of not being able to restrain myself further. I vaguely wondered what I could have done. I asked my hostess what the disturbing news might be. Then she told me that word was out that a military coup was to take place at midnight (that night). No planes would be flying and I would be there for no telling how long as there would be street fighting. I asked if I could get a plane out now — ahead of the coup and the answer was "No". Then I learned that this had been brewing for sometime. One of the husbands came in shortly who spoke a little English and he told everyone to remain calm — he thought it might not come off — it was a 50-50 chance. He said Prof. Uysal would be there shortly and to see what he thought. I don't believe I am exactly a coward, yet there is something about awakening to the realization that you are "alone" with no familiar voice or surroundings that weave an inner sense of lack of security which brings you face to face with reality looking you squarely in the eye and in anticipation of someone or a hidden enemy making a first move. I took a deep breath and awaited dinner at Prof. Uysal's home. The meal which had previously always held delightful conversation was strained. Piecemeal I learned that I couldn't go to the American Embassy for protection for our Ambassador was not enjoying protection himself. He had a few nights before my arrival, been invited to the new Turkish ruler's palatial residence for dinner and while he was there, someone had taken the gasoline out of the car's tank, poured it over his new Cadillac and set it afire. Three other Americans had their cars burned in the last few days. The college just out of town to which the United States endowed several million dollars, I was told, was being threatened with destruction. In fact, Prof. Uysal was wary of driving his own car which he had purchased while in the United States. I wondered why he had allowed me to walk into this and then I understood that there is an eastern rule of etiquette so far as hospitality is concerned that could only permit his making me welcome and safe, guarding me as best he could. Undoubtedly, this was why he was so insistent that I should not go to a hotel but remain quietly almost unseen in a friend's home.   A true and gallant gentleman of eastern culture!

His decision was to rise early and take me to the airport himself — which he did. Upon arriving, I found I had missed my plane — after much confusion, the decision was made that I should take a plane to Vienna, Austria — wait there and then get a plane from there back to Rome. With these arrangements decided upon, Prof. Uysal left me alone at the airport as he had classes to which he had to attend, for there had been several uprisings there too and he, with other teachers, were striving to calm the restless element. So, I bade him goodbye.

Only those who have been very lonely can know how empty and large a small room can become, much less an airport without the teeming life usually found there. Very few airline ticket offices are in Ankara, although it is the seat of the Turkish government, and that morning, I believe only two small airline representatives were on duty. A man with a dirty, mud encrusted mop was swiping away as I strolled around trying to find something of interest. The unpleasant odor of an unclean rest room wafted its way to my nose as I passed by — and then one of the loveliest ladies I've ever met walked past, garbed in an Indian sari. She was English, I felt sure, but from her tanned skin and attire, I thought she might be Hindu. As I was speculating on her background, I heard the typical voice of an American tourist from California, most attractively "put together" but given to the sole purpose of expressing her discontent over inconveniences as well as the seeming threatening spot we all faced. I remembered that the young boy at Prof. Uysal's dinner table the previous night had blurted out that airports were the most dangerous places of all because they were the first to become targets to be fired upon. His father had hushed him up just as the youngster reminded him of the one that had been attacked only a few days before.

My thoughts were suddenly jarred out of their wanderings by "a blare" of horns that proved deafening and approximately a hundred military men appeared whose legs seemed

- 87 -

to be slightly bowed due to the weight of the medals with which they were burdened, no doubt. They were representatives from all the surrounding foreign countries in their finery, being driven in their private cars in order to embark on the special plane which was awaiting.

Imagination is certainly the motivating force in our lives. I awaited a wild shot from some trigger-happy finger that would set off action in all directions — but none came. As these generals and men of high government positions left on their plane, I walked timidly over to the lady who had arranged for me to go to Vienna and inquired as to the meaning of this. She said they were as surprised as I was, as they had not been alerted to the possibility of such an august group of visitors.

It is in times such as these that barriers are always broken which hold people apart who might otherwise become warm friends if they only really knew and understood one another — so, I became friends with the lady from India.

Our plane came and the traveler from California — the gentle English teacher who had lived in India for 20 years and I all breathed a sigh of relief as the plane soared into the sky that bright sunny morning. There wasn't a hostess on the plane but a man in uniform who acted as an airline representative, and of course, our first questions to him were in regard to the plans to depose the present president of Turkey. He assured us that they had no warning of this serious situation but he did know that leading foreign correspondents from London and all over had been abruptly flown in the night before as some eminent news was expected.

Always bear in mind that Turkey is a great melting pot, for the Greeks, the Romans, as well as invaders from Asia, European areas and many others all had a role in shaping the destiny of those fascinating people who were to inherit this strange land.

I left behind a land of mystery, a truly entrancing land which holds things of infinitely greater value than our modern world of material man-made concepts — and, so I said "Goodbye" to minarets, the wisdom and beauty of works of Art to which only this part of the world has given expression. May they live on!

Turkey, a land of silent mystery, until fifty years ago governed her daily life by astrology! It was the genius of those who lived in that general area of Mesopotamia who gave Geometry to the world, as this reproduction proves. Their teachings were studied in the great universities of Europe.

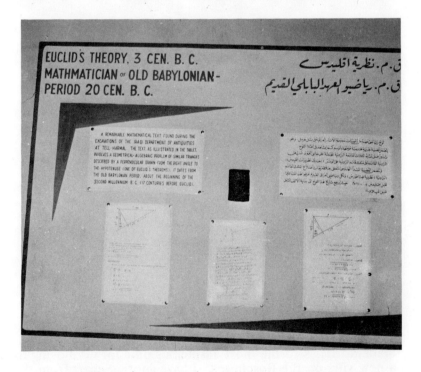

This cuneiform tablet recording a "Euclidian" theorem which led to quadratic equations, has been dated accurately at 19 centuries B.C. — about 1600 years before Euclid. It is in the old museum of Anthropology in Baghdad.

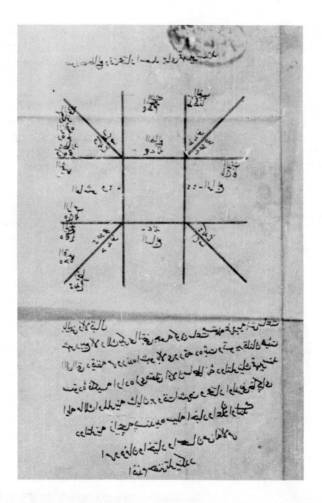

Above is a reproduction of the prediction made for Sultan Mahmud II, as to the most auspicious time for his moving to a new villa on the Bosphorus. I have another chart from the state archives in Istanbul showing a prediction by their astrologer as to the most auspicious time for his Majesty's navy to move on the 25th of rajab (Lunar Calendar) Wednesday at 1:45!

Prof. Uysal and his wife with city of Ankara in background —
capital of Turkey. The professor's help was invaluable to me
in many ways. He possesses knowledge which was particularly helpful in my area of study. He has recently published
the ONLY book on Turkish folklore which has been written
in English.

Kashmir

Mankind has followed many roads in an attempt to grasp
an answer to the eternal inner stirrings of his heart — Kashmir
is a place where the azure sky meets the snowy, lofty moun-
tain peaks and the smiling valleys beckon those who are tired
in soul. The pine-laden breezes, the murmur from the rushing
streams and singing of the birds all combine to instill in the
wayfarer a sense of TIMELESSNESS and a desire toward
meditation — something we in our bustling western lives
strive to kill. In certain months "when the planets favor" religious acts — the people of India and Kashmir come to the

famous spring near Pahalgam to remember their dead. The name of the spring is Mattan, being dedicated to "the sun", and therefore, thought of as an intermediary who channels good wishes on to those who have departed.

This is a photograph of a religious spot which urges each visitor to turn his eyes heavenward toward the stars who stand silently as sentinels promising fulfillment to all who seek.

Foreword
To Your Sun Sign by Decan

The following pages hold the entire KEY to your forecast, in my opinion. While you may have other planetary influences which will shade or alter these characteristic personality traits, the descriptions I have endeavored to clarify in this work will explain the true "inner YOU", I am certain; it is the face you do not turn to the world. In many instances, there may be things here of which you are unaware — but I know that as time moves on you will be awakened to this "seed" which lies buried deeply within you, and was planted at your birth.

What is your Sun Sign? The zodiac is a circle of three hundred sixty degrees, which we divide into twelve segments of thirty degrees each, called "signs". These are Capricorn, Gemini, Scorpio, and similar names with which you are no doubt familiar. In the course of a year, the Sun passes through all of these signs — and your Sun Sign simply means "The sign in which the Sun was located on the day of your birth". The beginning and ending dates of these sometimes vary, because there is a slight change of condition from year to year that alters the exactitude of these dates. People who have birthdays at one of the "changing points" between signs (or decans) will usually discover that they have some of the characteristics of each, owing to the nearness of the Sun to another sign or decan.

The Sun is the giver of all life — every living thing is dependent on its vital rays. Therefore, it is considered to have cardinal significance over your life in the astrological "scheme of things". As it is in approximately the same place on the same day of every year, its motion is predictable, while the various planets follow more indeterminate courses which must be calculated to a specific year. These are significant (as is the Ascending Sign) but are not considered here since your decan of the Sun is the most important of all — even in bringing a delineation of planetary influences from a general to a personal level.

What is your Decan? On the following pages you will find your Sun Sign broken into three segments, called "Decans". The dates that generally apply to each decan are given below the name of the sign, so that you can easily find which of these three segments holds YOUR birthday, and, thus, whether YOUR birthday is in the first, second or third decan of your sign. These "decans" are still finer "breakdowns" of a sign, dividing its thirty degrees into sections of ten degrees each. The use of decans refines the characteristics of a sign; other material you read about your Sun Sign will be perfectly applicable. In this respect, I have deliberately tried to concentrate my efforts on tendencies or events which might NOT ordinarily be considered in monographs on the Sun Signs, in the hope of giving you another perspective to be added to such information.

Your Ruling Planet: You will notice that the name of a "ruling planet" is given with each decan. This is a planet which is said to have special significance over your particular sign and decan. There are two methods of locating the "Ruler" of a decan. One considers the "triplicities". If your birthday is within a "Water Sign", for instance, then by this method the "rulers" ordinarily given to the Water Signs in their natural sequence will be considered as the rulers of the decans. I discarded the use of decans some years ago, because I could not find ample credence in this method to feel that it was worthwhile.

The Method I use: I now use a procedure which is generally referred to as "Sepharial's Method", because it was advocated by a man named W. Gorn Old, or "Sepharial". The only reference I can find on its origin is that Sepharial took it from the Chaldeans. Obviously, I subscribe to it absolutely.

You Are an Individual! This outline is necessarily a

generality that describes the qualities which are most likely to appear in the personalities or lives of individuals in any particular decan — but because you are DISTINCTLY, IN-DIVIDUALLY YOU, you might find that certain things apply more than others because of YOUR OTHER PLANETARY positions at birth. Remember, you may have planets in other signs and decans, or your Ascending Sign might be another besides your Sun Sign, enabling you to notice traces of "yourself" in several of the sections.

A Message to the Student: STUDENTS OF ASTROLOGY SHOULD FIND THIS WORK PARTICULARLY VALUA-BLE. I sincerely hope that these descriptions will shed upon your endeavors a whole new insight into the meaning of planets, Moon or Ascendant as they relate to the decan in which they are placed, promoting your placement of questionable times, as well. You will notice that consideration has also been given to the placement of the Sun's Solstice Point.

To All Readers: The chart on the following page gives for each sign and decan ANOTHER CORRESPONDING SIGN AND DECAN. This is a point which I consider to be sensitive to the one given. It will have influence over events in your life as well as indicate whenever planets transit over its place, and probably represent the sign and decan under which some important person who comes to touch your life will be born. By reading the corresponding section for your birth date, you are apt to gain additional insight into your own personality, as well.

IF YOU WERE BORN:	READ:
1st decan of Aries	3rd decan of Virgo
2nd decan of Aries	2nd decan of Virgo
3rd decan of Aries	1st decan of Virgo
1st decan of Taurus	3rd decan of Leo
2nd decan of Taurus	2nd decan of Leo
3rd decan of Taurus	1st decan of Leo
1st decan of Gemini	3rd decan of Cancer
2nd decan of Gemini	2nd decan of Cancer
3rd decan of Gemini	1st decan of Cancer
1st decan of Cancer	3rd decan of Gemini
2nd decan of Cancer	2nd decan of Gemini
3rd decan of Cancer	1st decan of Gemini
1st decan of Leo	3rd decan of Taurus
2nd decan of Leo	2nd decan of Taurus
3rd decan of Leo	1st decan of Taurus
1st decan of Virgo	3rd decan of Aries
2nd decan of Virgo	2nd decan of Aries
3rd decan of Virgo	1st decan of Aries
1st decan of Libra	3rd decan of Pisces
2nd decan of Libra	2nd decan of Pisces
3rd decan of Libra	1st decan of Pisces
1st decan of Scorpio	3rd decan of Aquarius
2nd decan of Scorpio	2nd decan of Aquarius
3rd decan of Scorpio	1st decan of Aquarius
1st decan of Sagittarius	3rd decan of Capricorn
2nd decan of Sagittarius	2nd decan of Capricorn
3rd decan of Sagittarius	1st decan of Capricorn
1st decan of Capricorn	3rd decan of Sagittarius
2nd decan of Capricorn	2nd decan of Sagittarius
3rd decan of Capricorn	1st decan of Sagittarius
1st decan of Aquarius	3rd decan of Scorpio
2nd decan of Aquarius	2nd decan of Scorpio
3rd decan of Aquarius	1st decan of Scorpio
1st decan of Pisces	3rd decan of Libra
2nd decan of Pisces	2nd decan of Libra
3rd decan of Pisces	1st decan of Libra

Aries

March 20-March 30
Ruled by Mars

1st decan

Some of the most phenomenally powerful people I have ever known were born in the first decan of Aries, as you were. Like a sun-kissed island in the midst of an everchanging sea, this decan seems to give great brilliance to the mind and warmth to the personality, while inspiration and sensitivity of soul are often marked characteristics I notice among my friends who are under its influence. I believe that you have an ambitious and enthusiastic nature that leads you to drive yourself forward at a faster pace than many people would — although your life is apt to be changeful, it is likely to be equally remarkable. Your talents might branch in many directions, because of a keen cultural awareness, and you no doubt prefer being "on your own", in challenging undertakings that will permit you to climb the "ladder of success", "several steps" at a time.

I have frequently observed that people born in this decan are particularly adept with instruments and tools, or in using their hands in some unusual manner requiring skill, and that they appear to have an innate understanding of everything having to do with the head, such as psychological principles, or dentistry, or cerebral functions. You may have a tendency to act on impulse — but I am confident that you have found it necessary to learn the value of patience, and that belligerence or argumentativeness gain you fewer advantages than the preservation of your true dignity. Having a basic comprehension of artful procedure, combined with an inherent spirit for "pioneering", your abilities are unquestionably well suited for "newer" undertakings that require fearless leadership, because in all likelihood, competition itself appeals to you more strongly than management of details or the following of habitual routines. You may very well approach life in a responsible, resourceful and productive manner, sometimes appearing to be parsimonious in small matters and "spending liberally of energy, time and resources in large amounts". One occasionally meets individuals who have birthdays around this time of the year who display a definite austerity: rather self-righteous, self-centered inclinations — but I trust that YOU make better use of the paradoxical combination of extravagance and economy that is no doubt evident in your nature.

There is little question that the position you attain in the world is particularly important to you, but in spite of "hidden opposition" that may delay your progress, from time to time, you are likely to earn in return for your conscientiousness more than an ordinary degree of favorable recognition, provided you staunchly follow your highest principles.

While I feel that you prefer to design your financial interests in such ways as to realize "long-term security" constructed on solid foundations, you will first have a number of changes — practical experience being for you a better teacher than purely "technical" learning, in all probability. Striving with deliberation for the most sensible course to follow to steadfast security won't always be easy, for you are apt to spend on impulse. Real estate, mining, and other enterprises involving property, frequently appeal to individuals born in this decan, from an investment standpoint, although "speculative" undertakings are likely to prove less gainful for you than those you enter with more certainty. Other people may think it obverse to many of your other characteristics that you sometimes resist new ideas concerning your assets and possessions, apparently hesitating just at the moment when they believe that you ought to "make a move". This inclination to "hang back", so to say, is probably a result of your wish to think material matters through with some profundity before you jump at conclusions.

"Services" you personally give in carrying out your daily routines ordinarily bring back to you greater returns than do your mutual endeavors, in my opinion. I have rather often noticed that when people born around your birthday become closely involved in such things as estates, "partnership accounts", insurance, or taxes, dissensions arise on at least one occasion, and not infrequently these are even accompanied by some degree of "bitterness" or cunning. It might seem a rather natural reaction for you to "even things" by taking a kind of "revenge" that seems fitting for the occasion — but I am confident you've learned that a more magnanimous attitude is always more gainful; otherwise, the only person you would ever really hurt would be yourself.

Being highly intelligent and quick to receive impressions, you may be quite capable of having several different opinions on the same subject at the same time, which no doubt gives you an appearance of being broad-minded, and enables you to "skim the surfaces" of a variety of fields of interest. You are apt to show talent in a number of directions, although DEVELOPMENT OF YOUR TRUE CAPABILITIES will be the "key" to your success, I believe. I have known people of this decan who became "crafty" to such an extent that they sometimes appeared indiscreet, or even not entirely honest; or had a diffusion of interests, scattered to a point of seeming "lost in the wind". Properly used, your mental restlessness provides you with every necessary means for constructively touching upon many endeavors, which might be a reason why such a large number of individuals from your decan become outstanding diplomats, brilliant speakers and television personalities, or professional people. A resolve to complete what you begin is almost certain to insure more gratifying results from your accomplishments. I am sure that you will find your ideas are well received, often in areas distant from your usual locale, when you devote your adaptable energies to pursuits you feel are helping other people, or performing necessary assistance. Few people will surpass your capabilities, I feel.

I think that you make a sincere effort to display a spirit of charity, sympathy and benevolence for individuals who come to touch your daily life, although there are times when your preoccupation with several enterprises you consider "pressing" brings you to appear somewhat abrupt, or even "thoughtless" of courtesies that might not at the moment seem important, but are in the minds of people around you. Nevertheless, you surely try to earn admiration and public approval, although you are apt to approach your interests with such an air of confidence that others neglect to show you the degree of appreciation they inwardly feel and you honestly deserve.

Mistakes you sometimes make in your choice of associates may not always seem necessary to admit, because you have a flair for turning many mistakes into advantages. I believe that you are ordinarily attracted to acquaintances who appear refined, yet somewhat detached from actual "domesticity", being more strongly drawn to intellectual pursuits, the progress and problems of the "times" in which they live, and the possibilities of contributing to the betterment of these. While you no doubt develop "friendships" that earn in return for your own generosity many courtesies or favors, your true confidants are likely to be relatively few.

I consider this to be one of the major points overlooked in regard to people born in your decan of Aries . . . that your deepest instincts prompt you to find appreciation, sympathetic understanding, admiration, and a keen sensitivity to your personal needs — yet your assured manner and inherent capabilities are apt to be strangely magnetic for relationships that are more intellectual and impersonal than otherwise. Being ambitious yourself, you may quickly lose regard for people who are not, while those who have less definite aspirations are apt to expect an overly amount of devotion, time and effort than you think your "busy schedules" can afford. Equally ambitious people are almost bound to have strong wills of their own that at least now and then tend to challenge some of your interests. Examining your personality in depth, I conclude that where your feelings are involved, you sometimes tend to be more idealistic than practical, holding on a pedestal cherished concepts that are almost certain to be too fragile for ordinary day-to-day "pressures" that inevitably develop in an imperfect world.

While some individuals might consider your manner too "businesslike" in certain situations, you are apt to appear blind to the faults of people for whom you feel affection. I believe that your loyalty to what you feel are your "obligations" is essentially strong, but when large enterprises attract your notice, you will probably incline to compensate your loved ones with the finest "material" advantages, while inadvertently overlooking their wish for additional amounts of "your time" and personal attention. Your interest in their welfare is no doubt sincere, although you probably avert many problems by displaying it quite openly, for generosity and devotion are qualities you admire and earnestly endeavor to cultivate in yourself. There are likely to be fluctuations in your closest relationships, from time to time, but I believe that the associations you form with people of cheerful, well-balanced dispositions, who are receptive to your finer capabilities; who gracefully reflect rather than challenge your "glories", will always be rewarding. The appearance of your associates is unusually important to you, in all probability, giving you a fondness for people who observe rules of etiquette and show good taste in dress and manner, in private as well as in public.

Children, younger people, or a particular person younger than yourself, are apt to seem a disappointment to you. Alliances you form with some younger or less experienced individual may result, to a degree, from a sense of "duty", or responsibility, whether real or fancied. Harmonious relationships are an essential part of your inner peace, in my estimation, but when you promote conditions as pleasing as those you wish for, you'll be truly seeking those conditions, and individuals who come to touch your life should give you a growing sense of contentment, because you will FIND what you seek!

You are probably particularly appreciative of beautiful surroundings, especially in your home environment, where you are likely to prefer a luxurious atmosphere that sustains a feeling of domestic felicity. People born in this decan of Aries almost always shine as hosts and hostesses, while I have noticed that one of their outstanding characteristics is a desire to display respect for their parents or guardians. THIS CAN LEAD THEM TO FEEL INWARDLY DISTURBED WHEN THE PARENTS DO NOT MERIT THEIR RESPECT.

Your versatile mind and frankness of expression is probably stimulated quite favorably by educational pursuits and frequent associations with places or work that encompasses some element that is distant from your usual environment. I think that you cherish knowledge and learning, and look upon almost every new experience with a view to gaining from it information of importance. These tendencies may bring you to an inordinate degree of telephoning, writing, or similar activity, and might make all other forms of "mass-communication" of particular importance to your achieving success.

Religious, philosophical, political and legal concepts give constructive outlets for many of your energies, and while you are likely to change your personal opinions regarding these and the "social values" you think are important not only to your own interests, but for the betterment of mankind as a whole, you are very apt to inspire in those around you greater effectiveness with respect to "their sense" of direction. Because I trust that you always keep sight of the principles that have historically proven themselves an asset to humanity, you can be instrumental in improving conditions around you from whatever substructure you choose to build your life upon.

Your decan of Aries combines perception and sensitivity with true might. When you recognize the wonderful capabilities, talents and abilities that are within your immediate grasp, and determine that you will cultivate them to their fullest by pacing yourself in a "budgeted" use of your energies that draws only from your better judgment, I believe that you are capable of reaching "the summit" of even the loftiest accomplishments! I feel that you have a gift of enthusiasm for participating in circles where you are, to such an extent, that you rapidly reach attainments that might even seem out of the question in view of comparisons in original advantages with other people who have equalled your accomplishments. By displaying a sense of humor and accepting any minor limitations that may ever be placed upon you by the "sands of time", your popularity is likely to grow abundantly, bringing more and more pleasing returns.

Aries
March 31-April 10
Ruled by Sun

I think you are acutely aware of the opportunities life holds for you, and of the capabilities you have to contribute to the world's betterment by taking your place in the mainstream of its activity. I have always found that people born when the Sun was in the second decan of Aries radiate an "aliveness" that sparks enthusiasm in individuals around them and seems to re-energize undertakings in which they participate, which may be characteristic of you, as well.

In all probability, you have a generous nature that makes GIVING more pleasurable for you THAN RECEIVING — although WHAT you give is almost certain to come back to you in at least equal measure, and your finer efforts may well be rewarded, from time to time, by LEGACIES, or SOME OTHER VERY WELCOME ASSISTANCE FROM PEOPLE WHO COME TO TOUCH YOUR LIFE.

Many people born in your decan have innate tendencies toward combativeness and forcefulness, that often makes their manner appear brusque and their outlook selfish — but because I am confident that you devote your energies to constructive outlets, I believe that you display enterprising qualities which gave early indication of a certain singleness of purpose you would carry with you through the years. You are apt to have an enterprising spirit that usually expresses itself somewhat assertively, if not "boldly".

Your spring birth may evidence itself in your nature by prompting you always to burst forth in newer blossom; to bring fresh life into endeavors that have previously been dormant. From time to time, you may have associates who consider your ideas unworkable, but when you make an earnest effort to continue in one channel, even in phases that appear to bring results less rapidly than you would really like, you surely have every necessary talent for fulfilling even your loftiest ambitions in daringly original accomplishments that are webbed within a practical framework.

While you might hold more than one point of view on a particular subject, or change your opinions from time to time, I believe you find it distasteful for anyone to interfere with your ideas. In the expression of some of your more challenging instincts, you are likely to consider that "the pen is mightier than the sword", so to say. This may result in messages you have written playing a dominant role in a particular area of your life — although I'm sure you've discovered that your "debates" gain more favorable responses when you enter them with an uncritical attitude, and soften your words with tact and diplomacy.

Your motives are apt to be misunderstood rather frequently by people who think your manner less careful or cooperative than their own — but I earnestly feel that your reasons for climbing toward the top of enterprises that intrigue you evolve out of a sincere desire to serve all of mankind that you can reach, by encouraging hope and faith, and offering an outlook you consider enlightening. Snobbery or underhandedness is contrary to everything you strive for, in all probability. When you like someone, it is no doubt because you are interested in hearing their ideas — even when these are somewhat "avant-garde" according to "ordinary" standards. You may even think of entering into more substantial mutual endeavors with "friends", upon occasion, although your most satisfying associations are likely to be with people other than "neighbors" or "relatives".

You have a strong creative sense, in my estimation, that gives you more than the usual degree of enjoyment from entertaining pursuits or the practical arts. Undertakings that have "undetermined outcomes", such as sports, are sure to appeal to you, while I know you have a special rapport with children and younger people. I think enduring and highly pleasing relationships with some people who hold your esteem highlight the happiness you receive, because your affections are deep and loyal, but close associations and "partnerships" are sometimes apt to seem limiting to a few of your personal aspirations. Many of my friends who were born in this decan of Aries along with you have found some of their most gratifying alliances among individuals who were either older than they, or seemed older because of their wise understanding and an unusual degree of maturity in their attitudes.

People to whom you are closely attracted are originally likely to appear dignified and big-hearted, but they settle into more impartial, tactful and particular dispositions later on. I believe that you feel a strong responsibility toward those immediately around you, or upon at least one occasion have found it necessary to be responsible for another. Provided you maintain a comfortable "distance" from those who are impractical, insincere and austere, the majority of your more cherished affiliations should prove strong and beneficent, although there may be some conditions involving a few of these that display sinister touches now and then. I am quite sure that you prefer to be around people who hold a good balance between conservative and concentrative force, and who display capabilities for caring for themselves, exercising both tact and judgment in the management of their personal affairs.

You are apt to have more changes to your home surroundings than many people, but in every new environment, you probably endeavor to add imaginative touches that give tribute to antiquity. A tendency to "lose yourself" in pursuits involving your usual locale may bring you to appear somewhat "reclusive" to a few of your associates, or others might consider you too much of a "bookworm" — but I believe that this is because you prefer an "intellectual" atmosphere to a purely "domestic" one. Sometimes your mutual activities are apt to become so enthusiastic that you incline to let things accumulate at a faster rate than you can deal with them, although it is no doubt a well-ordered "confusion" that enables you to find what you are looking for, when such a need arises.

I have frequently noticed that people born in this decan of Aries, as you were, are quite mechanically-minded and display an intriguing agility of mind, provided they channel their fine mental energies to avert excitable and irritable tendencies, so as to promote the true power of which they are capable. It is very likely that there were some stresses, as well as a "duality", in the years generally considered "through high school age", when you attained your "earlier education"; later on, distant places or countries foreign to the location in which you were born probably became more attractive. I should expect you to take a keen interest in philosophical, religious, educational, legal and political concepts, although it is rather improbable that you will remain with those in which you were reared. Once you have decided upon a certain conviction, you are rarely apt to display great plasticity of attitude, although you surely strive for a sense of tolerance that will temper some of your more direct methods.

I believe that you find it somewhat easier to break habits than many people — although this is due more to a capacity you have for accomplishing what you make up your mind to do than to any real simplicity in altering your accustomed patterns of living. You are apt to enjoy better-than-average health, when you take measures to prevent "excesses" and direct your nervous energy to constructive undertakings. Most people of your decan realize substantial benefits from a practice of well-regulated "schedules", because they are often inclined to "overdo", but when they are guided by their better judgment, they ordinarily have an innate understanding of the importance of maintaining wholesome, dietary practices and getting sufficient rest.

You are apt to have an "authoritative" approach to life that gives you an unusual degree of self-reliance and ambition. Triumph over every endeavor is probably your motivating force, where many of your "outside interests" are concerned, but your determination may occasionally be interpreted as a "sledge-hammer method", owing to your strong sense of resolution, combined with your tenacity of purpose. At the same time, people who know you well learn to find the sensitivities I feel certain are below a more stern appearance, recognizing that your true talents and capabilities are well suited for real diplomatic achievement. Courtesies you extend bring back to you particularly trustworthy people or services that reliably aid you in advancing your efforts, I'm sure.

I have noticed that people born in this second decan of Aries have a natural understanding of banking principles and finance. Although they seem to experience a few rather drastic major changes in their monetary interests, these appear to disturb them only momentarily, since they are less interested in rapid returns than long-term gains, where choice must be made between the two. Material stability is no doubt significant in your objectives, which might give you an affinity for "durable" enterprises, such as mining or real estate. Compared to some of your more impulsive characteristics, it may occasionally surprise your associates when you display slower reactions in security matters, pausing to quietly reflect — or even "sleep on a problem" — before committing yourself more definitely. Generally, enterprises you enter in a cautious and reserved manner prove to bring you the greatest successes, in my estimation, although when you combine this with your shrewd "business sense", even your more "speculative" undertakings often prove gratifying, indeed!

It appears to me that younger people frequently play a fortunate role in your interests, probably because of your own youthful attributes that make you aware of the wisdom that might be contained in their opinions.

Although you probably prefer to keep your quite sensitive emotions hidden, insofar as possible, you have, in all likelihood, a basically sentimental nature that shines forth admirably in creative endeavors, or hobbies, in which you can pour forth your innermost impressions with little restraint. Dramatic talent is frequently a marked aptitude in people of your decan, which may be a reason why many professionally enter various fields of entertainment, or become active participants in amateur theatre, where they seem to be as effective "behind-the-scenes" as on stage. This quality may also be an underlying secret of success for many of the proficient athletes born in this decan.

Travel and other "mass-communications" are likely to have strong appeal for you, probably because you know that these give wider scope to your outstanding qualities. I am confident that when you give consideration to other people and your own well-being, and you COORDINATE your energies, you will have growing peace of mind. Through the constructive direction of your extraordinary abilities, you will find doors that lead to the realization of your cherished hopes — and I feel that the keys for opening these doors lie in "universal love" you can give to dispel darkness in a troubled world, and in the gratification you will thus richly receive.

You have ideals many people would consider "unusual" or especially "futuristic", in my opinion, owing to a keen intuition that prompts you to know, sometimes without knowing quite how you know, that the possibilities for better serving Humanity are boundless, provided only that these first be envisioned and then turned to tangible advantages. Your inherent inquisitiveness might give an appearance of unpredictability to your true goals and objectives, from time to time, although your basic aims are no doubt resourceful, logical, and perhaps somewhat ingenious.

I think that the development of a stronger faculty for steady application holds for you many of the solutions for making your life one of remarkable accomplishment, in the area you earnestly choose — but because I trust that you endeavor to make this a permanent condition in carrying out your daily routines, I anticipate that you will no longer regard happiness as a destination, but as a DAILY way of travel!

Aries

April 11-April 20
Ruled by Venus

3rd decan

The Sun having been in the third decan of Aries at the time of your birth, I believe you have a warm and pleasant disposition, with strong preference for everything representative of harmony and beauty. This characteristic "refinement" probably gives you a keener awareness of your personal appearance and presentation than many people have, and inclines you toward investigations into "self-improvement" fields, (such as those designed to fortify one's ability to public speaking) which you then put into practice in carrying out your daily routines.

Lofty ambitions are likely to comprise a second, and equally powerful, part of your nature — and because your desire for realizing these aspirations is combined with the necessary capabilities for making them realities in your life, conflicts may occasionally arise between these and some of your "domestic" objectives, giving you the feeling that your endeavors bring less fulfillment than you would really like. Coordination between the ethereal and material is imperative to your true happiness, in my opinion, and when you place these qualities in balance with one another, you are almost certain to enjoy a growing sense of peace.

You are inwardly likely to gain a feeling of "complete-ness" only when you consider yourself in close association, or "partnership", with other people — although you may occasionally act against your own better interests by keeping such relationships apart from the most "public" areas of your life, or centering so much of your attention on "outer activi-ties" that anonymities inadvertently begin to develop that then require correction.

Being secretly impressionable, you may tend to form attachments with a certain degree of impulse, from time to time, but as a general rule, those you amply consider in ad-vance prove more gratifying. When you display an amiable and generous manner, people who truly have your better interests at heart are almost bound to enter your life, and I believe they substantially aid your progress. You probably prefer individuals who have enthusiasm at least equal to your own, but it may seem to you that these expectations are satisfied all too rarely.

You may once have tended to "skim the surfaces" of many subjects, but I think your desire for penetrating deeply specialized endeavors is now keener. Art, poetry, sports, music and entertaining pursuits are likely to have strong appeal for you, but you are apt to be uncomfortable around people who seem to you less or more knowledgeable than you are. This characteristic tendency of people born in the third decan of Aries makes educational furtherment so im-portant as to become a necessity, in my opinion, yet I have noticed that it is seldom attained easily. An unusual degree of "commuting" is occasionally required, while opportunities for training on a college level often appear limited to indi-viduals born in your decan — but because they recognize that "where there is a will, there is a way", they frequently sur-mount even seemingly impossible obstacles that temporarily stall their efforts, going on to unquestionable accomplish-ments.

Frequent changes may mark your "home and family" life, upon occasion, but I think that you have quite well-defined "domestic" inclinations. A fondness for children is one of your more outstanding qualities, no doubt — and while to some degree your associations with them may seem to you a disappointment, or YOU MAY HAVE HEAVY BURDENS IN THIS AREA OF YOUR LIFE, your active participation in the betterment of younger people's lives is almost certain to meet with success.

I believe that you strive for a sense of permanency in your financial interests, with the future security of your loved-ones your prime concern, yet it is likely that a true sense of satisfaction with your holdings, or assets, is less easy for you to attain than for some individuals. I have known many people born in this decan who always felt that they could have "gone farther" in the world if they had enjoyed better circumstances — but I am confident you are grateful for what you have, and that you assuredly move forward, certain that your efforts will become more and more gainful. When you hold this constructive outlook, I know you find conditions surrounding your interests steadily improve, often through "gifts" or other courtesies extended by other people, who appreciate your kindness toward them.

You are apt to approach your material affairs with a certain intensity you hope will earn more stable securities, taking a somewhat more restrained, practical and steadfast view of your holdings than many people would have — because I'm sure you aren't the parsimonious type one so often meets among those born in this decan, who actually bring denials, restrictions and limitations upon themselves, owing to their "fearfulness" of financial failure and resulting hesitancy to share what they have as generously as they might. "Speculative" investments, or some field that is "chancy" will probably touch your life to some degree. A conservative approach to these areas will serve you better than a more impulsive one, in my opinion, as will placement of funds into "fixed" or "long-term" enterprises.

People of your decan usually receive "public recognition" with seemingly little effort, but I think this is because you display an essential restraint, approaching your major interests with a basic reserve that earns admiration from people who hold "authoritative" positions and assures others that you will manage undertakings capably through an enterprising ability you will use in practical lines. There are occasionally people who have birthdays near yours who feel too inhibited to express themselves according to their true abilities, and this brings them to approach their "outside interests" too slowly for real accomplishment, or to display so much "self-centeredness" that they lose opportunities for improving their reputation — but when they learn to be less worrisome, holding faith in themselves and hopefulness for their futures, their "standing" invariably increases, bringing favorable notice and even pleasing "honors" their way.

You probably have a strong sense of self-respect that makes you more aware than many individuals of the advantages to be found in serving well the interests of other people and maintaining efficient routines in your daily practices. For this reason, you may have quite gratifying associations with persons who share your usual surroundings, although it is likely to disturb your sense of productivity when those around you appear to "talk unnecessarily", or to chat with one another at times when you believe there are more important matters to attend. This might well be one of your more notable characteristics: That little things often please or displease you with far greater intensity than many which would to anyone else seem larger. You may have observed that a thoughtful gesture on another person's part frequently touches you much more deeply, because of its heartfelt meaning, than even quite grandiose displays.

In health matters, you are apt to realize substantial benefits by cultivating constructive mental concepts of the perfect conditions you earnestly seek, in the knowledge that nothing unfavorable can penetrate to where you are unless you give it a channel in your thoughts first — and in your thoughts I trust that there is room only for concepts of improvement. It very often seems that the majority of ailments that disturb people of this decan, result from nervousness, although a more serene outlook generally insures continuing physical betterment. While you are basically likely to enjoy a "strong constitution", it may appear to maintain itself in a somewhat delicate balance, reliant upon sensible habits that include sufficient rest and moderation in food and drink.

In choosing your associates, you are often likely to prefer the society of people who hold somewhat dispassionate views along imaginative lines. Although some such individuals may occasionally prove to be a little bit more erratic or unpredictable than you would really prefer, I think that the majority of people you call "friends" are courteous, and just detached enough to respect the privacy you value so highly. In all probability you have an aversion to taking your "business problems home with you", so to say, dividing quite distinctly your usual "day-to-day" activities and your "personal life". I feel that your acquaintances frequently are responsible for supplying you with some of your more progressive, or far-reaching, ideas — not necessarily by suggesting them to you directly, but, rather, by saying or doing the very thing that starts the "wheels of your mind" spinning toward newer channels of endeavor. Although many of your attachments are apt to be somewhat fleeting, you long remember the contributions they have made to your life, in all probability, yet this is rarely due to any real sentimentality, rationalism, or emotionalism, resulting more from an objective outlook that reminds you that even less pleasing experiences provide something you can learn, when you earnestly seek to know what these lessons might be.

Owing to this characteristic, you probably become more receptive and sensitive with each passing year, which gives you a stronger awareness of benefits that can be found in an harmonious "domestic" life filled with tradition and "hearthside warmth". When you display openly the sincerity of these inner feelings, showing how very much you truly cherish the people who complete the more satisfying conditions within and around you, you are almost bound to earn growing contentment with your immediate surroundings, combined with a deepening perception. By finding peace within yourself, you will surely create greater tranquility in your environment, as well — and, thus, I anticipate that you will continue to play a larger role in the mainstream of the world's activity as a result of the sense of security you gain from your "home" atmosphere.

Some people born in your decan tend to become too dependent upon their domestic influences; many develop a complete interest in "self" — but I am confident that you devote your energies to the betterment of your country, as well as the circles of society you consider more "intimate". Peculiarly, however, I have noticed that individuals who are born in this third decan of Aries often have at least one experience with "a woman" they consider "problematical" during their maturing years. On the other hand, when you endeavor to improve conditions around you, your favorable returns should amply compensate you for any situations that prove contrary to your true wishes.

Many, many individuals who have birthdays close to yours are active in politics or similar "public affairs" — and they have an ability to accomplish almost phenomenal results from their efforts. I believe that you have an exceptional gift for promoting, more or less from "behind-the-scenes" even great enterprises that will aid people who are less fortunate than others. By applying some of your energies to activities that will benefit hospitals and similar institutions, or give comfort to singular individuals who are "confined", I am sure that you will earn in return growing inspiration that will spark some of your finest successes.

I strongly believe that all you seek, which is right for you to have, will become yours when you make a practice of looking for "the good" you can find; praising that good in your thoughts; blessing every person who touches your life, as you would someone greatly loved . . . then, goals you envision will increasingly become realities in your daily living; peace, harmony, love and happiness will be surely within you, as well as in your surroundings.

There is little doubt that you hold certain viewpoints that are sometimes considered "too idealistic" by a few of your associates — but I think that you have your own reasons for these attitudes, because you inwardly know that lofty ideals are the first objective necessary to achievement of better circumstances. I believe that you understand that you are the dreamer, and not the dream. Thus, your knowledge should be serene that you do not have to bow to circumstances. YOU create and control the circumstances which surround you, in my opinion, and you have every necessary capability for making these circumstances at least as perfect as even your more towering concepts!

Taurus

April 21- April 30
Ruled by Mercury

 **1st decan**

Of the three decans of Taurus, I consider yours the most "mental" and flexible prompting you to have a fondness for travel and new experiences, to such an extent that you are frequently apt to learn more from these than actual study. I believe that you like to feel you are "communicating" with the world as an active participant in its ideas; its wisdom, and in the planting of "firm roots" that will better serve Mankind in the future. You are rarely likely to act on impulse, because you no doubt prefer to think things through in advance before jumping to conclusions. Some people who were born in this decan carry this characteristic to an extreme, becoming stubborn or too set in their ways from time to time, but I am confident that you make an earnest effort to accept newer ideas and other opinions with the same degree of open-mindedness you like for YOURS to receive, recognizing that these may well prove helpful to your own interests. I think that you try to maintain a realistic approach to your personal affairs, managing them with as much thoroughness and deliberation as you can, and trying to do the things that seem to you most sensible under the circumstances in which you find yourself. Because these qualities are usually combined with a particularly attractive personality, most Taureans who have birthdays near yours are known for their "salesmanship", having not only the "know-how" for convincing people who come to touch their lives, but also for earning their trust.

In all probability, the majority of your efforts are motivated by material concerns, because financial security is especially important to you. You are likely to have a strong sense of responsibility as a "provider" for people close to you, or toward whom you feel a duty, although you are apt to display a great deal of patience, even when it takes you longer than you would really like to solidly develop, for time yet to come, as much freedom from financial doubt as possible. This is probably one of the reasons why people born in your decan almost invariably grow to a stage where they enjoy more than one source of income, and show more than ordinary versatility in their manner of accumulating assets. Transactions and personal "manipulation" of large undertakings may mark some of your major activity. You are no doubt alert to opportunities; curious and responsive to circumstances favorable for your purposes that you might find within them. I know Taureans of your decan who hold interests or possibly stocks in communications fields — AND enterprises having to do with the air AND artistic pursuits AND real estate, property or mining. The combination of manual and mental dexterity not infrequently brings them into athletics, such as trapeze artistry, that require absolute precision between the mental alertness as it is conveyed in physical response. THE SAME "PRECISION" HOLDS TRUE TO WHATEVER THEIR VOCATION OR AVOCATION MAY BE.

Duplication of possessions may sometimes seem to others one of your "idiosyncrasies", but I feel that this is due to your belief that if something serves you well, TWO can serve you twice as well — and might bring DOUBLE value later on. Associates are often likely to consider you "lucky" in your financial affairs. It is true that the regard you earn from other people may lead to "inheritances" or other very welcome "windfalls", upon occasion, and that however uncertain your material outlook might be SOMETHING always seems to "come through" for you at the last mintue – but in all probability you make your "luck" by advancing your interests in such ways that at least one benefit will always be available when you feel a need for its use. In emergencies, you are apt to put all your resources together in an effort to find constructive solutions – and, because you seek, you do, indeed, find that which you seek. You are very likely to be as adept at managing other people's financial interests as your own, although in this capacity you probably act with somewhat less optimism and more practicality, owing to the responsibility you feel toward their concerns. "Speculative" enterprises may also appeal to you rather strongly, and earn for you in return quite gratifying results – although I believe that you find useful and "down-to-earth" undertakings more attractive than many others.

In spite of a basic "fixity" you are almost certain to display in carrying out the majority of your activities, sufficient diversity and change which seem to you imperative to your true happiness, in my estimation, and, aside from your inherent aversion to a sense of "confinement", variety is essential to your well-being. When people of your decan permit the "scales" that weigh their daily routines to become over-balanced in one direction or another they frequently respond by losing their feeling of having emotional equilibrium – and for this reason, your true fulfillment is dependent upon your pursuit of interests that satisfy a wish for accomplishment and worth in the directions of your greatest capabilities, I think.

There are times in every life when one feels somewhat less "composed" than usual – and when you respond to these by making pleasing visits or extending a little kindness to people you feel will benefit from your help, you are apt to gain a growing sense of contentment. When you hold steadfastly to thoughts of peace, harmony, love and happiness, "within you" and in all conditions surrounding your life, I am certain that these will quickly become permanent conditions in your life. With inner calm as your guideline, I feel that you will take greater pride in your achievements, and earn in return the gainful results they deserve.

Deep within your spirit is a strong feeling for humanity, in my estimation, which enables you to take rather far-reaching views on its behalf. In this respect, however, it is probably easier for you to recognize ways of promoting a more comfortable, or "luxurious" existence than purely "scientific" or "mathematical" advancement — but this is because of your own deep appreciation of all those things that make life more enjoyable. In all probability, you sincerely try to approach your more "public" interests with geniality, but at the same time you maintain a clear-sighted-ness that enables you to remain "detached" from involvements you consider "binding". For this reason, you no doubt enjoy greater successes when you feel that you are somewhat "on your own", because the formation of too close "partnerships" frequently seems to deprive you of your usual adaptability and restricts a few of your broader objectives, bringing dissensions which occasionally could become quite serious, in your opinion.

You may tend to select associates who appear courageous and earn your admiration for their devotion to "matters at hand", owing to a feeling that they will encourage you to find better direction in your pursuits, although the promotion of harmony is particularly important, in order for you to feel that you maintain your own personal expression, as well as "a sense of trust". I believe that at least one person has appeared revengeful toward you — and that you were the last to learn of this situation. It will always be helpful for you to protect your better interests with somewhat more discretion than many people would, to avert any possibilities of being accused of something you haven't done, as this happens to individuals born in your decan now and then.

Although you may give an impression of being convivial, you are apt to have a certain degree of reclusiveness to your nature that makes your "privacy" more appealing with each passing year. When you balance this tendency with equal effort to have occasions that include the society of other people in your activities, you should reach a pleasing "middle ground" which is favorable for purposes you hope to accomplish. You are likely to feel an "obligation" toward individuals who seem less fortunate than you are, or to offer your own strength and cheerfulness to those whose outlook is less optimistic — but it appears to me that with this as the basis of many of your acquaintances, they all too often prove a disappointment to you. When you learn from the lessons any such experiences teach you, I am confident you will gain a wisdom that holds vast rewards for the great inspiration you contribute to those who are "confined", or in need of a cheerful word.

Sometimes, your true wishes probably seem simpler to choose than achieve — or, rather, many appear decided for you through opportunities in directions other than those you originally anticipated. While I consider these "swerving points" in your life more advantageous than otherwise, they can distract you from your original intentions, leaving a "vacancy" deep within you, silently implying little satisfaction with effects. Also, you may occasionally tend to stall your efforts just before you reach the threshold of success. When you concentrate your efforts upon what you have to give rather than returns, holding as a picture in your mind the exact image of what you WANT to achieve — just as it will be in its most perfect state — I know that this area of your life will improve, making your future prospects even more hopeful.

First decan Taureans like yourself are ordinarily quite discriminating and practical in their affectional relationships, although they are sometimes affected by the magnetism of others. People who have modest habits and "methodical" intellects are apt to seem especially attractive, either as social companions or in deeper alliances. You might display tastes some of your associates consider "puritanical", now and then, owing to your preferences for "quieter" forms of entertainment you can share with individuals whose refinement and reserve you admire. I think a reason for this characteristic restraint in some of your attitudes is a certain shyness in your disposition that prompts you to hold at "arms length" many possibilities of too deep attachments.

These qualities are often likely to reflect in your management of younger people. You no doubt have a fondness for children, but you are more apt to approach them with logic and reason, than by being overly sympathetic, accomplishing what you intend on their behalf quietly and unobserved, with a display of few pretensions. You should enjoy quite gratifying alliances with individuals who are younger than you, provided that you encourage them to use their own resources, instead of over-supplying their material wants.

I have noticed that people of your decan very rarely encounter the obstacles some persons meet in trying to advance their knowledge. Even in situations where all else appears to fail, scholarships and similar aids are almost invariably received, or near relatives offer their help. This is occasionally against their better interests, however, when it discourages spiritual development that often results from needing — and having to seek — answers to some of life's more pressing problems. I feel assured that YOU place your personal values far above the material plane, even though you are probably more conservative than emotional in your viewpoints; therefore, I anticipate that your efforts will continue to become not only more gainful, but productive, as well.

You may already have noticed that whenever you are anxious to settle "issues", or close matters you have pending in your mutual activities, delays very frequently occur that temporarily stall them, preventing you from reaching the agreement you anticipated as quickly as you first expected. By making advance preparations for such eventualities, you ought to be able to avert many of the more "limiting" phases of your endeavors.

I have observed among my friends who have birthdays near yours that they are inclined to cherish their relationships with such people as brothers and sisters, cousins, or certain neighbors with more sincerity than many individuals. This might be characteristic of you, too. I feel sure you enjoy a popularity among people in "neighboring areas", when you endeavor to find it, which brings others to seek from you "maternal or paternal advice" regarding their problems, in return for your protective sensibilities toward them. Pure "domesticity", as such, is less likely to lead you to complete contentment. In my estimation, you have high regard for the responsibilities you think your home surroundings imply, but you have moods from time to time when you consider these "RESTRICTIVE" TO A FEW OF YOUR MORE MAGNANIMOUS OBJECTIVES. Your outlook in this respect may result from a parent, guardian, or certain circumstance you thought overly-strict, or similarly a restraining influence upon you, during your earlier years.

By centering more of your attention on philosophical, religious, legal or educational concepts that will serve to continually strengthen your faith, you will soon hear the knock of "opportunity" upon the door to your future — and you need only to open it, to find the abundant successes, I know, awaits!

Taurus

May 1-May 10
Ruled by Moon

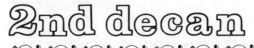

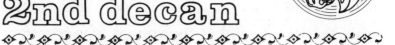

I consider your decan of Taurus one of the most reliable of any, because people born under its influence, as you were usually establish "the course" they will follow, and then display real determination in their will to attain their objectives. Disliking change, you are sometimes apt to await with apparent indifference the rap of opportunity — but when you "hear" its friendly sound, I believe you patiently move forward toward success, in spite of any and all obstacles. You are less likely to act on impulse than to plod along with patience, devoting much time and effort to the accomplishment of both your ideals and ambitions, and preferring to "think things over", or "sleep on them", in advance of making definite plans, decisions or agreements. This inclination for you to have slow response to impressions may bring occasional misunderstandings with people you know — because instead of showing intense reactions to new circumstances that come to your attention, you no doubt absorb them, carefully reflecting upon any apparent alternatives within the depths of your mind until, perhaps several days later, you feel you have come to your conclusions. Startling news is likely to produce very little, if any, display of excitement or distress at the time it reaches you — although you might have a great deal to say about it in days to come. Similarly, it may be some time after words are spoken to you before you begin to feel anger or appreciation with respect to them, or occasions in which you participate are long past before you think of the most appropriate retort for comments made to you.

These tendencies may bring you into occasional encounters with people who consider that you are one of the easiest of all individuals of whom to take advantage. In actuality, I feel that there is a definite "tolerance point" to your good disposition that can never be crossed. With kindness and gentleness, you will unfailingly give your complete cooperation and benevolence — but when you think you've been "pushed", you are apt to react in a stubborn anger with intensity equal to your sustainment in every other situation, a characteristic that makes it imperative for every person of your decan to develop the POWER OF FORGIVENESS.

Yours is apt to be an artistic and peace-loving nature that values the convenience of "luxury" and takes pride in the sense of achievement you earn through good, hard work. This may give other people an impression that you have an almost indefatigable endurance and perfect self-possession, because you are rarely apt to become distracted from your goals, or to frivolously throw "caution to the wind" in a moment of impetuosity. When you make a commitment, I'm sure you have every intention of keeping it; therefore, you promptly meet your engagements and can be depended upon to give in full measure whatever you've previously promised, even when the ultimate result proves a "hardship" to you, personally, or your return for a "guarantee" must finally come "out of your own pocket", so to say. Some of your greater disappointments no doubt result from a discovery that another person has acted with less integrity than you, yourself, would have attempted in the same situation.

The "fly now, pay later" plan probably appeals to you very little. Long-term security is important to you, I am certain — and you always feel uncomfortable in situations without a predetermined outcome. In all likelihood, you are something of a "do-it-yourselfer", preferring to see to matters personally rather than delegate them to other individuals whose methods are less well known to you. When you do place your trust in another, it is apt to be complete, because you will base your conclusions on experience, in assurance that good past performance will bring at least equal returns again and again. The fixity of your approach may sometimes hold you to patterns of living a few associates refer to as "ruts", because you no doubt incline to remain with those things and people who have proven their worthiness in time gone by, preferring the same simple foods day after day and following an identical route to any given place, even during temporary inconveniences, such as "construction" or changing weather conditions. You like to conduct your daily routines according to unmodified schedules; you would rather have one true friend than a hundred acquaintances — and you feel greater pride in a "small" accomplishment you can say you've attained on your own than in far more massive achievements that are "handed" to you by someone else. It surely takes great convincing to bring you to change brands of products you use, or experiment in territory unfamiliar to you — which is a reason why you alter your habits less easily than many individuals, in my opinion.

Once you formulate a purpose, you will persist in your original intention no matter how wrong you may be proven to be, resenting any intrusion, however well meaning, in your affairs. Provided you recognize "blank walls" when you come to them, this characteristic is more of an asset than defect, because it is almost certainly combined with a particularly placid and charming personality that earns great admiration from people who come to touch your life, and wins from those who know you, lasting faith, in your ability to responsibly "produce" in a manner parallel to your promises.

You are apt to find more personal expression when you arrange your routines with allowance for a certain degree of "independence" from close direction — and, provided you have a "home base" to which you can return, some travel is likely to be compatible with your regular practices. Slow, romantic music (such as the "old favorites"), as well as singing, may be so "therapeutic" in its effect upon you that it seems to dissolve almost any pressures you tend to feel, enabling you to view more truthfully "cares of the moment". You might find that sleep also brings you to a better awareness of correct solutions, or even appears to "cure" many temporary ailments, when you take it in abundance at their onset.

The early environment of people born in your second decan of Taurus is extremely influential in the values you are likely to carry into your more mature years, because you are seldom apt to succeed in efforts to shake off the fundamentals of your family training, ideals and tradition.

Although you are apt to dislike "idleness", insofar as possible you will design the course of your life in such a manner that your necessary activities will interfere as little as possible with your secure enjoyment of what you consider the "good things" for which you have a fondness. Of all things which might be abhorrent to you, the thought of taking a cold bath or shower is probably one of the first. I'm sure you prefer to be in a position that requires little budget for food, entertainment, and pleasing surroundings — yet you'll gladly make even seemingly enormous sacrifices when it seems necessary to do so, in order that these privileges can become a more enduring part of your future.

Some people may find it hard to fathom your mental processes — but I believe that you are ordinarily, exceptionally diplomatic; sometimes shrewd, canny, taciturn and inquisitive. You are quite apt to devote your energies to enterprises that will bring financial security — and while I have observed that the "upward climb" of individuals born in your decan is frequently a somewhat difficult one, bringing at least one phase when property owned is threatened to be taken away through loss of employment, difficulty through a member of the family or similar circumstances. Realistic application along constructive lines usually results in satisfying agreements or outcomes. It very often happens that people of your decan over-reach themselves in some area of their lives and so fall victims to their own plotting — but I am confident that YOU approach your interests more realistically, and thus enjoy gratifying returns.

You are apt to display a certain duplicity in your acquisitions, having more than "one" of the same types of possession, and maintaining a position that will bring income from more than one source. Oddly, in view of your steadfast qualities, your material technique is occasionally likely to be somewhat thin, owing to intermittent efforts that do not always bind. When you strive for quality rather than quantity, in developing your assets, and you use the same sense of caution you exercise in most of your other interests, you will probably continue to achieve the most gainful returns. Investments into holdings that offer permanency may appeal to you rather strongly — such as real estate, mining, construction, banking or farming. You might have a particular affinity for industries originating from "earthly" sources, possibly because you like to have your own "feet on the ground", and feel an inherent appreciation of enterprises that have either direct relationship to the land's natural resources, or the growth of prosperity for the world's fellow inhabitants.

- 125 -

Every decan has both its strengths and weaknesses, and a fair analysis could not be made without our considering one as well as the other. Until they are overcome, the faults that must often prove detrimental to the best efforts of people of your decan are PRIDE AND STUBBORN-NESS. Because I trust that you earnestly endeavor to remain flexible to other opinions, adopting better, or more advanced methods when trends indicate that it is advisable for you to do so — and you take a "helping hand" with the same sense of gratitude and compassion you have when you offer another your aid — you substantially improve your prospects of realizing continual promotion of conditions that concern you, thus increasing your promise of attaining from your endeavor greater and more lasting satisfaction.

In my estimation, you inherently feel that your whole life's purpose evolves out of a tranquil "domestic" situation — and unless you fulfill this inner need by joining your efforts with those of associates who can appreciate your finer qualities and thus give purpose to your daily activities, you are apt to feel somewhat "lost at sea", functioning with little sense of reason, and conducting your interests "mechanically" rather than with heart-felt enthusiasm.

Because I believe that you earnestly endeavor to contribute to the happiness of those around you in at least equal measure to that which you receive, and to prove yourself a good provider with respect to your own responsibilities to an association, I anticipate that your closest alliances will usually prove highly rewarding. I have friends who share birth in your decan of Taurus who attribute their major successes to the steadying "guidance" of at least one particular "business partner", while they almost invariably establish better-than-average marriages that often serve as examples for many of their acquaintances. Even unhappy experiences are frequently followed by relationships that prove more rewarding.

I think that this is because your loyalties and affections are intensely deep, bringing you to place them "forever" in a true spirit of wishing to "love, honor and cherish until death". Close associations with "flighty" or highly impulsive individuals are likely to disturb your sense of balance, while it is also more necessary for you than many people to bring into your life persons who share your points of view with respect to issues you consider most important. Many, many of my friends of this decan display little interest in romantic attachments over many years — but when they feel that they have discovered the "right person", they are inclined to respond with such a surprising intensity that some of them almost "frighten away" the very individual they are most anxious to win! Once they know they are victorious in their pursuit, however, they settle into a placid adoration that they'll gladly "announce to the world", and it becomes the foundation for everything upon which their futures will rest.

In your management of younger people, you are apt to be a strong disciplinarian, but because you combine your practical approach with a display of great affection, you are likely to realize from at least one such person who touches your life, some of your greatest fulfillment in compensation for another who brings some disappointment.

In all probability, you have strong preferences for beautiful and spacious surroundings. Even when your having these proves less practical than a more utilitarian residence, you are likely to reconcile yourself to even sizable inconveniences in order that you can live in a manner more to your true liking. I have known individuals of your decan who carry this to an extreme, sometimes passing up greater opportunities, merely because these would require of them relocation in areas or climates they consider less suitable than those they presently have, although such decisions are almost invariably followed by deep regrets. When you want anything, I believe that you intend to acquire it. The strength of this conviction may be a reason why people born in this second decan of Taurus often meet with the "problem" of "inheriting" a home or property in a distant location that causes temporary conflicts with respect to holdings they already possess. It seems strange, but someone born in December and another person born in June is often apt to play a dominant role in a Taurus native's life.

Second decan Taureans, like yourself, usually REALIZE their most cherished hopes and wishes — and when you use your wonderful inherent characteristics to the fullest, I feel certain that you will, too.

Taurus

May 11-May 22
Ruled by Saturn

3rd decan

This third decan of Taurus ordinarily indicates a methodical and stable person, as you may be, who displays a great deal of constructiveness in undertakings and endurance in carrying them through. You are apt to be somewhat less optimistic than many Taureans, but when you make a practice of viewing life more cheerfully, giving equal consideration to benefits you can realize for other people as well as for yourself, you no doubt earn abundant admiration and respect, not only for your firm character, but your steadiness and patience, also. I believe that you hold steadfastly to your purposes or beliefs, although this quality is such a well developed part of your nature that it is sometimes seemingly impossible for you to discard those that come to have little use.

You are rarely likely to display great ostentation — instead, you silently work with persistence, method and solidity until you reach whatever goals you have set. Being patient and economical, you probably conduct yourself with such system and prudence that you create an impression of being serious, calm, grave and faithful. I have known individuals born in this decan who tended to be brooding, sullen, stern, gloomy and severe at times; who were greedy in food or drink or other areas of their life, or who exercised little control over their physical appetites that their materialism overshadowed their more excellent attributes — but because I trust that YOU are careful and saving without begrudging areas of your life that bring slower returns than you would really like, I'm sure you receive favorable recognition for your penetrating mind, worldly wisdom and persistence, combined with a practical ability that brings other people to consider you worthy of honor and credit.

It is very, very rare to find moral instability among individuals born in your decan, but it does happen where certain planets other than the Sun have a dominant influence. You are apt to set an unbreakable "code" by which you intend to guide your life — and, at times when someone else might frivolously turn away from even great opportunities in silly and light-minded pursuits, YOU show that YOU are capable of overcoming obstacles by sheer determination.

Circumstances in their earlier environment often prove somewhat limiting to people who have birthdays near yours, making a "slower start" than many individuals would have, and developing a seriousness of mind which appears overly mature for a young age. Health problems, such as sore throats, frequently add further restrictions. Through high school age, a number of changes ordinarily affect education, although I have noticed that at least one woman is usually strongly influential over this period of the third decan Taurean's rearing, owing to her innate understanding of the sensitivity and domesticity which is ordinarily characteristic of such children, giving them a fondness for tradition and family unity.

Even though your reaction to newer situations is occasionally slow and uncertain, I feel that you possess a keen receptivity; your senses reflect with extreme accuracy the impressions presented to them. Perhaps there are times when you consider yourself almost too perceptive — and when you made your first adjustments to these tendencies, I think you occasionally met with misunderstandings or tended to "blame yourself" for events that happened which you had previously anticipated, sometimes wondering whether your own imaginings actually caused them. This, no doubt, led you to mask some of your more delicate sensibilities. Even today, you are occasionally likely to act as if you think one thing when you really think another, and to otherwise cover a few of the more fragile effects produced upon your mind. In your more formative years, you may well have found "a need" for discerning carefully what you would share more openly with others and what you would prefer to keep to yourself, although people such as close relatives or "neighbors" gained some of your trusts, as they probably do now.

You are apt to maintain a rather reserved and practical attitude toward your spiritual, educational, political, philosophical and religious concepts. While I believe you have quite definite opinions regarding these, many of which result from your "post high school age" experiences, and because you hold these viewpoints devoutly, finding within them growing strength, it may be somewhat antagonistic for you to discover in your associations people who hold different opinions on the same subjects. This is a reason why I consider it imperative that you develop within your relationships mental understanding, based on similar outlooks.

In my opinion, you are happiest when you feel that you can give constructive outlets to your practical energies, because your capacity for hard work is one of your strongest characteristics. Although you may incline "TO NEGLECT SOME MATTERS", surely you are able to temporarily then "PLUNGE IN" AND ACCOMPLISH THEM ALL AT ONCE, approach interests that concern you with little emotional impulse or veering toward sentimentality, when these have to do with your more material and "public" activities. Now and then you may encounter people who think that you are selfishly preoccupied with your own interests rather than sympathy toward others. In actuality I doubt that this is so; it is merely that you tend to stress your mental sensitivity rather than the emotional, owing to your nervous awareness toward every passing impression. In many ways you are probably something of an idealist, inwardly concerned with the needs of humanity and ways of aiding its progress. You might display spurts of vivaciousness, or even some enthusiasm and excitability at times, though your disposition is ordinarily steadier, seldom inclining to extremes.

With all of your usual conservatism, a marked unconventionality of temperament that stamps your over-all approach is sometimes likely to baffle people who are in your close association. Some may even consider your methods "eccentric", now and then. I attribute this to a desire to live according to your own standards rather than those designed by other people, although great degrees of independence rarely serve your interests as well as those that enable you to make use of people and things that aid and balance your efforts, because these almost invariably benefit your undertakings in abundance.

In carrying out your daily routines, you probably display many sympathetic, charitable and just qualities, which earn for you admiration from those who wish to respond by advancing your interests even further. I believe that you make an earnest effort never to betray a confidence — and should you inadvertently do so, it would only result from the confusion of the moment. By nature, I feel that you are a builder, with a simple good judgment that is sensible as well as inspired. For this reason, your popularity is almost always promised in situations where dispassionate judgment is a factor, and your efforts can be helped by comradeship and association. You are also likely to display more than an ordinary degree of talent for mathematics and other mechanical pursuits. Many, many expert judges, bankers and realtors belong to your decan of Taurus.

I am quite sure you have known at least one time when assets and possessions seemed less easy to acquire than you preferred, or when those you had appeared to "waste away" — but owing to your ability to push steadfastly forward, and conquer opposition that appears to block your way, I consider that your frugal manner will ultimately prove more of an advantage than otherwise, when you hold steadfastly to a belief that by sharing generously of what you have, your needs will always be taken care of.

You might have a tendency to expect that financial success is one of your birthrights, but you are no doubt perfectly willing to earn your way. In all probability, you feel most contented when you think that you are accomplishing these ends — and you go about them communicatively and inquisitively, displaying more adaptability than in almost any other area of your life. There may be occasions when you incline to be somewhat too diffuse in your material efforts, thus diminishing the stability of your returns. By adopting more positive policies and devoting yourself responsibly to gainful endeavors, your assets should increase quite substantially. Dual ventures are likely to have more appeal for you than those which are purely singular, because by maintaining more than one dominant interest, you increase your prospects for acquiring from multiple sources, that can counterbalance one another during less promising "times". When you become involved in other people's financial concerns, you endeavor to prove that you are trustworthy, in my estimation, generally acting with thrift. On the whole, your larger returns are more likely to come from expenditure of your own time, energy and resources than those of other people, while there are strong indications that at least once you'll assume financial responsibility for other individuals.

The society of other people may bring to the fore, your sympathies more often than genuine compatibility, leading you to approach this area of your life in a rather faint-hearted manner, owing to inner misgivings based on timidity or reluctance. On the other hand, certain acquaintances may remember you for some of your more valorous deeds. You have surely known some individuals who secretly "work against" your better interests while appearing to offer their "friendship" — but when your own feelings are magnanimous, such people generally fail to accomplish their purposes. In this respect, however, I must conclude that a few acquaintances you know well and are fond of, usually prove more satisfying for you than larger circles of "casual" associates.

I have great confidence that you endeavor to realize inspiring objectives and to maintain harmonious relationships; therefore, there is little reason for me to mention "the difficulties" people of your third decan of Taurus encounter when they indulge in "excessive behavior" in a certain area of their personal life or dissensions.

People born around your birthday ordinarily form their romantic attachments around mental companionship, because they have high regard for cultural entertainment and individuals who display intelligent, prudent characteristics. In more serious "partnerships", they frequently experience deeper feelings that are stimulated by great magnetic charm. I think you want to devote yourself with staunch faithfulness to one person, although jealousies and similar hurtful situations might arise upon occasion. When you take measures to avert misalliances, you are likely to realize exceptionally favorable returns from your closest relationships.

In your management of children and younger people, you are apt to be somewhat practical and analytical, but your successes are often dependent upon your displaying more openly your true affection and minimizing some of your more critical findings.

I have frequently observed that the domestic lives of third decan Taureans are turbulent, and finding a reason is difficult, because I feel that you cherish the thought of love and happiness. It appears to me that you will have little difficulty in any interest that concerns you when you earnestly determine that you will continue to develop the qualities of vivid warmth and generosity that are inherently yours, instead of giving play to the obstinacy and haughtiness that so often becomes, among individuals of your decan, a way of asking for greater understanding from associates. Many display arrogant and dominating characteristics to those who share their "home environment" — and while you and I know that this is only because they feel that their other efforts to earn appreciation they seek have proved inadequate in the past, I'm sure we also realize that this approach rarely brings gratifying results.

Everyone born in your decan will find it beneficial to take more than the usual number of precautionary measures against fires in their immediate surroundings, in my opinion.

I believe that you are a person who wishes more with each passing year to act according to open and honest methods, and to respond to "problems" with indomitable courage. I know that you sincerely try to be a model of vigor and grace; to take pride in and give splendor to your work, and to let your more good-natured qualities serve as an example for those around you, in breadth of action and kindness of expression. Thus, I anticipate that you will continue to find growing happiness, love, contentment and peace.

Gemini

May 23-May 31
Ruled by Mercury

Your decan of Gemini is known for its adaptability. Almost without exception, people born under its influence display more than an ordinary degree of broad-mindedness, curiosity and mental restlessness or changeability; a ready and clever wit, as well as a remarkable alertness to new situations. Of all groups of people, yours is the most shrewd and when the power of this phenomenal mind is channeled to constructive outlets, your receptivity to new ideas can be your key for opening doors to outstanding successes and achievements.

I have known individuals from every walk of life who were born in this decan, yet I feel that it can be said without qualification that they show a "super" intelligence, according to their "relative" planetary positions.

A definite dispersity is usually evident in the natures of first decan Geminis, making them some of the most charming and intriguing personalities of all people. You may notice that there are at least "two of you" inwardly pulling in different directions or finding attraction in varied pursuits. You are likely to have so many interests at the same time that it is frequently hard to choose between them: You want to go, but you can see advantages in staying at home; you care a great deal for someone, but, on the other hand, you are awfully fond of someone else, too; you are happy about a certain thing, yet sad about another. This characteristic variability sometimes makes it seem that people of your decan run "hot and cold" in the same breath, although the real reason is probably that you simply find it too distracting that there are so many different things going on at once — and you would like to participate in every single one of them.

Although you have surely learned that it is necessary for you to better coordinate your efforts, you still may find that you occasionally begin one endeavor when it suddenly dawns on you that you've forgotten to complete another; you've no sooner turned your attention to the newer one than it occurs to you that there is something else you must be sure to do, and so you move on to it — then another . . . and another . . . and unless you stop right then to continue these undertakings you originally "launched", you soon discover that your energies have become lost in a series of fitful starts which arrived at no end. This tendency is so inherent that it is really out of the question for you to try to overcome it, in my opinion — but for your sense of inner well-being, it is imperative that you CONTROL it. The way you can do this is to determine for yourself a definite set of GOALS — the first of these for the course you wish your LIFE to take; the second, with respect to your DAILY achievements. Pick out four or five objectives you INTEND to realize. You can go back and forth among these as much as you like, provided you make sure that you never turn to others beyond them until ALL OF THESE are completed according to your original aims. This practice will give you growing returns from your efforts in every condition in and surrounding your life, I believe, and as your pride of accomplishment develops, your satisfaction with your attainments and other assets will, also.

You no doubt have a superb capacity for skimming the surfaces of many different fields of knowledge, and for descriptively relating your findings to other people. Because it is usually less easy for people of your decan to remain for long periods of time with a single endeavor than it would be for some individuals, you are likely to be better suited for "transitory" endeavors, such as "selling" or short story writing, that enable you to touch upon a subject briefly and then go on to newer "scenes" of activity. I'm sure that you set as high standards for yourself as you do for other people, so there is little reason for my mentioning those first decan Geminians who do otherwise — but in all probability precision seems important to you in carrying out one's daily routines. You are apt to feel that there is a PRECISE answer to every question, or that there is a definite way of doing certain things that must be minutely exact for accuracy, which leads you to find vague generalities unusually disturbing. Some individuals become cruelly critical of associates' methods, when these differ with their own, but I trust that you conduct yourself in a manner that will serve as an admirable example others will admire and automatically want to follow. Thus, you should have fewer difficulties than many of your contemporaries in this decan.

I feel that you are especially aware of the impression you make, and that you frequently associate "success" with material prosperity. Among people born in your decan, this attitude frequently evolves out of earlier environmental conditions that bring a notion that one parent, or guardian, is limiting to personal expression, or overly strict — but this is usually due more to a dislike of anyone exercising a seeming "authority" that appears to demand of you certain codes of behavior than to actual severity of outlook on that person's part. Nevertheless, it occasionally brings individuals born around the same time you were to expect that other people OWE them more than they have previously known, and to find within their present possessions or holdings little more than momentary gratification. You may have observed that you want whatever you don't have, more often than not, but that when you finally attain that, which has looked so appealing, you soon feel a certain disappointment with it, wishing that you had, instead, acquired something different.

"Luxuries" probably appeal to you very strongly, making you alert to the "latest" fads and styles, and quick to try the newest brands reaching the market. Although first decan Geminians like yourself ordinarily enjoy more than ordinary success in their financial affairs — being recipient of at least one inheritance or similar most welcome endowment from another — their capacity for spending amounts even greater than they have available for their use is ordinarily stronger than ability for saving or "budgeting" for an even brighter "tomorrow". Until they learn wiser management of their time, energy and resources, this is often one of the areas of greatest dissension in close relationships. On the other hand, it is usually said that "experience is the best teacher" — and because people of your decan prefer to enjoy as many experiences as possible over any given period of time, life itself, frequently serves as your finest teacher, when you are alert to the "lessons" it has to offer you, enabling you to develop greater practical insight than almost anyone.

A "whimsical" trait may very well be yours that prompts you to venture into conversations, modes of dress, or forms of decoration a more conservative individual would sidestep — and, owing to this quality, your closest associates are rarely apt to feel able to predict in advance your actions. When you maintain a consistency by always acting according to what you know is your BEST, you should encounter few serious difficulties as you travel "life's road". I have known a number of people who have birthdays in your decan who permit themselves to be swayed strictly by the "mood of the moment", so that they radiate charm, dignity, poise and kindness when they are lifted by phases of optimism, and, conversely, let themselves go to the depths of untidiness when trends seem less cheerful. Your desire for displaying your finest characteristics in all situations is almost certain to grow when you occupy yourself with abundant interests, putting to use your marvelous creative and other talents, and participating in activities that will give adequate expression to your kaleidoscopic abilities.

The earlier years of education often represent to youngsters of your decan the very authoritarian policies I mentioned previously that are so adamantly against your "grain", bringing to the fore, a strong sense of rebellion, that is accompanied by an absolute refusal to abide by established rules and regulations, and even to learn! The primary reason for this is an inherent "fear of failure" that may occasionally hold you from participation in competitive undertakings, or bring you to display resistance for which you give other reasons (such as dislike for the stupidity of other people, or an excuse of ill health) in an effort to avert circumstances you think might challenge attributes that you "inwardly" know are more superficial than you would like others to notice. Certainly there are individuals who never mature beyond this attitude, but I have great confidence that you recognize any like tendencies and take proper steps to replace them with constructive responses that are certain to earn favorable attention.

Generally the years following "high school age" are more rewarding for people of your decan, because the independence they offer is more compatible with some of your less conventional ideals. This is ordinarily the point in a first decan Gemini life that begins to earn the greatest "scholastic" accomplishments, as well as deserved popularity. Because you are likely to be considered by some a "late bloomer", this is frequently a more "romantic" cycle that brings into focus within your own thinking the true potential you have within, for finding the degree of appreciation you feel you deserve for your more attractive characteristics, and giving scope to the more charming aspects of your personality that you have previously held in abeyance except in situations where you felt most certain of receiving approval.

Marriage and business partnerships usually seem essential

to people of your decan, although they are generally entered into for REASONS rather than deep feelings of affection. This is because love, as other people define the word, is usually more a matter of intellectual understanding, among first decan Geminians, than heartfelt emotion. You are very likely to have an illusory quality about you that makes you especially appealing to other people; like mercury, they can only get so close to you, and then you give an impression of "darting away" — coming near, yet always being somewhat beyond actual grasp. For this very reason, you are apt to find your greatest happiness in alliances that leave you "unfettered", at least to some degree, yet bring with them promise of financial and emotional security. When you base your relationships on mental understanding, choosing among your closest associates those who will remain flexible to actions or thoughts you have that seem disconnected, or promises you make with sincerity that you might inadvertently overlook later on, you are likely to enjoy quite successful results.

Although the physical constitutions of individuals of your decan are usually quite strong, emotional serenity is frequently somewhat less easy to attain. When you dismiss from your mind all thoughts of ill-health for yourself and your loved ones, turning instead to outdoor activities and other vital interests, you are apt to gain greater productivity from all of your efforts and find worthwhile solutions to any "problems" that appear to occupy your present interests.

Many Geminians of this first decan display few maternal or paternal characteristics — but when they become parents, or involve themselves with younger people, they ordinarily respond quite favorably. A feeling of accomplishment frequently seems to evolve out of these associations, providing opportunities for giving the keen cultural background you think any young person deserves as a foundation for life. You might tend to follow the "textbook rules" more often than your own intuition, but I believe that you earnestly want to be a good influence in the lives of others whose path crosses your own.

There are apt to be periods when little enmities seem to crop up. Dissensions are sometimes likely to mark your relationships with acquaintances and especially relatives or a particular in-law. Although when you make your way to circles of society that appreciate your qualities for leadership, and you strive for confidence in the position you hold to mutual activities instead of regretting honors you haven't yet achieved, your originality can give the "spark" that makes even grand successes of undertakings in which you participate and brings you into "public prominence", in recognition for all of your esteemed attributes.

The only recommendation I would make to a person of your decan is that the singular fault to be averted is that of being your own worst enemy. I have never known any Geminian of this decan who took an interest in worthwhile activities and gave freely their wonderful, wonderful, personalities, phenomenal knowledge and exceptional talent for the benefit of Mankind who was not highly esteemed and regarded by others an outstanding success. Because I hold absolute assurance that you earnestly determine that you will manage your life responsibly, putting the needs of your cherished associates before your own, I feel sure that you, too, will gain greater satisfaction with your efforts each passing year, and earn the steady advancement this constructive approach will warrant.

Gemini

June 1-June 10
Ruled by Mars

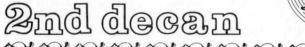

Some of your more notable characteristics are reactiveness and impulse, in my estimation. You are likely to have about you a dynamic and energetic quality which is seldom in question, your liveliness and agility giving an impression of enthusiasm for forging ahead in the world, in conquest of newer realms that will bring appreciation for your knowledge and be filled with activity. When you direct your energies to constructive pursuits, your keen, quick intellect should serve you exceptionally well in enabling you to master with almost phenomenal success more than one language, or put onto paper a few of your most honest and outspoken opinions in situations where another person might mask real facts. You may occasionally have associates who consider that this forceful approach, which is sometimes apt to be touched with SATIRICAL AND CAUSTIC COMMENTS, is little more than sheer bluntness — but because you surely modify your conclusions, giving favorable trends you think noteworthy space at least equal to those you feel are less appealing, you ought to have "a perception and insight" THAT WILL MAKE ACCURACY A KEYNOTE OF YOUR SPEECH OR WRITINGS. I have known a number of people in your decan who are highly successful in such endeavors as chemistry, aviation, science, invention, or some field where the use of words, written or spoken, were a dominant factor in their success, and I feel sure that you take an interest in these areas yourself.

There is frequently a tendency among individuals born in this decan to disperse the great force behind their energies in such ways as to become highly-strung and argumentative, depleting the great brilliance with which they are inherently endowed to outright excitability and irritability. By determining that they will develop continuity in their efforts so that they can persist with any policy they adopt, they quickly find the vast rewards to be earned by advancing with compassion, good humor, benevolence and geniality, and I have strong confidence that you endeavor to do this also. Therefore, I do not anticipate that you will display the ingratitude and wantonness which is often characteristic of this decan . . . I know that instead of useless strife your life will be filled with purpose, and that your discussions will be tempered by kindness and wisdom, proving helpful to all those who have the privilege of hearing them. Owing to this refinement in your over-all technique, you are almost certain to place your interests in worthwhile channels, and beneficially apply your very acute faculties so that you will realize from them the most profitable returns.

Being born in this second decan of Gemini, you are no doubt fond of reading, lectures, travel and similar pursuits, but you are likely to feel most expressive when you turn some of your more imaginative impressions to gainful undertakings that will increase your assets and possessions. In this regard, you are apt to display a certain disregard for actuality, from time to time, but, on the other hand, people who know you well may often consider that you have a "nose" for detecting an opportunity favorable for your purposes without being told, or quite knowing "how" you know. There are likely to be changes in your financial interests now and then, some of which RESULT FROM DISSENSIONS OVER HOLDINGS IN MUTUAL CONCERN with other individuals or "corporations", such as in taxes, insurance, estates or "partnership" funds. When you have reason to manage other people's resources, you are apt to be even more bold and ambitious than you ordinarily are with your own, sometimes preferring to "negotiate" your own interests under another's "backing" or through the use of credit.

The earlier years of education, or those generally considered introductory to the "whys and wherefores" of the world, are particularly important to people born in your decan, I have observed, owing frequently to sisters, brothers or relatives who prove helpful. Occasionally one such person will seem overbearing or intolerant, or a challenge to recognition you wish to gain on your own merit, but in many instances it appears that such alliances promote favorable notice more often than not, where your own interests are concerned. You are very apt to meet this period of your life with a full, frank and expansive outlook that earns popularity and enables you to use quite abundantly your more generous, magnanimous and theatrical attributes. Opportunities you have during this phase are sometimes likely to prove some of the most fortunate of your lifetime, owing to people you meet or appreciation you receive for your talents that you can then carry with you through the years.

You might observe that growing inquisitiveness marks the "chapter" beginning around your late teens, bringing you to take somewhat more progressive and original views from those you held before, and even to occasionally admire attitudes others think of as being "eccentric" or contrary to popular opinion. You are very likely to make important changes at this time, with respect to your personal appearance, as well as your over-all environment, while even quite radical alterations in your religious and philosophical concepts are probable. I notice that among my friends in this decan, this stage sometimes brings great intellectual concern over the needs of humanity as a whole — and, evolving out of these trends, some display of rebellion from the "childhood beliefs". When, instead, the mind is turned to science and devotion to promoting the welfare of Mankind through merciful, humane and philanthropic pursuits, this can be a "turning point" to phenomenal accomplishment that will be accompanied by lasting renown.

I believe that you take an almost obsessive interest in matters pertaining to health. Certainly there are notorious hypochondriacs among all Geminians, including those in your decan, due to the attention they feel they receive for their "complaints" and "the escape" from challenging situations these appear to provide — but because I'm sure you are above such "childish" practices, I trust that you endeavor to serve people whose physical or emotional well-being is impaired, through selfless donation of your knowledge, abilities and other resources to charitable causes. Individuals who have birthdays around the same time you do are almost invariably mechanically and mathematically inclined. When this is combined with the natural adeptness, dexterity cleverness and insight, it often provides all of the necessary ingredients for an excellent surgeon, diagnostician, researcher, lawyer or in the field of dentistry.

One of the ironies of your decan, in view of the "showy" personality one ordinarily expects to find under its influence, is that when inner confidence is developed, through a feeling of pride in genuine accomplishment that gives assurance of favorable attention without the need for ostentation and display, some of the most remarkable achievements originate "behind-the-scenes", or in "background positions" that originally are somewhat away from public notice or where the work is performed in some small space.

Individuals who have somewhat "fiery", or ambitious, temperaments are likely to number among some of your more helpful acquaintances. I believe that you often attract the notice of "authoritative" people, who admire your capabilities and are intrigued by your initiative. When you contribute generously to the harmony of your surroundings, you are apt to find among your "neighbors", or even those you consider "relatives", at least one person who will become a lasting "friend" and have the "know-how" for substantially advancing your over-all standing in circles where you are. I think you admire those who have "executive" ability, and that one of your fonder wishes is to equal or surpass their apparent competency and efficiency by discovering new "territories", or pioneering ideas that will become imperative in their usefulness.

Because I trust that you seek to contribute more to alliances you form than you are personally apt to gain, and that you refuse to let sarcasm, suspicion, criticism or revengeful practices have any part in your life, I feel that you will achieve your greatest hopes.

The romantic interests of people born in your decan usually seem somewhat slow in their development, owing, ordinarily, to inner doubts. Probably because you find tactful, particular, impartial and serious individuals especially attractive, you are apt to gravitate to at least one relationship WHERE THERE IS A RATHER REMARKABLE AGE DIFFERENCE. Since you are apt to be somewhat less creative than many Geminians you know, you may prefer for company in your entertaining pursuits individuals who display well-developed religious and philosophical temperaments, yet who seem ambitious. It occasionally happens that people who have birthdates similar to your own feel "pushed" into at least one such alliance, or experience what they consider to be a rather deep sorrow when their expectations of marriage are "fatefully" thwarted.

As a rule, you second decan Geminis are less inclined toward marriage, or feel less need for it than your contemporaries born in the first decan of this sign — but when you do select a partner (OR PARTNERS, AS IS OFTEN THE CASE) you are very likely to choose someone quite different, indeed, from the "types" you've generally appeared to select in courtship. In business relationships, as well, you are apt to have preference for optimistic, sincere, alert and cheerful associates who share your own restlessness and "duplicity" to at least some degree. Educators or individuals with heritages quite removed from your own are often likely to seem attractive to you in these alliances, while their independence is apt to disturb you little, owing to your own wish to be free from serious restrictions. Above almost any other consideration, you will probably seek a person of "affluence" — although your closest associations are usually more harmonious when you display a cooperative manner toward mutual financial interests instead of trying to dogmatically gain control, as some people will.

I believe that you feel a duty to have children, rather than a strong desire for them — yet at least one disappointment marks this area of the second decan Gemini life, or they prove less easy to have than you originally anticipated. More satisfaction is generally attained later on — sometimes through the adoption of step or foster children, and similar arrangements.

Because of the swiftness with which you are likely to carry out some of your undertakings, you may be somewhat more "accident prone" than many people. By curbing your more temperamental and impetuous impulses, you probably avert many mishaps, although individuals of your decan are more inclined to break an arm or have some affliction to the lungs than some individuals. I think you are basically endowed with great will power, when you put it to good use, which enables you to find within yourself growing peace and harmony, when you but seek.

With each passing year you will become more and more refined, cool, neat and modest in your manner and outlook, in all likelihood, although it might be advisable for you to hold your perfectionism and fussiness to a minimum. You are quite apt to be something of a "home lover", taking pride in your surroundings and being rather fastidious about hygienic practices within the maintenance of your dwelling place. It very often occurs that people of your decan decide upon a particular location they think of as "ideal" in climate and other standpoints, and this or a nearby area is where they prefer to remain insofar as their day-to-day routines are concerned. You might be more inclined than some people to hire "services" for attending to certain "household tasks", so that you can more fully enjoy some of the more "luxurious" aspects of your daily interests, while an "intellectual", or mentally stimulating environment is almost bound to have appeal for you.

In summing up the characteristics you are most apt to display, I think it important to mention that you will always benefit from your efforts to develop your sympathies so that your more tender feelings will never become overshadowed by pure mental reasoning — but when you do this, and combine it with an earnest endeavor to constructively coordinate your activity, I'm sure you'll become known for your big-hearted and generous deeds; your benevolent influence upon all who come to touch your life, as well as an extraordinary perception others call "wisdom". In return, you will achieve a growing sense of happiness, I am absolutely certain!

Gemini

June 11-June 22
Ruled by Sun

3rd decan

Your decan of Gemini is one of most desirous of giving warmth, brightness and happiness to other people, I observe, bringing you to display real kindness, sympathy and sensitivity to the feelings of those who ordinarily come to touch your life, particularly your relatives. In fact, your decan is noted for helping sisters or brothers or in-laws and afterward receiving little "thanks" for it. You might not always consider that you understand yourself as well as you do individuals you meet, although with each passing year it should become more comprehensible for you to analyze reasons behind your attitudes and behavior in such ways as to gain a stronger sense of inner solidity.

You probably have a certain degree of dignity to your personal appearance which impresses those whom you contact, this being further enhanced by a sunny disposition that makes you seem generous, proud, quick of perception, stable and firm; free, ambitious and outspoken. There are individuals born in this decan who become over-confident, which leads them to seem combative, but because you surely feel humbled by the many great blessings with which you began this earthly life, you are apt to be more imaginative and idealistic. There is little doubt, however, that you have phases when you question your true motives or reactions to situations in which you find yourself, owing to a duality within your nature that frequently makes it almost impossible to explain, even to yourself, some of your responses. You might wish with all your heart that a certain person will call, yet, when they do, find yourself dismissing them abruptly . . . you are apt to make carefully laid plans for going somewhere, and decide at departure time that you would rather stay at home. It may occasionally happen that you absolutely determine that you will follow a certain policy . . . but suddenly discover that you are doing the exact opposite! This characteristic variability is probably one of the greatest secrets of your charm, because other people are ingratiated by your fascinating qualities they think never quite predictable — but at the same time it is likely to be the trait you most need to control.

Deep within, I believe you know that there is one "part" of yourself you like better than "the other", so to say, and that you always feel happiest when you can consider that you are acting according to your "better self". There is little question that even the features of your personality which you think of as being more "negative" than others still require expression. By providing for these CONSTRUCTIVE outlets, you'll find your real key to success, in my opinion.

You ought to be exceptionally artistic, or, at least, deeply appreciative of everything representing beauty and symmetry. When you devote your energies to creative pursuits, you are likely to enjoy not only exceptionally pleasing results, but a uniqueness of style, as well, that evolves out of your ability to display from your changing moods almost kaleidoscopic impressions.

When you feel that you have enough to do, you are rarely apt to be disturbed by serious difficulties, which might be a reason why you are sometimes said to be at your best in emergencies. Even your health is likely to improve during times another person would consider "stressful", because you are so preoccupied with "matters of the moment" that you turn your thoughts away from "self". I think it advisable for you to concentrate your efforts to the extent that you will focus your attention on fewer undertakings until you bring them to completion, so as to sidestep the tendency of your sign and decan to "scatter your energies" — but with this exception of carrying through to achievement several well-chosen endeavors, your efforts to "keep busy" will almost certainly bring a growing sense of satisfaction.

One idiosyncrasy I have observed among my friends in this decan is that they frequently use "ill health" as an excuse for averting challenges. I believe that this is because you earnestly want to maintain a favorable appearance in every circumstance, and you sometimes feel unsure of your capacity for doing so in specific instances. The over-all constitutions of individuals born around your birthdate are generally especially strong. When they refuse to dwell on little "aches and pains" and anticipate unhealthy conditions that will probably never really occur, their abundant resources invariably serve them exceptionally well — and because I have confidence that you follow this practice, I'm sure that YOU revel in a more pleasurable and gratifying life. There will certainly be temporary phases, now and then, when you'll feel like the ostrich, an inclination to "hide your head" and pretend that a situation no longer exists — but when you view such trends more realistically, I'm sure you'll realize this method only prolongs or worsens an agony a constructive approach would readily eradicate. In the alternative, when you truly SEEK worthwhile solutions by "facing up" to issues that displease you, I feel that you will FIND what you seek.

The financial affairs of third decan Geminis are ordinarily rather changeable, while in one manner or another it seems that these often attract some attention. You might receive publicity concerning certain possessions you own, from time to time, or acquire a belonging that becomes known as something of a "show piece". I believe that you have an inherent instinct for "taking in" whatever you think is available for your use that will serve practical purposes, and to collect items which are of special interest to you, protecting these somewhat more carefully than another individual might. Being "penny-wise and pound-foolish", you may incline to remain passive when you learn of ways of making more substantial gains, being indecisive, or slow to act on information you receive, yet once your conclusions are formed you are apt to manage your interests with a high degree of thoroughness.

You are frequently likely to develop friendships with kindred and neighbors, among whom at least one may seem outstanding because of a certain accident or affliction to the spine or heart. I think that your loyalties to such individuals are intense and unbending; in fact, what you consider to be a betrayal of their better interests will bring you courageously into battle (even when you know that the person who holds your affection is wrong in some respects), and this is an area of your life where you may either win a few of your more noble victories or go gloriously down in defeat, confident in the knowledge that although it has seemed necessary to lose certain advantages you, yourself, might have gained, you've magnanimously held to the great-hearted principles' that seem to you so very important.

In writing or speech you may tend to be deliberately evasive, upon occasion — and because of "a shrewdness" for anticipating what other people will do, particularly "clever" in laying plans to outwit them, thereby entrapping those who would deceive you; your efforts in this direction sometimes boomerang, although this is seldom.

Oddly, your approach to some of your more general and "outside" interests is apt to be less decisive, bringing you to converge upon an undertaking according to one policy, and then swing around "mid-stream" and reverse yourself completely. When you endeavor to apply some of your more "fiery" impulses, giving the same staunch devotion to every concern you would gladly give to any true friend, your wish for improving conditions for people who are lonely, confined, or otherwise less fortunate than most, will gain great promise of fulfillment — and, associates who have previously accused you of aiming at totally intangible goals will remark that you do, indeed, relieve suffering you find around you!

It appears to me that you have a strong sense of drama, theatrics and staging. During your earlier years of rearing, you are apt to be considered even something of a "ham", owing to your uninhibited enthusiasm for acting out a role that strikes your fancy. As you grow older, you are likely to take to heart petty jealousies that result from some of your more shining achievements, becoming silently admiring of good humored action, but overly modest where displays of your own talents are concerned. When such efforts meet with approval from individuals around you, you can use this encouragement for a prompter to quite outstanding accomplishments in creative and humanitarian lines.

My feeling with respect to your inherent nature is that you earnestly hope to live your life in such a way that it will prove helpful and inspiring to the world around you. You might express yourself in hundreds of different ways in order to accomplish this single purpose, but to find true peace within yourself, you no doubt think that you MUST direct your energies to enterprises that will, in some measure, improve conditions for Mankind, even at the sacrifice of a few of your personal desires. The Gemini friends I have had who have gone against this part of themselves are among some of the most inwardly miserable people I know.

Your idealistic spirit holds a great deal of romanticism, in my estimation, that leads you to attain particular enjoyment from "entertaining" pursuits, especially the telling of humorous situations. Because your thoughtfulness of others usually earns numerous favors from acquaintances, you are apt to have almost too many opportunities for participating in pleasurable pursuits that "while away the time" without bringing you to any particular "destination". It isn't that I think you really intend to procrastinate — it is simply that there are frequently so many different activities going on at the same time that you tend to "put off" other things that will contribute more definitely to your progress. THE ROMANTIC AREAS of Geminians of your decan ARE OFTEN MORE GRATIFYING than are some of their more permanent relationships evolving out of marriage and business partnerships. I observe that these closest associations are very frequently delayed or avoided altogether, and when they are entered into, it is often more with a feeling of fulfilling an "obligation" or "duty" than through a strong wish to do so. I believe that the real reason for this is the degree of responsibility a closer alliance implies that appears to you more restrictive than pleasing. When you do set your sights in this direction, you are very likely to take notice of individuals who are older than you, or at least who seem so in view of their moralizing, trustworthy, ambitious and dignified natures.

INSINCERITY AND TACTLESSNESS MAY BRING DISAPPOINTMENT FROM ONE OR TWO CLOSE RELATIONSHIPS, or you consider that another person's coldness and selfishness places upon you disciplines which are not entirely to your liking. Differences in religious or philosophical attitudes occasionally arise, in all probability, seemingly taking away from you some of your more progressive and changing viewpoints, as compared to those in which you were originally brought up.

You might have little inclination for "family life" that is restricting or limits your freedom, but I observe that when people of your decan do have children of their own, or associate themselves with the interests of younger people, they ordinarily earn abundantly satisfying returns.

Probably because you find long-range decisions difficult to make, action you take somewhat "speculatively" may often prove some of your most fortunate, endeavors with undetermined outcomes bringing to the fore some of your finest attainments.

At least some of your "MATERIAL" successes will come from your associations with other people, in my opinion. Writings and other communications of various kinds, particularly the use of spoken words, as well as trips or journeys may earn for you numerous acquaintances as well as increases in your holdings. Individuals to whom you feel especially closely related are also likely to benefit your holdings now and then.

Some people might consider you too "meticulous" because of your apparent "pickiness" over little matters of hygiene, diets or certain methods you consider unalterable. Provided you take measures to prevent yourself from carrying this characteristic to an extreme, you ought to be quite practical in your judgment of your "domestic" environment — and this should grow with each passing year — in spite of at least one basic difference you have (or have had in the past) with a certain person influential to your primary interests. I think you are so sociable that you feel "a need" for having other people around you, disliking being alone or finding yourself in surroundings that seem to you "isolated" — so that a loving and uncritical attitude toward those nearest you, even at the compromise of minor points, will surely always be to your advantage. You are apt to desire to reside where there is elevation or in an apartment above the ground floor.

I am convinced that anything and everything you truly wish for yourself, which is right for you to have, CAN and WILL become yours when you endeavor to control the circumstances which surround you.

Cancer

June 23-July 2
Ruled by Venus

1st decan

Being born in the first decan of Cancer, as you were, you are likely to have very deep-seated, quiet feelings that often seem to permeate the whole atmosphere. I have observed that people who have birthdays in your decan have sociable and amiable dispositions, generosity of character, kind and attractive natures that earn many friends, as I'm sure you do — but you are ordinarily apt to display a certain degree of reserve in your day-to-day associations, withholding a "special personality" that belongs only to your few cherished loved ones. For this reason, people may occasionally consider that you are difficult to "know", although I believe this is because they have never had the privilege of being accepted into areas of your life that might be considered more "confiding".

You may have a tendency to be unusually (even "hyper") sensitive, although this characteristic can serve as one of your greatest assets when you use it perceptively, as a measure of other people's sensibilities, weighing your words and actions with the tact and diplomacy you, yourself prefer to receive. I believe you know that you are more "vulnerable" than many people to blunt criticisms, situations that are less harmonious than you would really like, and other conditions you think of as "hurtful", which might lead you to wear a "shell", or give a surface appearance, that will conceal the fragility of your emotions. Upon occasion, this may bring you to give an impression of "not caring", or even of being less amiable and cooperative than people around think you ought to be under the circumstances, at the very times when you most wish for appreciation and attention! Individuals who come to know you well no doubt learn that they can easily bring you to agreement by taking notice of your finer qualities, appealing to your ready sense of humor, and looking below the surfaces of your apparent "moods" to understand that they must not take these personally. Disliking "surprises" or unexpected changes, you may show a more favorable response when you are prepared in advance as to what you should expect in a "new" situation or there are alterations in your usual "routines". Even when some individuals have less insight into your true nature than others might, you are very likely to endear them to you without their quite knowing why it should be so, owing to an indefinable charm that results from the gentle and ingratiating method I feel certain you have.

I believe that a deep, quiet sentimentality frequently cloaks the depth of your intellect and the enthusiasm of your ambitions — you might wait a long time, but when you want something, I think you tenaciously pursue it, until you have securely brought it into your own sphere of activity where you will privately glory in the pride of your accomplishment. One of your more outstanding qualities is apt to be a capacity for subtly acting from "behind-the-scenes" to get your own way without arousing opposition. It is very likely that even when people intend to harm your better interests, their efforts will inadvertently act in reverse, bringing favors or advantages to you instead!

In all probability, you have a few inner misgivings where your material interests are concerned, and while you no doubt appreciate "comfort" and "luxury", you may incline to deny yourself enjoyment of some of the better or more costly things you can afford, in the event of future adversity that, in all likelihood, is but a creation of your imagination. There may also be times when you incline to collect or keep things that at the moment serve little purpose. Through a more constructive, optimistic approach, and earnest endeavor to make your efforts more gainful, I feel that your assets will grow more rapidly. In the management of money, as well as in the care of your possessions, you are occasionally apt to display a somewhat cold, or critical attitude that appears thrifty to such a degree that some of your associates think you overly "money conscious". A few individuals I have known who were born in your decan of Cancer are unusually restricted and limited in their material outlook, to such an extent that they will calculate ways of taking "emotional advantages" in order to advance their own returns; sometimes they have phases when they are suspicious and fearful — this often results in their saying "no" to anything suggested almost immediately — ("No, I can't; No, I won't") only later on agreeing to do what they had reacted negatively to at first. But because I have confidence that YOU strive for more self-assurance, I believe that you are reliable in your monetary interests, generously sharing what you have and otherwise displaying a sense of responsibility to unselfishly give, in at least equal measure to what you, yourself like to receive. When the management of other people's assets is left up to you, you no doubt take a detached and clear-sighted view, earnestly endeavoring to provide the same protection you would wish for your own belongings.

A few of my friends in this first decan of Cancer tend to be somewhat curious about the affairs of others, or meddling; sometimes worrisome and fussy. I'm sure that you make better use of your capabilities, and thus manifest your greatest vitality on the mental plane, being reasonable, practical and logical in your basic opinions. I have little doubt that you are efficient in the management of details; discriminating and practical — although you might find it necessary to make a stronger effort than many people to avert critical tendencies. During the earlier years, people with birthdays in this decan ordinarily enjoy a degree of popularity that will continue to grow throughout their lifetimes, even though they are inclined to be somewhat more studious and conscientious of small facts, figures and statistics than some people their age, which might be true of you, as well. A retiring and somewhat solitary manner throughout these formative years sometimes leads to a feeling of "competition" with close associates such as "brothers and sisters", diminishing the confidence first decan Cancerians would otherwise carry.

Maturity to what is generally considered "college age" frequently appears to lead individuals born around your birthday to a temporary period of "hardship", that often makes a higher education either difficult to attain or entirely out of the question. In studying the reasons for the seeming "denials" sometimes accompanying this period, I conclude they usually evolve out of personal disappointments in "LESSENING FAMILY TIES" and other affectional relationships, in such ways as to PRESENT STARK REALITIES QUITE SHATTERING TO MANY CHERISHED DREAMS OF IDEALISM WHICH WERE PREVIOUSLY HELD. You are rarely as likely to approach "adversities" combatively as you are to "withdraw" from them. This characteristic occasionally brings people of your decan to at least one phase when there is vastly lowered regard for self, accompanied by strong feelings of confusion, moral, and spiritual betrayal. I have observed that there are great lessons to be learned from any such experiences, but the length of time involved in their discovery; also the duration of the reversals that originally brought them into being, depends upon whether a person of this decan reacts with cynicism and moroseness; worry and self-pity, that ultimately deteriorate the majority of their life's interests to untidiness — or whether they determine to move constructively forward in a manner that will improve, if not erase, the reflections mirrored in their past. This is accomplished, I feel, through determination to solve existing problems by giving of your finer qualities for the benefit of all of Mankind you can reach, in tangible lines of endeavor that will give expression to your true talents and abilities. When you SEEK, you will find balanced relationships with individuals who are on a high spiritual, moral and intellectual level that will encourage your more faithful sensibilities, and otherwise compliment your real attributes, I know!

I believe that you prefer to make acquaintances among individuals who are mentally alert, although you are at least equally responsive to those who have cheerful, level dispositions and practical, dependable outlooks. True harmony in your closer alliances is apt to result from your making the happiness of people around you, rather than "self", your first interest, even at times displaying optimism, devotion and consideration you do not really feel. When you endeavor to concede minor points in dissensions and show through your actions your genuinely high regard, your own inner contentment will abundantly grow, I am certain.

You are sometimes likely to follow singularly "fitful" undertakings, owing to an inner restlessness that is no doubt evident in your nature, but when you truly become interested in any endeavor, even purposes others think of as ignoble or petty, they are surely executed, in all probability. You are apt to require a certain degree of variety in your routines, as well as independence for carrying them out according to your own concepts. You should have ample energies for matching your enthusiasm, while you are almost certain to prefer mastering every technique that will better serve your enterprises. Close observers are seldom likely to question the brilliancy of your approach, although they might occasionally challenge your methods. Generally, people who have birthdays in this first decan of Cancer are attracted to fields of endeavor that will enable them to "oversee" many different concerns — but they rarely feel real happiness with their accomplishments unless these are contributory in some way to the welfare of others. Regardless of their particular sphere of activity, they invariably display rather outstanding oratorical abilities, taking as a personal responsibility the instruction; the teaching — the uplifting — of those around them. You have probably noticed that you, too, are more convincing than many people, not so much because of what you say or do, but because of "the WAY" you go about it.

Cancerians who have birthdates similar to your own require a secure environment that will be a center for all of their other activities, in my opinion. You are likely to add "homey" touches to any surroundings in which you find yourself, and to have strong preferences for any time you spend in the place where you consider you reside. You might have somewhat solitary moods when you care little for the company of other people — but when you have close associates who take equal pride in your "household interests", with YOU as their first concern, you are apt to realize a growing sense of inner contentment that makes all of the other conditions of your life appear more worthwhile.

While you may often be attracted to "independent types" with abundant interests, in the selection of your close companions, enduring happiness is more likely to result from your relationships with individuals who might be termed "domesticated", in the "good, old-fashioned" sense.

Although you probably show a tenderness toward people for whom you feel affection that might be regarded as "paternal" or "maternal", your actual associations with children are sometimes likely to bring more than an ordinary number of stresses. Apparent problems can often be solved by recalling your own actions when you were a certain age.

With each passing year of life, "balance" will seem more and more important to you, I believe. Everyone born in your decan needs to correct any tendencies toward contemplating knowledge without turning it to immediate account, or building up more great ideas than are executed — but because I trust that you use your powers of introspection not only artistically, but actively, I'm sure that you earn the abundant returns that are rightfully yours to have.

I think that you will continue to enjoy betterment in all of the conditions that directly concern you when you share them with "one particular" person who thrives on a feeling of pride and admiration for you and closely shares with you the fullness of experience life has to offer. When you find a sense of tranquility with the world around you as well as within yourself, all that you truly wish will more easily yield to your grasp, I am certain.

Cancer

July 3- July 12
Ruled by Mercury

You are apt to be somewhat more impressionable than many people, owing to a keen intuition and strong imagination. I believe that you often appear to know things without being told, and without knowing how you know, but you might become so "absorbed" that you occasionally overlook actualities, and, above all, originality, having more of a singular retentiveness for such things as historical matters, facts, or figures, than an adaptability to newer ideas. For this reason, individuals who were born in the second decan of Cancer, as you were, frequently receive particularly beneficial results from a conscientious effort to maintain "breadth of view" in their attitudes so that they will assimilate more than mere reference to antiquity or statements that will serve as good examples later on, thus maintaining the strength of their excellent memories.

Because I trust that you have learned to be less passive by bringing your emotions into harmony with your immediate associates and surroundings rather than permitting yourself to be "swayed" by the "moods of the moment", passing these periods of not wanting to talk, thereby, "closing a door" to others, so to say, you no doubt have greater stability than one might sometimes expect, which gives you less likelihood of falling into a habit that appears "stubborn" to people who come to touch your life. I have generally noticed that when this characteristic does display itself in individuals of your decan, it usually results from subjection for long periods of time to a single stress.

Although I feel that you are extremely sensitive, having strong "likes and dislikes", now and then even to a point where you think you cannot endure the company of associates who are not in harmony with you, you are more tolerant than another person might be inwardly as well as in your outward display, because you consider that opinions are not, after all, of supreme importance. Should anyone try to argue with you, you will probably react with obstinate resistance, yet by appealing to your perception, persons with powerful wills can often bring you quite easily to agreement with their views.

I have observed that birthdays within your decan of Cancer frequently imply that an education is more easily attained than is true of those in other decans, sometimes through another's help, such as an aunt, uncle, or other relative, even when a parent or guardian seems overly "strict", or you are aware of similar "limitations". These "earlier" years of your life are apt to give you some of your fonder memories as time passes on — and aside from actual "book learning", your experiences in the "school of life" may be particularly abundant, through places beyond the locale of your birth or the "travels of your imagination" into philosophical, religious, legal, political, and similar realms.

You are very apt to have somewhat stronger spiritual feelings than you always outwardly display, because you mask these by a "scientific" spirit. It is quite unlikely that you will remain always with the religious concepts in which you were reared; you might incline to follow rather unconventional, or even "mystical" principles, based primarily upon somewhat psychic or receptive impressions, at least to some degree. You may recognize almost too vividly the "pain and suffering" of the ages, yet your over-all outlook no doubt holds an inner optimism that will always earn, for you, advantages.

A certain "refinement", such as that necessary for a nurse, may be evident in your nature, that enables you to express yourself quite convincingly, by showing a degree of tenderness without diminishing the efficiency of your opinions with traces of emotion or pity. I have known women born in this decan who quickly discover that they can gain their ends by telling falsehoods, "tattling", or dramatically reducing themselves to tears — but you surely approach your interests with greater maturity. Your close association with someone during your more formative years may have influenced many of your more admirable qualities. I believe that you have more than an ordinary capacity for advancing your relationships with "neighbors" and "relatives" by distributing your tenderer feelings through intellectual channels in such ways as to promote harmony among them without becoming more deeply involved than you would really like to be.

In your basic instincts, you are likely to be dignified, bighearted and generous. I have known some individuals whose birthdays are in this decan who are extravagant or "overly self-centered", or even seem inordinately selfish — although I have complete confidence that you are humanitarian and tenderhearted, perhaps even too much so when your gentleness and generosity of feeling leads you to people or situations less appreciative of these nobler qualities than they might be. Your greatest material successes are more apt to come from your own efforts than your alliances with other individuals or "corporations", as these are rarely likely to be entirely steady or predictable. Those who know you are frequently likely to consider you especially fortunate, when it appears to them that a "protective hand" always seems to rest over your "pocketbook" to "come through with something", even in your darkest moment!

Changeful occupations that enable you to follow more than one particular pursuit at a time, and touch frequently upon territory distant from your usual base of "operations" are almost bound to appeal to you, giving vent to some of your more restless impulses and enabling you to display more openly your alertness, cheerfulness and sincerity in carrying out your daily routines. I think you have an admirable capacity for focusing your mind perfectly upon sharp, well-defined goals, and then bringing these into being exactly as you originally envisioned them. You are apt to resent any confusion of issues, inwardly being somewhat afraid of being cheated by the introduction of facts which are foreign to the subjects under your scrutiny, but this may also be one of "the secrets" of your success, which you obtain by attending to one thing at a time, even when this leads to an occasional accusation from others, that you are being narrow or one-sided. I feel that the necessity of having enough independence and variety in your daily activities is the real "key" to your well-being — because I have known so many people in this decan who, under different circumstances, became offhanded in their manner; careless and restless. Even physical ailments occasionally appear to result from "a deficient degree of diversity". You have probably noticed that the thought of travel or similar alteration in your routines almost immediately gives you a stronger sense of tranquility, especially if it takes you near a lake or body of water.

Every decan of every sign has its strengths and its weaknesses, and in my opinion, these are ours to develop or overcome, so that we may achieve continually improving conditions in all that concerns us. The only real enemy a person born in this decan of Cancer ordinarily encounters is himself or herself! When any highly-strung tendencies are turned to mechanical pursuits or other constructive undertakings that give better direction to your mental energies, and you fulfill an absolute resolve that you WILL carry these through to completion, your happiness is almost bound to grow, as well as the pride of accomplishment you will gain by earning, through your most persistent policy and hopeful attitude, greater achievements.

I feel that you are inherently ambitious and have talent for managing your ideas particularly well along "executive" lines, or somewhat independent of close direction by other people. Your approach to any endeavor that captures your attention is apt to be distinctly enterprising, sometimes even "bold". There is little doubt that you will have singleness of purpose in carrying out your undertakings, which you hope will bring immediate results. There may be times when you incline to display an assertive quality that not only surprises your close associates, but also proves less favorable to your better interests than you originally expected. Under ordinary circumstances, however, you prefer to use methods, or explore territory, different from the "usual", yet along practical lines, in my estimation.

In all probability, you developed your basic aims, hopes and wishes at an early age, and have since changed these very little. You are likely to adhere to rather conservative and conventional principles, which are acceptable to present-day "society", and evolve to a large degree from the fundamental attitudes in which you were brought up. This often results in your saying "no" to a new suggestion or "I can't -", and later agreeing to try whatever you responded to negatively at first. "Long-term security" is apt to seem especially important to you, as well as an enduring "home and family" life, – for this reason, I think as an instinct to protect yourself, you "shy away" from a possible hurt and will spurt out a "No" in self defense.

- 162 -

With these as your underlying motives, I believe that you seek in your acquaintances people who have reliable temperaments that guide them with staunch purpose, faithfulness, and singular dependability, yet are "domesticated" in their outlook. These are likely to be particularly successful when you endeavor to be a good listener. I have noticed that the romantic lives of people who were born in this second decan of Cancer are frequently kept somewhat "secretive", but are passionate and intense. Magnetic feelings of "romanticism" often promote the initial allure, which occasionally leads to relationships productive of some jealousy or even vindictiveness. In close attachments, such as marriage, or business partnerships, individuals of your decan very often select associates who are rather dour, displaying self-reliance, ambition, authoritativeness and industriousness, but this can also lead them to be somewhat commanding, willful and determined as compared with your impressionable temperament. Thus, I must conclude, in this regard, that from time to time there will be stresses in a few of your more "personal" affiliations.

You are apt to feel a stronger need for children than many people, but in your alliances with younger people, you might occasionally find it less easy than many individuals to encourage independence of attitude among them, or to accept readily their development of viewpoints that appear to be in contrast with your own. When you make a special effort to show respect for their individuality and to act as a subtly-guiding influence, contributing to their confidence in, and enthusiasm for, using their real aptitudes, talents and capabilities, I know that you will enjoy increasingly pleasing results as these and similar relationships grow.

In your immediate surroundings you have deep appreciation of balance, artistry and beauty, in all likelihood, yet within somewhat conservative boundaries. I am inclined to believe that you tend to think of your "home" environment as a "possession", or to feel a responsibility and duty toward it. Most second decan Cancerians inwardly sense that this area of their lives is often rather "restrictive", or less satisfying than they would really hope, because of a lack of fulfillment through another person.

- 163 -

People who have birthdays around the same time of year as you do, advancing through life, frequently find that they grow more self-contained and "reclusive" with each passing year, or that they display greater "secretiveness" with respect to their personal interests. Because I have complete confidence that you will always make a special effort to show a genuine interest and concern for other people's welfare, and display a real pride in their accomplishment, I am certain that a very harmonious, beautiful attitude toward yourself will increasingly develop, mellowing in strength to give your more lovable qualities continual expansion and bring back to you the peace, harmony and contentment I'm sure you will earn.

Cancer

July 13-July 21
Ruled by Moon

3rd decan

People who were born in the third decan of Cancer, as you were, frequently have unusually changeful lives, bringing them into touch with many fascinating places and experiences, either through travel, or in their imaginations, by way of an abundance of newer ideas. Being keenly receptive, domesticated and sensitive, you are likely to react somewhat uncertainly and slowly to new impressions, because you prefer for these to sink into your mind and dissolve completely so that your senses will reflect them with extreme accuracy. This might lead you to appear rather "meditative", upon occasion, but anyone who knows you well, will recognize that this is never due to your being mentally idle.

Upon at least one occasion you are apt to be aware of an effect produced from "within" that cannot be attributed to circumstances around you, or seems "psychic" in its origin; in any event, I feel certain that your memory is especially good, although you realize greater benefits when you also endeavor to act upon information your sensitive, intuitive mind receives.

Many people who have birthdays in the sign of Cancer give an appearance of being cold at times or unpredictably "changeable". Although some display terrifically unstable, clannish, moody, or emotional tendencies, I have observed that when another person might seem filled with the intense energy associated with strong creativity, individuals of your decan can usually blend into complete harmony, somehow, the placidity, sensuousness and receptivity that are ordinarily evidenced in their natures.

Although you are apt to feel less desire for acquiring than readiness to do so, balance and breadth of outlook will be necessary before you are likely to enjoy the fullest development in your material interests. I believe that you intend to be generous and great-hearted with what you have — and most of all, that you feel it impossible to express yourself in mean ways when you recognize that an advantage can be won, even though there are people born in this decan who occasionally display a degree of haughtiness, or even obstinacy, in their methods. You are apt to be interested in many things beyond the "business of the moment", preferring involvement in the "mainstream of financial activity", so to say, creatively cutting away newer avenues for gain. "Speculative" enterprises probably appeal to you to some degree, although "long-term" investments are likely to capture your attention more frequently than those requiring rapid turnover, owing to a certain "fixity" you prefer to have in your purposes.

In instances when the management of other people's possessions or assets is within your control, you are apt to follow your intuition more readily than pure facts or figures. It is very likely that maturity will bring with it a growing gift for comprehension of and correctness in higher mathematics, or a sense of impartiality you will develop that is the mark of a good judge or banker, for instance. Returns you receive from close associates, estates, or similar "mutual endeavors" will rather often prove to be erratic, in my estimation, making it less easy for you to predict in advance outcomes you hope to achieve. Such things as electronics and futuristic enterprises may capture your fancy for investment purposes from time to time, or you might investigate fields of entertainment and sports. Provided, of course, you maintain always a strong sense of personal responsibility in financial matters, as I trust you will, these should generally prove more gainful for you than otherwise.

A few individuals who are members of this decan of Cancer tend to be worrisome and hypercritical, sometimes even meddlesome and sarcastic — but because I have confidence that YOU earnestly endeavor to use your finest characteristics, I believe that you are more inclined to be discerning and analytical. You no doubt have a pronounced gift for absorbing and incorporating information that comes to your attention; then "digesting" it for future use. I feel that you recognize the importance of developing your intellect, although it may sometimes appear that you do so with a degree of detachment or coldness that results from placing pure reason before sentiment and emotion. From time to time, people who know you might think that you give too much attention to minor details, "not seeing the forest for the trees", so to say . . . or that you take so much notice of the interests of "relatives" and "neighbors" that you ignore some of your larger opportunities. YOU ARE APT TO BE AWARE OF EVEN THE SLIGHTEST FLAW IN ANY UNDERTAKING, AN ATTRIBUTE THAT CAN BECOME A REAL ASSET, when you constructively apply it to the betterment of an enterprise and improved efficiency in all other matters that directly concern you.

A characteristic that probably presented itself in life is your quickness for learning, although this might occasionally tend to prove something of a defect when it enables you to learn so easily that you overlook the necessity of concentrating sufficiently to retain knowledge you acquire. Other than this, you ought to have an excellent memory. People of your decan ordinarily feel an attraction for writing (having a special fondness for satire and critique), while most have a capacity for becoming particularly adept linguists or speakers, who enjoy the "know-how" for combining scientific inquiry with fertile fancy. You might also be especially clever in such things as the handicrafts, as well as "a story teller". There is a strange ability here to relate a circumstance so that the listener actually sees the picture drawn in words.

It is always helpful for individuals who have birthdays in this third decan of Cancer to strive for greater tolerance of "points of view" which are not entirely like their own or to guard against embellishment of true facts, and to see the world as it actually is instead of as they think it should be. Because I'm sure you hold confidences that come to your attention with the same respect you would wish another to have for your more private concerns, I do not anticipate the difficulties for you many people have.

The over-all emotions of third decan Cancerians, like yourself, are ordinarily exceptionally intense and generous, and because these deep feelings are combined with a magnetic charm that is apt to encourage attractions of the strongest sort, it is probably more necessary for these than almost any other people to raise and maintain on a permanent level not only the depths of their emotions, but their altruistic feelings, as well. Because I'm sure you genuinely display an unselfish concern for other individuals who come to touch your life, maintaining for yourself values at least as lofty and idealistic as those you expect of them, the moderation with which you conduct yourself is almost certain to earn gratifying alliances, while your tact and diplomacy will serve as a brilliant example others around you are likely to follow.

I feel assured that you accept compliments with the dignity they deserve, and constructively direct emotions that would otherwise be as dynamic as "a sea in a storm". Because I sincerely believe that whatever we think and do come back to us in kind, your efforts to display genuine trust in people who hold your affection, and to send selfless thoughts of compassion, devoid of all personal needs, will continually bring back to YOU happiness, loyalty and the preservation of that which you most deeply cherish. By earnestly striving for steadfast spiritual beliefs, based upon practical principles, which you will unwaveringly follow, and accomplishing what you set out to do not through force and vengeance some people would use, but through NOBLE means, newer and better beginnings are almost bound to be yours, that hold within them golden opportunities for finding all that you seek, which is right for you to have.

You are apt to display a somewhat "thrifty" disposition with regard to your "daily routines", with a particularly pronounced insight into human nature. I have frequently noticed that people born in this decan of Cancer feel impelled to assume responsibilities for themselves, and, often, close associates as well, thus performing their tasks more from "a sense of duty" than of pleasure. Owing to the "promptings of necessity", it occasionally seems that finding their "niche" in the "work-a-day" world is somewhat delayed and discouraging — but when they conscientiously prove their trustworthiness, progress invariably offers a "helping hand", frequently through the esteem of an "influential" person — yet those born at this time almost always acquire a home that has the comfortable look of "a nest". Because you are apt to recall at least one phase when it seemed that more was asked of you than the returns you received would indicate, you are probably aware that the preservation of your health is somewhat more imperative than that of many people, and that it generally improves when your undertakings are relatively independent of the close "requirements" of other individuals.

You are frequently likely to attract, in close association, people who are reserved and practical in their outlook, and have as one of their stronger qualities self-respect. The strength of their moral character; THEIR SENSE OF THRIFT, CAUTION AND PRUDENCE, are often apt to prove beneficial to your better interests, bringing to you rewards that might otherwise seem out of the question. Surely your disappointment in a few acquaintances has sometimes led you to a preference for "older" or more mature companions, but, in all probability, you will find that, overall, your greatest "inner fulfillment" evolves out of a sense of being in close relationship with another person.

Although I doubt that your mind is as restless as it is very sensitive to impressions, you may consider that extreme thoroughness of reflection is necessary before you begin to give out again in a new form your deductions from facts which you have absorbed. Individuals who know you very well are apt to discover with little effort that they should not seek to upset your basic mental concepts, even for your own good, because you will merely dislike them for doing so. Of course, I'm sure you recognize this characteristic and now make a stronger effort to give more leniency to your attitudes.

From time to time, it no doubt seems to you that many of your realizations fall somewhat short of your original expectations, but improvement is almost sure to come as return for a more optimistic and less materialistic goal.

You probably feel that you require some "time to yourself", thereby going through "moody periods" where you prefer to withdraw and not be drawn into conversing with others, even possibly going into your own room or some place where you can be alone. Your efforts, after these moods have passed, to reach cheerfully forward will bring growing benefits with each year, I am certain. The more you develop your sympathetic understanding, just attitudes and charitable instincts, the more expansive, harmonious and balanced the conditions in and around your life will become, without any question. I have frequently observed among my friends in this decan that a confused, and even dualistic, battle with morals and values is followed by the deepest spiritual faith — and this seems to bring with it "a renewed gentleness" of countenance that appears almost to "brilliantly glow" in the eye of the observer. Because I know that you guide your life by your more simple and sensible discernments, this magnificent endowment is also yours to have and keep always.

These are a few of the reasons why I anticipate that your journey across the sea of life will be a glorious and beautiful one, guiding you surely to the "ports" where you will most easily find popularity with many, enhanced by "special" associations that substantially add to your personal sense of fulfillment! It is rare indeed to find those born in the sign

of Cancer who do not enjoy security above the average in the
late years of life!

Leo

July 22-August 2
Ruled by Saturn

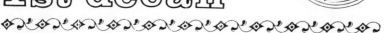

1st decan

I feel that yours is the most changeable of the Leo natures,
bringing you to display forethoughtfulness, deliberation and
energy that often make you appear somewhat more optimistic than you will always be in every situation. An ingratiating
personality no doubt wins for you many, many immediate
friends and admirers, while your inherent, forceful attitude
outwardly, renews confidence in people you meet. I believe
that you have an absolutely uncanny knack for "sizing up"
either environmental moods or persons, and knowing the precise response these require; you can bring to almost any circle greater unity, or make an "occasion" of a gathering,
where none previously existed, by adapting yourself to the
highest or the lowest of societies . . . the educated or the
uneducated alike . . . among the staunch or the meek. We
shan't mention all of your secrets, but, between you and me,
your faculty for adding discomfort could equal your ability
for improving conditions around you, if you were a less
magnanimous person than I'm sure you are, because you can
just as easily determine the necessary ingredients for creating
absolute havoc!

You are likely to present yourself in a manner that gives
others assurance "you have complete control" over your
own interests, and because you frankly give your honest
opinions when they are requested, individuals who come to
touch your life believe that they may turn to you with their
problems to receive sympathetic understanding and good,
common sense advice that evolves out of your indepth comprehension of their SPECIFIC needs, emotions and reactions.

- 170 -

Even when they mention more superficial issues than those actually weighing on their minds, you will almost invariably see to the root of their disturbances, and give your honest counsel according to this conclusion.

The irony of your great insight is that it is ordinarily extremely difficult for you to apply the same principles to your own affairs. I think you are actually sensitive, and that you all too often take generalities personally. You are apt to incline to moods of uncertainty and depression that make your own outlook seem particularly bleak — and because you are regarded as something of an oracle by others, you discover that at these times of "personal crisis" there are few people to whom YOU can turn, who display perception equal to that you show for them under like circumstances. There are a number of individuals born in your decan who have phases when they rather delight in feeling sorry for themselves or entertaining vague doubts and imaginings, but I feel so certain that you have within you a phenomenal POWER to accomplish ANYTHING you truly wish, I earnestly believe that by practicing what you would "preach" if another person laid an identical problem before you, you will enjoy unquestionable success in maintaining greater balance.

In all probability your first wish is to have everyone happy. Having a fun-loving spirit, you are apt to give an impression that you live your life in a whirling, dazed state that is concerned only with trivialities, but in truth you are exceptionally deep, in my estimation. You may sometimes have forebodings you can neither account for nor escape — and your dread of these might grow with each passing year, when experience proves that even some of your more morbid premonitions are correct the majority of the time.

I have observed among my friends born in your decan, who hail from all walks of life, that there are frequently conditions in their earlier and formative environment that seem restrictive or limiting to a real sense of contentment. These delays, or impediments, to self-expression often mark the future with a tendency toward over-independence and, quite frequently, self-punishment. You may notice that you occasionally have an inclination to act in the very manner you KNOW will be detrimental to your favored interests, or to place a damper on activities that give promise of a joyousness you inwardly feel you do not deserve; you might take on unnecessary responsibilities that seem to you a real imposition, or assert your independence at inopportune moments. The reasons, in my judgment, are that earlier disappointments — or your estimation that you have, in the past, fallen short of expectations other people have had of you, even though you've tried your VERY best to please them — have brought you to feel somewhat distrustful of other individuals and lacking in self-confidence. Another of the more remarkable qualities I have noticed in people who have birthdays near your own, however, is that they look themselves "right straight in the eye", so to say — therefore, I know you are inwardly aware of any leanings you have in these directions, and I trust that you earnestly take measures to correct them by using your abundant assets. When you understand that you are often driven by a desire to be perfect in an imperfect world, as I think you are, and to be so sensitive to what you believe are the wishes of people you cherish that you place upon yourself impossible requirements, you may gain some tolerance of what you consider to be your own "failings", recognizing that excellence, both within and in conditions surrounding your life, will evolve out of a determination to make progress every day.

Your approach to routine undertakings is undoubtedly sensible, realistic, thorough and deliberate. You are apt to give special credence to opportunities communications hold, traveling to another place to present your ideas in person when someone else might send an ordinary "application", or discussing candidly your background and actual motives in situations where some people would, instead, use subterfuge. Once you begin something, there is little doubt that you intend not only to complete it, but to give it unparalleled attention. Thus, you surely expect as much in return. As everything is at least somewhat transitory, this trait is often likely to enlarge your disappointment in endeavors that prove less enduring than others. On the other hand, whatever is before you at any moment is apt to appear to you to hold these lasting qualities you anticipate, which occasionally leads you to consider incidental alterations or changes, that are only very fleeting, as earth-shattering events, because in that instant it seems to you that these will never correct themselves.

While there might be areas of your life where you express yourself too impetuously, there are probably others where you tend to hesitate too long. You are seldom likely to choose an objective casually; you prefer to think it over, weigh it, balance it, consider it and sleep on it before you commit yourself very definitely — but because you are apt to MAKE the most of your own opportunities, this characteristic may serve you rather well in the majority of instances.

It often seems that people of your first decan of Leo are really too talented. You may notice that you are interested in so many different fields, or demands placed upon you by others, that it is frequently difficult for you to choose between them, which could prompt you "to plunge" into just as many as you feel you can capably manage — and because there is very little likelihood of your being satisfied with half-hearted participation, "YOU ARE APT TO DRIVE YOURSELF ALMOST TO A POINT OF EXHAUSTION" a great deal of the time. Oddly, cold intellectualism, in its proper context, is rarely connected with your birthdate. Your successes result from "the way" you approach matters, in my opinion. When you decide you want to accomplish a feat, I believe you throw your "all" into it — even when you feel sure it will take you years to achieve what you set out to do — you willingly sacrifice your time, energies and resources to reach the purpose you have in mind, sparing yourself nothing. Yet, you'll manage to maintain an appearance of cool dignity in your ordinary exchanges with other people, and find, somehow, time for entertaining activities, which now and then earn for you a reputation of holding positions for which you are thoroughly unskilled, untrained, and unequipped. Moreover, you may very well permit your associates to maintain these viewpoints while you silently enjoy the pride of your accomplishments!

I think that you have a special "know-how" for acquiring almost extraordinary stores of knowledge, but your real forte will be found in the creative and "human fields". You rather anticipate that material assets are rightfully yours to have, in all probability, which may bring you to over-extend somewhat more often than you really should. While the warmth of your personality, alone, is apt to earn phenomenal favors from individuals who admire you, few of your more substantial holdings are likely to come from "mutual" endeavors. Many of these, because of another person asking so much from you, may actually seem more costly than gainful for you. When you review your talents and capabilities, you are almost always sure to find some means of achieving an income, and it is through this source that your strongest security will probably be upheld.

Some people might regard you as lavishly generous; others as hopelessly selfish. This accounting alone may well show your opinions of them. You probably give rather exuberant display to almost all of your emotions, although you are apt to react to your less tolerant feelings with a quiet stateliness some people consider "aloofness" rather than any desire to gain revenge. When anyone earns your favor, I believe that they also attain your profuse loyalty and your absolute devotion, "through thick and through thin", as the saying goes — and even when they appear to betray you, you always make an effort to understand and forgive their reasons for doing so.

I think that you are tremendously sociable; although you need a certain amount of time alone each day, you are happiest when you can share every possible moment with people you cherish. You will tend at intervals to put all sorts of stresses and strains on your closest relationships, sometimes just for the sake of testing the endurance of another's affection — but if, for even a flash, it appears you've acted too severely, you become overwhelmed with a sense of regret that leaves you feeling entirely "lost at sea", afraid and alone.

Even when people of your decan are, feature-for-feature, less attractive than many individuals, they nearly always have a "quality" that is handsome! Besides personal magnetism, they are invariably immaculately clean of their person and careful of their grooming, as you may be too. This is sometimes likely to bring more attention than will really serve your better interests, because you surely respond quite readily to flattery or adulation. You might have associates, now and then, who reproach you for maintaining an ephemeral attitude toward your romantic interests, but your reason is no doubt that you inwardly know your own feelings toward your "one and only" are true, regardless of your surface attitude. Being somewhat "possessive" of your loved ones yourself, you are likely to comprehend the rather unreasonable jealousies you often inspire in others, and surely you've learned that your utmost tact, diplomacy and good judgment must be consistently utilized in order for you to preserve the happiness you earnestly hope to maintain in your closest alliances.

Actually, I believe that your real motives are extraordinarily constant and sincere in love. Either in your business or personal associations, individuals whose devotion matches your own, will arouse within a feeling that you have found your "glory," although this unfortunately all too rarely happens. You are frequently apt to attract cold or detached associates who thrive on your warmth, or to acquire those whose weaknesses are strengthened by your vital powers. Because you tend to bring "new life" into the very souls of people who come to touch your life closely, you are often the last to notice any true faintness of spirit that might exist within others. This has no doubt brought you to at least one rather heart breaking emotional experience, and may be responsible for "a well-kept secret" you have known concerning a certain alliance.

I'm sure that you have the deepest regard for children, because your own "childlike" enthusiasm is in complete rapport. Some problems or difficulties are ordinarily attached to this area of the first decan Leo's life, although these often bring you to give your efforts to other younger people in such ways as to accomplish even more good than you might have if circumstances had favored your original expectations.

A younger person you "adopt", so to speak, is likely to bring you to some of your greatest rewards!

When you earnestly endeavor to leave in your PAST all temperamental outbursts and blunt criticism, and to turn every thought of SELF to selfless giving for the benefit of all Mankind, your every wish will soon be fulfilled, I am quite confident, earning for you growing concurrence, unity and amity!

Leo

August 3-August 12
Ruled by Jupiter

A kind, humane nature is one of the major characteristics you are no doubt known for. This second decan of Leo gives one of the few temperaments that can ordinarily claim complete inner tranquility, which preserves for the benefit of all of Mankind you reach more of the resources, energy and time another person might spend on self-discovery. The "life forces" within you, are apt to be so pronounced that they sometimes seem almost overwhelming; you may have such awesome regard for the privilege of your earthly sojourn that you consider it blasphemous to leave any talent or capability untouched, however small it might be. Being so acutely aware of your blessings, you probably have little reason for dwelling on regrets or contemplating any apparent limitations — because you feel an inherent obligation to take whatever gifts you might have, which are yours to use, and make of them as much as you possibly can. This is apt to be the quality which is most frequently misunderstood by other people, some of whom may think you ambitious for power, and overly confident of yourself. In my opinion, power itself means much less to you than the PRIDE OF ACCOMPLISHMENT you find by earning your way to "powerful positions". In your efforts to achieve all you think you must, you are often likely to feel quite uncertain, indeed, but you'll no doubt consider this all the more reason for calling upon the great courage with which you are also endowed; carrying your head high, and moving forward to the best of your ability. The fact that you never determine whether you can, but that YOU WILL is your whole secret of success, I feel. Many of my Leo friends of this decan tend to be overly modest in relating their achievements. Although their records might sound tremendously impressive, they often withhold any mention of what they think are their truly remarkable accomplishments, because they are afraid these will not sound believable! You might incline to do this also, from time to time. Your attire is dramatic and unusual so that at some time in your life you probably wear a large ring or quite unique piece of jewelry.

If you could choose, I doubt that you would trade one ounce of "love" for all the fame, fortune or position in the world, because this is your whole driving force — and, in your mind, you have no self-esteem and no motivation without an "inner sense" that you are becoming, through your "material" efforts, the person you feel is measurable to expectations of people for whom you hold affection. When you love, you are apt to love to the point of being pathetic — and your feeling for another human being, or even a pet, will be sufficient strength for surmounting absolutely ANY obstacle, in all probability. This trait may be as detrimental as it is virtuous, because when you feel a vacancy in this area of your life you are apt to lose all sense of direction; you mechanically carry out your routines without being able to give them any real meaning.

The sympathies of second decan Leos are ordinarily so warm, and the natures so generous, that they give sunshine and brightness to any circles of society where they are, or make a "party" out of almost any occasion. They have a capacity for appearing casually unconcerned with anything consequential while they are making phenomenal attainments, of which their associates are sometimes entirely unaware. You, too, may have this instinct for renewing courage in people around you and breathing "new life" into undertakings that attract your attention. I have observed that while the earlier years of the lives of people born in your decan are usually some of the happiest from an emotional standpoint, they are generally met with enormous disappointments and problems. These stalls in your original efforts may place dampers on many of your later enthusiasms, prompting you to curb a few of your more musical, gregarious or magnanimous characteristics and replace these with some of your seemingly more "serious" features. Besides limiting circumstances, you are likely to enter the world with such idealistic expectations and strong sensitivities that you take as a personal affront each new encounter with cruelty, selfishness, unfairness or jealousy. Quite frequently a feeling of responsibility toward such people as brothers and sisters, relatives, or individuals who neighbor your earlier surroundings, brings you to decline some of the more pleasing aspects of your rearing, or even to appear less talented than you actually are for the sake of strengthening their self-confidence. I believe that you abhor injustice.

During this beginning phase, you are apt to appear too much "older and wiser" than the majority of your contemporaries; many, mistaking the sincerity of your motives, may accuse you of being too kind, too happy, too humorous, too dramatic, too dominant, or too polite — and because you probably strive for self-perfection, every adverse comment leaves a permanent scar upon the "surface" you will later present. Being anxious to promote happiness in every situation, by relieving problems, YOU MIGHT REFUSE TO DISCLOSE TO ANYONE THAT YOU ARE PHYSICALLY ILL, OR YOU MAY INWARDLY SUFFER WHAT IS, TO YOU, A DEEP SORROW WITHOUT EVER SHOWING TRACES OF IT IN YOUR MANNER OR APPEARANCE. This "difficult start" I notice among people of your decan very often has a peculiar effect upon all the rest of the life, bringing a growing display of "aloofness"; an inner lack of confidence with respect to freedom for USING, openly, capabilities, and "a rather peculiar secretiveness" that seems all out of keeping with your frank, full temperament and deep hunger "to talk" to others.

These delays might prompt you to forge ahead on a "path" of your own choosing at a relatively "young age". While you are apt to have opportunities for a college education, you are likely to be your own best teacher for the practical purposes you will come to fulfill. Having an intuitive type of intellect, I think you absorb information in your own way, which frequently conflicts with accepted academic practices, and often prompts you to discard "trivia" that will not be directly applicable to your ultimate objectives. For this reason, the style in which you express your findings will seldom be brilliant; in all probability, you'll use practical terms anyone can understand and strive for "a humorous" approach, not only in "what" you say, but "how" you say it.

Although you are apt to re-adapt better than originate, yours is one of the most creative of all decans. Being domestically inclined, such things as interior decoration, cooking and entertaining are likely to be your favorite outlets, when your time permits, but you may be so actively engaged in other pursuits you consider more important, you rarely feel able to satisfy your true preferences along these lines.

The most outstanding thing I have noticed about your sign, and particularly your decan, is that it produces almost without exception people who will completely master at least one field of endeavor. Their efforts in this direction are apt to be so thoroughly concentrated that they make the most inordinate sacrifices to give them their "all" — and although they not infrequently become recognized authorities in their field, later on, at the onset of their original studies they usually consider them mere hobbies.

One such man I know makes his living by sweeping the floors of a drug store after hours. He rides a bicycle to and from work, filling the basket with old pieces of wire he finds along the way, or discarded automobile parts and other scraps of "junk" he can salvage. Out of these he makes elaborate inventions and usable mechanical equipment of all kinds. He devotes every moment he feels he can spare to a study of astronomy — and he knows the solar system from beginning to end! His comprehension of the physical workings of the universe is absolutely awesome! This is one example of the intense WILL TO LEARN which is invariably evident in Leos who share birth in your decan, and the creative methods of applying the results of these efforts.

Individuals born in this second decan of Leo often have rather modest incomes, and being generous to a fault, they give away most of what they earn or spend it on their libraries or other items they consider useful for more pleasurable pursuits. Owing to their cheerful outlook and resourceful attitude, they usually find a means for practically applying to gainful ends, activities they think of as entertaining rather than otherwise, while their kindness toward other people earns, in return, AT LEAST ONE "INHERITANCE" or other very welcome gift. This often seems to come through little-expected sources, or at a time that seems an "answer to a dream". You might notice that this is true of your life, as well — and that when you hold securely to encouraging thoughts, your needs always seem to be supplied!

Over-popularity is occasionally a problem that drives individuals of this decan to a somewhat "retiring" or "clannish" existence. Because people no doubt like and admire you, they are apt to make impossible demands upon your time and energies. You may gladly include in your circles, individuals who show respect for your more consuming interests, preferring confiding relationships with a few true friends to a million casual acquaintances. Bitter experience probably has taught you that unless a person is willing to help himself or herself, there is little point in denying your own concerns, to be of aid to others who will lean too heavily on your help.

YOUR EARLIER ROMANTIC LIFE IS APT TO BE

RESTLESS AND CHANGEFUL, bringing you into close association with some people who gain more than an ordinary degree of public recognition. Inherently you probably wish to devote yourself entirely to one person who will share similar interests and displays equal love for you, your home, family and pets. MORE OFTEN THAN NOT, THIS BRINGS PEOPLE OF YOUR DECAN TO YOUNG AND ILL-ADVISED MARRIAGES — quite frequently with colder and more unyielding temperaments, or individuals who recognize within your talents possibilities of realizing substantial material advantages. At least one very deep disappointment is likely to occur in this area of your life, while your most cherished wish for children may seem to thwart you even further, in one respect or another. I have heard it said that when a Leo heart is broken, it can never be repaired — and I believe this to be true, at least to the extent that a large disillusionment will seem for you, a shattering experience. No one should ever underestimate the ardency of your love nature. Being a real devotee of "togetherness", I doubt that you ever feel you can see enough of people you adore or do as much for them as you think they deserve. This patronizing attitude is at once the asset that earns for you many strong and magnificent alliances — and leaves you open prey for those whose motives are less magnanimous than your own. You might appear blind to the failings of people you love, because it is against everything in which you believe to mention these, but you are apt to recognize each and every one.

When future hopes fail to meet your expectations, you may incline to encase yourself in a somewhat reclusive "shell" that conceals from any but your very closest and most trusted loved ones your true personality — and, more especially, your sensitivity. Gaiety is a very powerful part of your nature, in my opinion, but frivolity is not. When you assume an "obligation", I think you fully intend to keep it, promptness and preparedness being two of your outstanding characteristics, although you expect as much of other people. I believe that you are so anxious to please that you incline to try to "live up or down" to what you think are the expectations of your close associates. Anyone who knows you well probably realizes that when you are "pushed" or criticized you become "all thumbs", as the saying goes — clumsily making inexcusable mistakes at every turn — and, conversely, when you receive even the merest indication that your own devotions are returned, peace, tranquility and happiness will perpetually reign.

Inwardly lacking confidence in yourself, you probably need constant assurance and reassurance from those around you. A series of disappointments, resulting from blind trust misplaced sometimes brings individuals of this decan to some suspiciousness or displays of possessiveness that are absolutely alien to their true characteristics. I'm sure you know that you never experience these when you truly feel that another's love for you is secure — but you are apt to be hyper-sensitive, and I have confidence that should you ever have these inner-promptings, you will react constructively, by either finding associates who are more compatible with your inherent needs, or directing your energies to worthwhile endeavors.

Every sign and every decan has its particular "cross to bear", and yours appears to be the denial of an "ideal domestic life". The quality of your love is apt to be so great as to find no equal, or when it seems that you have found a love to match your own, "the powers that be" may intervene, interrupting the endurance you would personally choose; ALMOST WITHOUT EXCEPTION, PEOPLE OF YOUR DECAN EITHER HAVE NO CHILDREN OR HAVE DIFFICULTY BEARING THEM; THOSE THEY HAVE ARE TAKEN AWAY, OR THERE ARE MOMENTOUS PROBLEMS CONCERNING SOME OF THEM — but I believe that this is "life's way" of placing you where you BELONG rather than where you would LIKE to be. You are likely to have an uncanny understanding of human nature; you can feel the very souls of individuals who come to touch your life and find exact solutions for bringing into them renewed hope, courage and enthusiasm. You probably accept another's pain as your own and become absolutely outraged over abuse of an animal or child. As writers, painters, social workers or psychologists, people born in your decan have a capacity for serving, on a personal rather than a general basis, some of the greatest needs of every living thing, in my estimation. I know that you have such great love to give — and when you nourish the children of your imagination with the tenderness you would give your own offspring, your reward is SURE to come . . . sometimes in ways unseen, like the echo of another's heartbeat.

Leo

August 13-August 22
Ruled by Mars

3rd decan

Fearlessness, independence, frankness, honesty and generosity are ordinarily some of the more outstanding characteristics people born in your third decan of Leo display. You are apt to have especially good business acumen, combined with a sense of humor, or appreciation of other people's badinage, at least. Yours is the most ambitious decan of Leo, but I doubt that you expect anything as your "due"; being an ardent and loyal worker, you very willingly give your devoted service, priding yourself on perfection in your finished results, and the practical means by which you've achieved them. For these reasons, you are capable of rising to positions of responsibility, authority, trust, control and management, in my estimation, although it will always be advantageous for you to take command over any tendencies toward being outspoken to a point of bluntness, which can otherwise prove embarrassing and humiliating to people who come to touch your life.

In work or in play you are likely to be energetic and enthusiastic, qualities that sometime incline you to either "overdo or act in haste and impulse", you later have reason to regret. There are individuals born in this decan who have fiery — occasionally even violent — temperaments that bring them to demand rather than ask for favors. In my estimation this is usually the result of an earlier environment that seems cold and unyielding, leaving small example of the "hows and whys" of diplomatically earning favorable attention they desire and earnestly seek — but, nonetheless, it brings such people to successive disappointments and sorrows instead of the sincere admiration they wish to receive. A slender "hurtful streak" is frequently evident in even the finest among those born in this decan, although close associates who treat them with loving adoration rather than fearful respect can usually "lead them by the nose". Because I have great confidence that you endeavor to modify your more assertive tendencies, I think that you infuse into whatever undertakings capture your interest a radiant energy, confidence and skillfulness that serves as an encouraging example for others. Being scornful of defeat, you are apt to display a "do or die" pioneering spirit with which you dauntlessly force an idea upon a reluctant world, by open and honest methods, compounded with indomitable courage, pluck and perseverence.

There is little doubt that you are basically greathearted. Your geniality is likely to win some of your greatest successes, because under most circumstances you probably remain a model of vigor and grace, taking pride in the splendor and range of your activities, and bending people around you through your warm persuasiveness. I believe that you have wide sympathies that give a great deal of breadth and balance to your actions, although you are less apt to concern yourself with betterment of animals than for Mankind. In all probability, you want happiness to reign over all the world, as well as in conditions around you, and you feel greatly disturbed by sly treachery or underhandedness. Even when you incline toward haughtiness, arrogance, melodrama or domination, as you may when you are pressed by more than the usual number of stresses, you'll strive for frankness, going into battle with your "flags flying and your bands playing", so to say, so that everyone will easily recognize their "opposition". This inclination may sometimes thwart material benefits you could otherwise receive, but you would probably rather magnanimously go "down in defeat" than feel that you have acted unfairly.

You are likely to have abundant interests which include

numerous people as well as in material things. Your style is rarely apt to be considered brilliant, owing to "the simplicity" or "common touch" with which you prefer to present yourself. Appearances may be ultra-important to you in some respects, but you might show little or no regard for them when your enthusiasm for a certain enterprise becomes aroused. I believe that elaborate descriptions will make my point less easily than living examples, so I shall mention, in this regard, some of my more typical Leo friends whose birthdays are also in your decan:

One is a regal, warm and charming woman — just "chock-full" of PERSONALITY. She lives in a gorgeous home that even includes a ballroom, where she maintains a staff of servants and entertains leading dignitaries who are professionally associated with her husband . . . but she loves nothing better than to climb into her "old" clothes and touch nature, or dissect any no-longer-living bug or animal she might find, checking against encyclopedias to determine pertinent details about the nervous system or muscle and tissue arrangements; sometimes she examines the botanical complexities of plants. This friend tailors expertly, making beautiful coats and suits for her family; she has waiting lists of people who wish to buy her paintings or take art lessons from her; she has written and published numerous children's books, books on poetry, and books on wildlife, which she illustrates herself. She personally helped the FBI break up a spy ring during one of the world wars; she is a devoted wife, and has reared four children plus several foster children.   One might find her building a wall or fixing a roof — or almost ANYTHING, just as one might any other Leo!

You third decan Leos seem capable of mastering ANY field of endeavor that appeals to you!

I know a man of this decan who was raised in the slums of New York. After a most difficult childhood, he was forced to leave school, at the age of fifteen, to devote even more time to work that would aid his family's support. When he could, he would walk miles across the city to a library where he could find information on his favorite "hobby", electronics and engineering. After a concentrated study, he took the graduating examinations of a leading university, which is noted for its severe academic requirements but issues a degree to anyone capable of passing these tests. My friend scored high on these — and went on to become a military authority on engineering and electronics, as well as an expert mathematician! He has made several of the more remarkable scientific inventions of this century, in fact.

Individuals born in your decan ordinarily use a somewhat "cautious" approach, because they prefer to methodically pursue enduring, stable and constructive objectives. You, no doubt, have this patience and moral force for pushing yourself steadfastly forward to conquest. Although you are apt to be overly-generous in most respects, there may be areas of your life where you tend to be somewhat selfish, emotionally — although I trust that you recognize this tendency and take measures to correct it. While you probably adore beautiful things and have a special "eye" for "quality", you are likely to be analytical, shrewd, assimilative and discerning in your outlook toward financial security. I believe that you strive for honesty in your concerns and faithfulness to your "obligations". You may have occasional phases when you tend to view your possessions as they "ought to be" instead of "as they are" — or decide that a certain course will be gainful, when everyone else appears unconvinced. On the other hand, you've probably learned, in your material reasoning, that it is sometimes less easy than it originally seemed, to draw logical conclusions from two premises.

The majority of people who share your birthday period or decan enjoy greater returns when they make "their own decisions" and choices than when they devote themselves to mutual endeavors, as there are frequently some stresses attached to these, and even "deception" upon occasion. You may have losses from "undetermined" sources, now and then, when other individuals or "corporations" manage your assets. There is almost invariably more than an ordinary degree of activity in this area of your life — and with few exceptions people of your decan realize at least one quite gratifying "endowment" that increases their personal holdings. I have observed also that questions arise over the estates of individuals of your acquaintance, sometimes, or that someone meets with strange "circumstances" near the close of life that never become entirely solved in your mind.

You are very apt to become known among relatives and neighbors alike for your sympathetic, charitable, hospitable and just disposition, which is almost bound to earn for you many pleasing favors. People who know you will usually remember your versatile, adaptable, inquisitive and communicative manner, and while this is likely to win for you numerous acquaintances, you probably have only a few cherished friendships, owing to the number of people who depend upon your strength to atone for their superficiality, diffusiveness, restlessness, excitability or inconsistency.

Because you are sympathetic, you probably "feel" another person's needs instantly — and you certainly have the "know-how" for renewing hope and courage in even the most distressing situations, and suggesting more realistic and profitable approaches to problems.

The only characteristic in the natures of third decan Leo people that is destructive rather than constructive is a tendency toward JEALOUSY — and until they learn to control it, they may now and then abuse their fine intuition by recognizing the weaknesses in certain individuals and making disparaging remarks they KNOW will be hurtful or put others at a disadvantage. I have noticed that they are rarely happy when they act in this manner, yet any seeming threat to their "dominion" can prompt tyrannical behavior powerful enough to devastate any promise of happiness or accomplishment. When they DETERMINE that they will NEVER express this part of their disposition, Leos of your decan have more potential than almost any other individuals for realizing perfection!

I wholeheartedly believe in a "law of return" that brings back to us in kind every thought and action we transmit. It often seems that Leos of this decan are thwarted or "thrust down" at their "moment of glory", or suddenly topple from high positions they've doggedly endeavored to attain. The tendency I just discussed might be a reason.

The romantic lives of people born in your decan are rarely as gratifying as they would really like them to be. You might be something of a "late bloomer" in developing an interest in this area, and find older or more serious individuals more attractive than many others. There is almost always some "coldness" or selfishness evident in at least one of these deeper relationships.

While you are probably attracted to the idea of having close relationships or partnerships, your strong and independent disposition is likely to make these seem more "binding" than pleasurable. When you promise to "love, honor and cherish", so to say, I think that you intend to do just that, and you will try your utmost to live up to any such promise or oath — but you will sometimes discover that you are either the entire "strength" of a close alliance into which you enter, or that by selecting associates who will yield to your own need for freedom to do as you please, you have also chosen those who do not easily invest themselves in another. I believe that your loyalty is steadfast, so that a disclosure that you and another person are not working faithfully toward a similar ideal is apt to be quite distressing for you.

Leos ordinarily love and want children with the deepest sincerity, but there is almost always at least some disappointment attached to this area of their lives. They may have difficulty gaining those they have or have none at all; they occasionally lose a child, or have problems through one. Sorrows of this kind often seriously affect marriages among people of your decan. On the other hand, these less happy experiences frequently drive some of you to do truly GREAT things for younger people — and while these might not appear to compensate you personally, in entirety, your magnanimous deeds will prove a distinct service to Mankind.

I feel that you take a strong pride in your "home" surroundings, although you rather easily become somewhat too tied to them, or such a "perfectionist" that casual alterations seem inconvenient.

I conclude that yours is one of the strongest and most powerful of all dispositions; you are so intensely gifted that by continually directing your dynamism to selfless undertakings that will IMPROVE conditions for every person who comes to touch your life, you will receive as one of your returns a sense of accomplishment and fulfillment you earn by radiating a genuine joyousness which is yours, alone, to give!

Virgo

August 23-September 2
Ruled by Sun

1st decan

A sunny disposition that gives an impression you are generous, outspoken, proud, free, ambitious, stable and firm is likely to be one of your more distinctive characteristics. Being born in this first decan of Virgo, you are apt to display more self-confidence than many other people of your sign, which may give you an apparent dignity that immediately earns the trust of individuals you meet. I believe this radiates from an inner-desire to serve and help other people, which will be so strong as to frequently bring you to sacrifice your personal preferences for the benefit of others upon whom you center your wide sympathies.

At the same time, you are probably something of a cynic, or at least less easy to convince than many people, because you approach newer ideas with skepticism that awaits further determination by your good reasoning mind. I think that you try to be discriminating and practical in carrying out your daily routines, and to apply logic that will reassure your inherent sense of causality.

Inwardly, you are apt to feel a certain shyness that prevents you from showing yourself as you are, or to present yourself with a reserve that conceals some of your sensibilities, although people who come to know you will no doubt have high regard for your "justness". Individuals born in this first decan of Virgo ordinarily have excellent and retentive memories, although they frequently allow garnered facts to repose unused. You should learn readily, although you may sometimes be slower to learn from experience than actual study, especially in the area of physical well-being, and particularly dietary matters. You are apt to have phases when you tend to seem somewhat worrisome. People who come to know you well probably realize that your reactions to situations are generally more superficial than they outwardly appear, but I trust that YOU endeavor to express your more HOPEFUL thoughts which will be encouraging to everyone concerned.

The earlier lives of individuals born in your decan are ordinarily happier than not, in areas that might be considered more "basic", although you no doubt have to make more effort than many people to "push your real self forward", so to say, owing to an inclination toward reticence. The cycle through "high-school age" is frequently responsible for the greater complexities you will eventually exhibit in your day-to-day interests, because of peculiar combinations within your personality of: "studiousness"; sprinklings of exuberance . . . a "super-flexibility"; staunch, unbending will . . . patience with stinging temper . . . generosity; self-centered quality and a desire to give all that you feel you can, compounded with a rather strong dislike of responsibility.

These opposing characteristics can be beautifully blended in mathematical, mechanical and technical pursuits, or similar analytical studies, although some people of this decan instead suffer untold privation and affliction; sometimes restraint or even confining or restricting conditions in their personal lives. In the development of your better judgment, I'm sure you've known a few problems you would prefer to have done without, but I have confidence that your EFFORTS are constructive. Therefore, I anticipate that conditions will improve for you with each passing year.

During these earlier times, there is almost always some feeling of competition between individuals of this decan and siblings or acquaintances who are "closer" than many, while there is usually a noteworthy "accidental" situation flaring for a time, involving others or attached to "a passing" cyclic trend that is related to transit or travel.

There are quite often, in the lives of individuals of your decan, some changes in the "immediate" or "parental" family structure which are not merely swift, but, in your thinking, illusory — and these may tend to increase your own restlessness. Nevertheless, you are likely to realize from at least one person who strongly influences your rearing, extremely favorable returns, perhaps sometimes more than are really beneficial for you.

I think that you hold a realistic, sensible, appreciative and thorough attitude toward a college education. Whether or not you attain your knowledge through formal means, as you probably will, your arrival at the "late teens" and "early twenties" ought to bring you into a less stressful period than the one preceding, giving more solidity to your manner and stability to your opinions. This is a time of your life when you may hesitate over an opportunity you will later wish you had taken. Some travel is also probable that will permanently sway a few of your attitudes. You might have occasional moods when associates will consider you brooding, stodgy or prejudiced in your outlook toward certain subjects, but in all likelihood this is due, in at least some measure, to your desire to be a cautious and profound thinker without jumping to conclusions. One of the characteristics others are almost bound to notice in you is that while you approach almost every new endeavor with curiosity and an appearance of dispersement, you are really apt to alter your original religious and philosophical viewpoints very little. There might be times when you tend to take an inordinate pride in your intellectual ability, but for the most part you no doubt remain cool-headed and even-balanced, making few pretensions as you carry out your routines quietly and unobserved.

Being mindful of "detail and very methodical", you will

be discriminative and keenly critical — but I trust that you also strive for tact, keeping your more unkind discoveries to yourself. In your way of thinking, there is likely to be one certain way various concerns should be undertaken — and it will seem intolerable to find that they are being done otherwise. When you endeavor to show appreciation for the manner in which other people conduct themselves, even though this is sometimes quite different from the one you might seek for yourself, you are almost bound to earn more and more favorable results in gaining their cooperation for "enterprises" which are of interest to you. I know people who have birthdays in this decan who are unusually revengeful and sarcastic when they meet with opinions that do not match their own, but I'm sure you've discovered that combativeness brings you fewer accomplishments than the courageous placement of your sharp, acute and capable mind in constructive efforts that will serve practical purposes.

The balance of your financial interests is likely to be quite changeful, principally owing to a fondness for possessions and pursuits that aren't really necessary, but increases the pleasure you receive in your usual activities, as well as a tendency to build up more ideas than you will execute. At most, you will probably find some way of gaining those things you really wish for most, while you should ordinarily receive "gratifying returns from services you perform" that will prove helpful to Mankind. A solid education is more essential to the "earning-power" of individuals of your decan than most people, in my opinion.

Close "partnerships" and similar mutual endeavors that bring your material interests together with those of other people are rarely likely to prove as completely harmonious or as successful for you as your more singular efforts. Dissensions are sometimes apt to arise in some of these, or it may appear to you that any assets you receive from others are quickly dissipated. It seems especially advisable for you to keep your material concerns distant from those of such people as relatives or "neighbors". Many of your more "speculative" undertakings will probably prove highly gainful, particularly those related to the earth, such as golf courses, mining or real estate. Flying and enterprises that are helpful to air travelers frequently attract favorable attention from people of your decan, while many involve themselves quite successfully in fields of communications or by expressing themselves through the use of words, written or spoken.

You've surely had to learn that your tendency to "dabble" in a variety of pursuits needs control, but when you select several consuming objectives upon which you will concentrate your whole attention, you should earn quite pleasing results from your efforts. A "DOUBLE LIFE" will no doubt mark your existence in one respect or another, not only in these "outside activities", but in those more personal as well. The majority of people in this decan marry more than once or enter into numerous business partnerships; they ordinarily live in a "multiple dwelling" at some time, or acquire "homes" in several different locations. Certainly, it does not seem natural for you to stay in one situation very long, which gives you a strong inclination for travel − often to strange places.

I notice that individuals born in your decan are almost always quite popular, and that they receive many favors from their acquaintances. The society of people distant from your usual surroundings is apt to seem more attractive than that of those nearby, or in "neighboring" areas. You have probably had at least one experience with a person in close vicinity you consider "bitter". On the other hand, when you endeavor to promote harmonious relationships with such people, by giving praise where you can and refusing to retaliate when you feel that they have acted against your better interests, you ought to have fewer problems in this area.

Of all the things you truly wish for, I believe that a happy "domestic" life is first, or at least a home of your own design. You might have associates who overlook this inherent quality, owing to your tendency to consider your environment restrictive to your independence, but I know, as you do, that this is only because you abhor a feeling of being "bound".

While your romantic life is apt to be abundant, you will probably approach it with a sense of responsibility, resourcefulness, conscientiousness — and in the hope it will be productive of marriage and children. This practical outlook surely earns its rewards, although your "purposeful" attitude might deny some of the more "lighthearted entertainment" many people relish. My friends in this decan seem to either be slow to marry, or choose someone older than they are; many never marry at all, or have a long period of bachelorhood between marriages. In some manner, you are likely to feel that you sacrifice yourself in very close alliances like marriage or business partnerships, so that you are apt to enter into them out of a sense of duty. You might have a loss or disappointment in this area, the origin of which you never quite understand, or a person who touches your life in this manner or you, yourself, may spend some time in a confining element, placing an apparent "burden" upon you. I must conclude in this respect that what you consider your greatest sorrows will come from more intimate association, although many compensations will result from your relationships with a particular younger person.

Emotions are not likely to play a great part in your disposition, but your sympathies may often prompt you to take additional responsibilities, and when you endeavor to give whatever aid you think you can without becoming too involved personally, you might prevent many difficulties. The motto "look before you leap" will always be well worth remembering, in my estimation.

You might incline to be extremely "secretive" about many of your interests, upon occasion, although you are generally likely to show directness in both expression and thought. The older you grow, the more you should make a practice of reflecting before you speak, so that you will better gain from life all that you truly seek. There might be things in your past that you look upon with regret, even at times without realizing that you do, which may bring you to show apology for yourself in many instances, by minimizing your accomplishments or making belittling statements about yourself you know are really not true. A display of confidence will always be more advantageous for you, because other people are almost bound to admire your dignity, when you make it a primary part of your daily life. Although you no doubt have phases when you seem somewhat solitary and retiring, I believe that you enjoy the companionship of other people, or at least being in the company of others. I have very great confidence in you. Therefore, I trust that you will devote all of your energies to constructive pursuits which are HELPFUL to other people. By making a practice of honesty, forgiveness, kindness and commendation, I am certain you will earn gratifying returns.

When you use the magnificent qualities with which I'm sure you are naturally endowed, and you determine that you will improve every condition within and around you, better coordinating your efforts, as well, circumstances will bend at your command, bringing to your reach the fulfillment of your fondest wishes!

Virgo

September 3-September 12
Ruled by Venus

Having your sun in this second decan of Virgo, I should expect you to have a kind disposition which you often express through bright dialogue. You probably display a genial and vivacious nature that is even further enhanced by pleasant allusions that often seem to fill your very being. Invariably, people of your decan have more than an ordinary degree of grace and attractiveness, owing to a sunny, cheerful, sympathetic and affectionate disposition, as well as an inclination to make the most of their personal appearance. These qualities no doubt win for you a great deal of admiration in circles of society where you are. I believe that you have a natural affinity for "staging" which enables you to produce a somewhat artistic effect in almost any endeavor you touch.

Although you might have a special fondness for music, singing, the theatre, and all refined pleasures, you are apt to be exceptionally clever with intricate design, especially in undertakings that require that the whole of your finished product will evolve out of "a number of separate pieces".

Instinctively, you have high regard for modesty, chastity and purity, in all likelihood, that prompts you to show deep compassion for certain pets or people who toil and for the sick, which may frequently turn your attention to work being done in large "institutions" or charitable enterprises where you think you might in some way be of additional service, especially in areas of health.

I have a few friends who share your birthday decan who are unusually shy, and so fussy that they become almost intolerable perfectionists, but I trust that you are merely CAREFUL, without carrying this excellent attribute to extremes. Individuals of your decan ordinarily entertain beautifully, spending many hours, when necessary, in an effort to contribute to the comfort of their guests; and while they are some of the most sociable of all people, they have an extraordinarily keen and accurate perception that inclines them to be fastidious in the selection of their associates, as you may be, too.

I think that a basic tendency toward indifference to many situations that would seem to require emotional response from some people gives you a special magnetism all your own. With the strong conviviality you are almost certain to display, it might seem to many who know you well an idiosyncrasy that you occasionally have a power of expressing sensibilities you do not really feel. You may be perfectly capable of giving a very convincing demonstration of sentiments that inwardly touch you very little, but this is no doubt because you tend to distribute your more delicate feelings through intellectual channels. Many marvelous nurses, speakers and actors belong to your decan, who can efficiently carry out their "routines", giving an impression of caring without actual involvement or pity.

You are likely to have stronger attachments to relatives or other individuals who influence the earlier years of your life than many people would, being not only popular with them, but even somewhat "clannish" in your outlook toward their concerns. I have friends in this decan who retain these close relationships with neighbors or schoolmates over years and years and years. Through "high-school age", shyness might bring you to "shine" more easily from "behind-the-scenes" than in the forefront of your major activities, although this is likely to be a cyclic period when you enjoy many "honors" and favors, about some of which few people know. Having a special knack for out-maneuvering your "opponents" you have probably found from the beginning that even when associates intend to undermine some of your interests they almost always prove to serve these even better! I feel that a reason for this is your desire to quietly promote better conditions for individuals who temporarily seem less happy than many others, which brings back to you in kind, favorable results from certain efforts which are particularly important to you. Critical opinions have almost surely filtered into your words and actions from time to time, although each passing year ought to bring greater recognition that you earn vast returns from your sympathetic understanding and true generosity, which make these more laudable attributes well worth cultivation at least equal to your refusal to exercise those others that only harm advantages you otherwise would receive.

When you reach the "late teens or early twenties", you should discover that you are becoming somewhat more reserved, slow-reacting and cautious in your responses, which adds steadiness to your endeavors and gives a greater appearance of your being reflective and quiet in manner. I believe that you hold quite steadfastly to many impressions you receive during these years of your life — and while changes you make will be within the range of your original values, you will alter to at least some degree a few of your philosophical and religious viewpoints. This is a phase when you may strongly resent any interference with your ideas, but for the most part you are likely to remain conventional and conservative.

True devotion is apt to seem even more significant to you at these ages — and you might gain special recognition for something you do or accomplish. Acquaintances you make during this period may hold importance for a long time to come; some of your favored objectives might well be fulfilled, and what you learn will almost certainly be long-remembered.

Owing to the promptings of an energetic parent or another person who similarly influences your rearing, you will probably approach life with a display of agility, liveliness and being career-minded. I know people born in this decan who are exceptionally argumentative and highstrung, and dissipate their energies — but most of my friends among them transfer their marvelous verve to assorted and tangible goals, as I am confident you do. You may have noticed a tendency to disperse some of your forces, from time to time, but when you do so, you are apt to become more irritable and excitable. I'm sure you have numerous interests in many different directions, which makes it imperative that you coordinate your efforts so that you may achieve in the fullest the many successes of which I think you are capable.

I feel that it is essential for you to maintain variety in the various aims you strive to achieve, yet continuity will be necessary before you can properly persist in any policy. I suggest that you determine that you will do several things, and then see them faithfully through to conclusion before acquiring newer interests that also appeal to you. Otherwise, some of your efforts may incline to become intermittent, bringing you to a halt just "short of the finish", so to say.

Many individuals who have birthdays similar to your own find great expression for their more inquisitive, original and inventive characteristics in fields having to do with "the air", although various realms of technical "know-how" frequently hold excellent possibilities. You do need to involve yourself in enterprises that benefit some of the needs of Humanity, in my estimation, before you can find your true happiness. The use of your "intuition" and experience will often advance undertakings that attract your attention, in all probability, although there might be occasions when you tend to lean neither to one side or the other of issues on which you are expected to take a stand. You are apt to have an admirable faculty for concentration, provided you earnestly apply yourself to "tasks at hand".

The majority of people born in your decan enjoy excellent health. When problems arise in this area, it usually seems that they result from "nerves" rather than actual constitutional defects. You might tend to think and talk about health matters often, or to anticipate illnesses that will probably never come to pass. In my estimation, you will find it beneficial to make a daily practice of concentrating your thoughts on PEACE, HARMONY and HAPPINESS, which you KNOW are "WITHIN" and in EVERY condition surrounding your life. As your optimism grows, your sense of well-being will improve, I feel quite certain!

Material concerns are frequently likely to appear somewhat more "weighty" or "restrictive" than you would really like, owing to reversals in the assets of your "family" and similar "stalls" that delay prompt returns from many of your efforts. I have observed among my friends in this decan that even when resources, as a whole, are quite abundant, there is often a "partner" or some other person who makes such an issue over expenditures that any real pleasure in spending which might otherwise be attained is limited, placing "out of balance" whatever assets there are. Nevertheless, your close associations with other people and large enterprises or companies are usually likely to be favorable for your interests, sometimes bringing even larger returns than many of your more personal efforts. "Speculative" paths are apt to have appeal for you, although it appears to me that these will be more gainful when you approach them cautiously, centering the majority of your attention on athletic and similar competitive concerns, as well as those having to do with properties, "real estate", mining and land. Impulsive ventures will rarely bring as gratifying returns as those you approach more conservatively, in my opinion.

I believe that you have stronger inclinations for making numerous acquaintances than confiding friendships, yet you will tend to be so receptive to people you meet that they rather easily influence your thinking. You probably have a good insight into human nature that indicates to you immediately upon meeting another person the basic character that lies within, which often proves helpful, no doubt. Although you might display a great deal of tolerance in selecting your associates, you probably find the company of individuals who are not in harmony with your basic views almost unendurable, so that when you do dislike, you incline to dislike quite intensely. A saving grace might be that you do not always try to apply the same degree of logic to your social affairs you would to other areas of your life, holding, instead, an attitude that opinions are not, after all, of supreme importance. You probably prefer the company of people who easily converse and seem intelligent, yet are "domestically" inclined, so that they can discuss with you such things as gardening or food preparation, as well as purely human subjects.

Romantically, individuals of your decan are usually tremendously magnetic and commanding, although they are apt to display a somewhat forceful and direct quality in their approach, from time to time. You no doubt know what you want and recognize it when you see it, which may fill you with will and determination that could almost be called obstinacy. There are therefore likely to be some stresses in this area of your life, or occasional "battles of will" — but because you have abundant charm, you are very apt to gain the triumphs that seem most important to you.

In your more entertaining pursuits, you may have frequent attractions to individuals who appear ambitious. I feel sure that you admire tireless enthusiasm for work and a strong sense of responsibility, which may often bring you into associations with individuals who seem to be good organizers and show promise of holding somewhat "authoritative" places in their mutual activities. This may occasionally prompt you to form relationships with people you think are capable of rising out of the environment in which they were born, into an even better one. Having a fondness for "sports and games of chance", you might often seek companions who share these interests, or while you are participating in such pursuits you may meet individuals who will come to give you many entertaining hours.

A contradiction in these selections may arise sometimes, when you then think of developing such associations into "partnerships", because in either marriage or close business alliances you are apt to find your greatest happiness with individuals who have benevolent, compassionate, humorous, genial and generous dispositions, even at the cost of some of the more ambitious qualities that previously held your esteem. There might be occasions when you inadvertently join your major efforts with those of individuals who prove to be unreliable, extravagant or over-imaginative, but even when a few of your closer alliances prove less satisfying than you would really like, they are, in some way, likely to bring certain advantages to your interests.

Multiplicities are apt to arise in many different areas of your life. I notice that a number of people born in your decan marry more than once, or become active in several highly dissimilar activities; some have business as well as marriage partners, or income from several sources. I know a few who have "step-parents" or are reared by people other than those to whom they were born, while some have multiple-births. Most of these friends of mine eventually maintain residences in more than one location, just as you may.

Although there are frequently difficulties or disappointments through at least one younger person, others almost always compensate. As a general rule, however, certain "domestic" dissensions will be evident in the lives of people of your decan, some of which are tied to relationships with children. Because I have confidence that YOU earnestly endeavor to give deserved compliments and otherwise attend as much to the emotional as material needs of youngsters you know, you probably enjoy more gratifying results from these associations than many people.

Being born in this second decan of Virgo, you might have

a tendency to become more and more restless with each passing year. When you center your energies in constructive activities, I am certain that other people will compliment your cheerful, sincere manner, and often turn to you for advice they consider almost "prophetic". By developing your aptitudes and pursuing interests that appeal to you, your pride of accomplishment will surely grow — and, accordingly, "your sense of inner peace" will increase also. Many of my friends in this decan love to travel, as you may, and I observe that this very often leads to many pleasing experiences. From time to time, however, you are almost bound to have moods when you prefer secluded surroundings, or to live a somewhat more "retiring" life.

In summation, I feel that you are gifted with many truly brilliant qualities, which are yours to use for the benefit of other people. When you make kindness and graciousness your first objective, I know you will win loyal "friends" among people who come to touch your life, many of whom will look upon you in a spirit of brotherhood, as a true patron of the "poor and needy" — you will be a person beloved by all!

Virgo

September 13-September 23
Ruled by Mercury

 3rd decan

An excellent memory is apt to be one of your finest attributes, because, being born in this third decan of Virgo, you may be, not only quick to learn, but almost "photographic" in your retention of practical information that comes to your attention. This might occasionally give some of your associates an impression that you are not paying attention at times that seem to them "critical". Actually, I believe that you have a faculty for "carrying on" one conversation while you are listening to another, and taking away with you all that you've learned from both, or doing two entirely dissimilar things at once, without any distraction to either. Your nature is apt to be alert and quick; restless and loquacious, but because you are likely to develop your greatest strengths in intellectual lines, other people who come to know you, may sometimes consider that there is a certain detachment and coldness to your disposition. I feel, personally, that this is primarily due to an inclination to try to regulate your life by "logical reasoning" in a world which is often moved by emotion, feeling, passion or sentiment.

The characteristic of your mental processes may make you suited to deal with practical affairs in either technical fields or in the area of physical well-being, possibly medicine, hygiene or diet because you are probably very adept at analysis. I think there is a very definite stability to your approach, even when it is touched by superficialities, that enables you to store within your memory information which appears practical for your present purposes, and discard, as if they never existed, facts which seem more trivial.

Regardless of circumstances that have brought you to the point where you are today, you are no doubt a grammarian, at least to some degree. You might scan a whole body of material and notice instantly every flaw, or you may tend to catch little errors in speech that substantially distract you from a point another person is trying to make. This superb knack for correcting that which you find around you may make you a valuable "efficiency expert" in circles of activity where you are, because I feel confident that you are also discerning, withholding your less kind judgments for situations that will benefit from your offers of improvement.

You are apt to have a special fondness for word games, or games using cards, although many golfers are born in the sign Virgo, because you combine knowledge with logic to shrewdly outwit your opponents. Although there is a great deal of plasticity and receptiveness to your mind, in my opinion, you are also keenly aware of everything going on around you. This might bring you to take notice of sounds which are too low or too loud; temperatures that are even minutely different from those to which you are ordinarily accustomed, or noises that are not in their proper place, such as "squeaks" and "knocks" — and you will no doubt feel compelled to see that these are immediately repaired. This is certain to make you a master for managing details in whatever direction you might choose — because there is little question that you will strive for perfection.

People of your decan are ordinarily the least domestically inclined of the "Virgo family". A somewhat more "public" life is apt to appeal to you rather strongly, although your approach is likely to be so versatile that you tend to diffuse some of your energies now and then. I believe that you are exceptionally inquisitive — although you like to be "secretive" about your own interests — and this prompts you to "try your hand" at a variety of enterprises that you feel will enable you to communicate your "real self" on a wider scale. Being highly adaptable, you may be well suited for a number of different pursuits, many of which you might undertake at the same time. There is a certain irresponsibility and vagueness to your approach, in all probability. Finding it hard to concentrate upon any one subject, or even to take any subject too seriously, you may occasionally appear to devote yourself to the prosecution of a particular object — but it will often seem as if there was originally no real basis corresponding to the observed effect. For this reason, one occasionally meets people born in this decan of Virgo who are so "restlessly excitable" that they appear highly inconstant, or even extremely superficial — but I have strong confidence that YOU direct the dualities of your nature to versatile and constructive activities that preserve your finer abilities.

While you are an enthusiastic "worker", I think, permanent projects make you restless and uneasy in a short space of time, bringing you to feel happier when you have "more than one" dominant interest. In carrying out your daily routines, you are apt to display some detachment, although you are almost bound to be imaginative and courteous, dispassionately organizing "tasks at hand" to the best of your ability. I am sure that you display something of a "scientific attitude", and you will combine this with great interest in other people. There is some humanitarianism in your spirit, I have little doubt, but while you admire in people you meet a sense of personal involvement, YOU are more inclined to function on a somewhat more impersonal plane, remaining unmoved by such things as emotionalism, rationalism, or sentimentality. This might be an explanation why individuals born in your birthday period "are rarely" known as extremists or fanatics.

I feel certain that you display to people you come to see from day-to-day a universality of views that earns for you a reputation as a marvelous conversationalist, always well worth listening to. You are likely to observe social graces, and infuse any gathering with an attractiveness which is distinctly and uniquely YOURS. This inherent characteristic may sometimes seem less favorable for you than for people around you, because you are apt to give more pleasure to others than you always think you receive in return. Although you are surely extremely social, you are seldom likely to feel entirely satisfied with any one individual, because your sympathies move in too many channels.

I have observed that individuals born in your decan ordinarily enjoy excellent health. When problems do arise, constitutionally, they are ordinarily of emotional origin. You might have a tendency to take alarm over small indications of ill-health, but when you endeavor to hold calming and peaceful thoughts, your nervous system should become quite tranquil — and as it does, circumstances surrounding your life ought to, as well. By merely seeking a "change", you may resolve many difficulties.

During the earlier years of your life, you might have a tendency to be somewhat worrisome or hypercritical, but very deep feelings and magnetic charm usually make this cycle one of popularity and scholastic accomplishment. Sometimes there are social troubles or competitiveness with such people as sisters, brothers and other relatives, or "neighbors", that make this phase rather "stormy" from time to time — but a strong rapport is often established with these same people later on. Favors and attention are likely to accompany this time, yet you might be aware of little "jealousies" over affection which is given to some of your associates, or one, in particular, upon occasion.

Among people of your decan, I notice that there is almost invariably a rather substantial disappointment over a relationship with one of the parents, and this experience sometimes leads to a life-long condition bordering on unhappiness touching your "home surroundings", some of which might be due to lack of trust and optimism, or a deep-seated suspicion that even when "things are going well", so to say, they may soon take a less favorable turn. By analyzing this tendency and making any adjustments that seem applicable to YOU, you are very likely to realize growing harmony in this area of your life.

In spite of this tendency, I think that you rather cherish the idea of having a home and family life free from contentions, which might be a reason why you incline to establish real "friendships" with your relations, and are so frequently attracted to maternal and paternal temperaments in selecting your closer acquaintances.

You are apt to take a rather reserved, cautious, calculating, conscientious and responsible attitude toward your romantic life, being more strongly guided by your ambitions than your emotions. I doubt that "frivolous types" appeal to you as strongly as those who show foresight and steadiness, and prove their trustworthiness to an objective, which should earn for you gratifying distinctions and even, sometimes, honors, through people with whom you share some of your more entertaining moments. Having simple tastes, I believe that you take strong personal pride in the attractiveness of your favored companions, but in your estimation "naturalness" is imperative.

At least one close union or partnership you form in business or marriage is almost certain to result in stresses or disillusionment, which makes it seem to me advisable that you select your closest associates especially carefully. At some time or another it appears that people of your decan become involved with a person who is prone to excesses of food, drink or drugs, or that there are deceptive conditions which are never entirely explained. A reason might be that you are apt to enter into these alliances with people who incline to be generous, but intensely emotional and tempera-mental, or are otherwise unstable. You are seldom likely to reveal to many around you the true facts concerning any such mismatches, owing to a rather magnanimous attitude you are apt to hold that will prevent you from making publicly known any little "enmities" that develop, although your greatest disappointments have probably come from these.

You will wish for children, in all likelihood, as well as a good education for them, and in one way or another they might play a rather fortunate and prominent role in your life.

I believe that your restless nature longs for change, prompt-ing you to travel as often as you feel you can, and to seek within your outside mutual activities sufficient diversity to provide outlets for your abundant energies. This might lead you to look upon your "home environment" with a sense of duty more than pleasure, or you may find its influences limit-ing to many of your preferred desires. People of your decan are ordinarily capable researchers, preparers and investigators; many realize their more phenomenal accomplishments from "behind-the-scenes" undertakings; others throw almost all of their efforts into "hidden enterprises", and then present an appearance of rather effortlessly enjoying returns these endeavors bring. This might attract you to a somewhat "retiring" existence, from time to time, although you are apt to enjoy the society of other people too much to become truly reclusive.

You may attain some of your greatest pleasures from trips you take to distant places, but responsibilities you feel toward interests closer to your usual locale will no doubt prevent these from being as numerous as you would really like.

There is very little likelihood that you will change during

your lifetime, your basic "childhood beliefs" to any great extent, yet "blind faith" or strong spiritual conviction is apt to touch you very little. In your over-all outlook, you will probably display quite a lot of patience and moral force, which are based more on material considerations than a sense of righteousness. When you are faced with displeasing conditions, you probably have an instinct for either sidestepping them, or ignoring these entirely, a quality that gives an over-all appearance of immense tolerance.

Financial and material affluence is extremely characteristic of your decan. I believe that other people are exceptionally helpful to your more gainful efforts, while those in which you participate more singularly will earn substantial rewards as well. You are likely to display particularly good judgment in matters involving your assets and possessions, perhaps because your approach will be simple and sensible, reliant more upon building for the future than immediate returns. Speculative ventures no doubt have attraction for you, as well, and bring back to you similarly gratifying results. It often seems that people of your decan are "just plain lucky" in these respects, because however desperate their circumstances, something appears to come unfailingly to their rescue, even when this aid seems to arrive "just in the nick of time"!

"Little things" mean more to you than most people, in my opinion, bringing you to feel touching sentimentality over a kindness or thoughtful gesture; in turn, you may extend more than the usual number of courtesies yourself. I am sure this earns for you a beloved reputation among people who come to know you. When you move forward with sincerity, striving for ways in which you may better serve your fellow man, I feel that YOU will continually RECEIVE even more advantages than you offer!

Libra

September 24-October 3
Ruled by Moon

1st decan

This first decan of Libra is exceptionally persuasive. Being born under its influence, you are no doubt quite shrewd and capable of handling other people and situations in general. This peculiar "maneuvering" ability enables you to be compromising, diplomatic and courteous — because I have strong confidence that you use it for the BETTERMENT, rather than hurt people who come to touch your life.

It is very, very important for you to strive for "equilibrium", in my estimation, owing to a tendency among individuals born in your decan to be too well balanced or the exact opposite, either of which leads to extremes in action or thought, or both. When you earnestly endeavor to find a "middle ground" upon which to devote your energies, your aesthetic perceptions will increase, I know, earning admiration for your great quality of balanced judgment.

You are likely to be fond of show, which brings you to take the "center of the stage" in circles of society where you are, or mimic rather easily professional stylists or "stars" who attract your interest. There may be times when, after only a brief exchange, you find yourself duplicating little mannerisms or an accent, or putting into your voice the same inflections used by someone you met. In your desire to create the "right" impression, you might spend days trying to determine exactly what you will wear for a certain occasion, frequently changing your mind as you do so — and preferring, within, for someone else to make the decision for you. I believe that you are meticulous about your dress and acutely aware of your general appearance, which prompts you to observe yourself in mirrors and similarly notice your reflection more often than many people.

Practicality is not likely to be one of your major attributes. A reason might be that you incline to relate everything to yourself, weighing one thing against another according to your personal experience. With your self as the "center" for all activity, you are apt to react to almost every situation according to your own emotions: "I can understand this, because I often feel this way myself", or, "I would probably do the same thing in equal circumstances, because, after all, I remember the time when I . . ."

I think that you feel little need for seclusion, largely whiling away your time in association with other individuals. This is an admirable characteristic that almost certainly wins for you many pleasing acquaintances, but it is also imperative that you develop definite PURSUITS that will give productivity to your existence, in my opinion, because you are brilliantly talented in many different directions that will prevent your grandiose schemes and magnificent ideas from going unused. When you make a policy of returning things you borrow and minimizing the number of appropriations you ask; you show a genuine interest in other people's concerns, and make a policy of DOING everything you SAY you are going to do, provided, of course, it is constructive, you are sure to enjoy growing HAPPINESS, SUCCESS, POPULARITY and FULFILLMENT!

Your moods are likely to be changing, occasionally swinging from the most excessive optimism to deep melancholy; a sense of inferiority might impel you to mention every compliment you receive and go to extreme lengths to win "a pat" on the back. I know a number of people of this birthday period who love to sulk over fancied injuries and feel abused — but I trust that you place at the forefront of your thoughts your appreciation of beauty, harmony, artistry and justice, thus enabling those around you to enjoy the real suavity of your disposition.

Being idealistic in nature, I feel that you often display a

manner which is graceful and gives you considerable social charm, while your methods of expression will similarly have some of this characteristic delicacy. You may tend to shirk coarse or dirty tasks, because of your dislike of them, although you are apt to prefer these tasks to people who act crudely.

Open-mindedness, foresightedness, frankness and versatility are likely to become evident in your personality at a very early age, to give you an illusory, transitory and lightning-like quality. You might be known for your question-asking, owing to an insatiable curiosity that makes your thoughts present themselves like shooting stars and gives you a rather pronounced air of simplicity. This is a phase when your impatience might prompt you to speak in haste and "repent at leisure", so to say. I doubt that you deliberately intend to wound; you sometimes forget to consider how your remarks may strike the hearer, or feel so certain of words still left unspoken that you introduce a newer thought.

Interrogations into religious and philosophical principles might occupy many of your conversations and a good deal of your time, bringing you to cross-examine people who share your day-to-day routines, in an effort to establish the over-all values you will take with you through the remainder of your life. Politics, law and geography are also likely to have special appeal.

It frequently seems that the earlier "home environment" of individuals born in your decan presents too few challenges; lack of discipline is often quite noticeable. While this will surely be an asset in many ways, it is apt to discourage a sense of responsibility that comes from making difficult decisions and surmounting, unaided, difficult obstacles, which may be a reason why some people born in this first decan of Libra appear in adulthood to lack character or "backbone", and find it hard to settle their own affairs with certainty. It can also make marriage and other close alliances unusually stressful, when these appear to present the first real challenges to their wants.

As you gain maturity, you will probably have opportunities for attaining a higher education, although you are apt to feel undecided with respect to your true objectives. I notice that the "late teens and early twenties" frequently prove expansive for people of your decan. For you, too, these might permit outward manifestation of plans, changes or ideas you have secretly held for a long time. A few of your associates might consider that there is a certain diffuseness, or even shallowness, in your activities, because of the fluidity of your interests — but when you seize circumstances favorable for your purposes and determine that you will improve upon your inherent gifts by putting to constructive use your many, many talents, these years of your life are certain to lift you toward the top of any "hill" you may choose to climb!

I believe that yours is a highly romantic nature — although your charming and enthusiastic personality will earn attractions that occasionally make it seem difficult for you to permanently settle your attention on one individual. Young, impulsive alliances are very often formed among individuals born in your birth cycle, frequently with material advantages as one of the underlying motives, but unless the other person's energy sparks your own ambitions to give better direction to your capabilities in mutual activity, there will sometimes be clashes of will that bring less gratifying results than you originally anticipated. This is probably a reason why many people of your decan are considered better "lovers" than marriage partners; better friends than business associates — because until they learn to control any tendencies toward fickleness, unsteadiness, vacillation or evasion of responsibilities, as I trust YOU do, their prospects for maintaining complete harmony are rather limited.

A few of your tastes, in your selection of close companions, may appear unconventional to some of your acquaintances, because your affections are developed on humanitarian lines, in all likelihood. Instead of giving your blind allegiance to one person, you are more apt to offer your "friendship" along quieter, more coolly-affectionate lines than many people. I doubt that domesticity will appeal to you as strongly as social rapport, which will often inspire intellectual attractions or attachments that offer mutual understanding without the fetters of deep personal attachments.

Because you are likely to approach all of your interests through gentle and ingratiating methods that radiate sweetness, sensitivity and amiability, you might create an impression of being more readily given to home and family life than you really are — but while you may be more attractive and more brilliant than many other people, you are less likely to have the "good old-fashioned" fervor for day-to-day routine counted upon by a person who hopes to have your complete devotion.

Your monetary interests are often likely to be closely linked to an alliance you form, while these considerations might prompt you to enter into many mutual endeavors which would otherwise attract you very little. It appears to me that your financial concerns will sometimes be stressful, owing to contentions that arise over them, or spending which is in excess of your income; you may discover that you are misplacing your energies, from time to time, in enterprises that prove less gainful than you hoped at the onset. When you approach matters having to do with your assets and possessions conservatively, balancing necessities against pursuits you consider more entertaining, and striving for permanent security, commensurate benefits should result. By following the opinions or counsel of trusted "advisors", you are often likely to realize substantial advantages, because in all probability you will tend to attract to yourself individuals who approach such interests sensibly, deliberately, realistically and thoroughly, using for their guide good, practical experience.

I think that you have a keen intuition which will frequently serve you well in "speculative" investments, as in other areas. Your perception may increase with astonishing rapidity, giving you an insight far superior to that of most people, when you endeavor to OBSERVE people and situations around you, projecting into them with no thought of self. I notice that individuals of your decan ordinarily have very strong spiritual resources, although these will invariably embrace a number of different religious concepts rather than a single dogma. This might be true of you, as well — and you probably have a special faculty for conveying inspiring messages in speech or writing that uplift your fellow human beings and earn for you esteem.

By channeling in this direction your idealistic intentions; that certain detachment from deep personal involvement which in my opinion you have; your imagination, and inherent feeling that your life purpose is, in some way, to become a "savior" of Mankind, the charity, diplomacy, benevolence and sympathy of your disposition will surely serve to promote better conditions in the world. Many judges are born in the sign Libra. I believe, absolutely, that WHAT you give will unfailingly come back to you in kind — so that when you emit generously these magnificent attributes which I feel are yours to share, your own success and happiness will be insured. I consider that your talents can be triumphantly directed in many different channels — you might dedicate them to betterment of the interests of younger people or to the entertainment world — whatever your choice, I URGE you to USE them always to the fullest.

Should you have moments when your hopes and wishes seem delayed in their realization, as you probably will, or people you consider friends and acquaintances appear to impose more limitations than pleasures, you might find it beneficial to weigh carefully every possible alternative, considering whether you are actually SEEKING in equal measure to your expectations and otherwise contributing as much as you believe you ought to receive.

The aggregate of your temperament is paradoxically economical and extravagant, in my estimation; you can bring together in PERFECT HARMONY your extraordinarily fine characteristics by remembering that your dreams are only as promising as the goals they set. The higher your goals, the more fulfilling the realization of your dreams will be, I feel, provided only you determine that from this moment you WILL STRIVE TO REACH THESE. You will receive property, or other very welcome endowments, I believe, but these will come through your associations with other people or their efforts.

Libra

October 4-October 13
Ruled by Saturn

I believe that you have a personality which other people consider singularly pleasing, because you generally display amiability, cooperativeness, friendliness and mellowness of strength. You probably have excellent concentrative powers which add a distinct conservatism to your nature, while a search for "balance" prompts you to turn more than an ordinary degree of your attention to such fields of interest as religion and philosophy. Being acutely aware of any inconveniences, "trials" or "tribulations" to which you feel you are subjected, you are apt to be quite sympathetic of Humanity's sufferings. Some of your more humorous, benevolent and genial qualities are substantially modified by a consideration that you are personally deified for the purpose of correcting injustices in the world, in all likelihood, which adds to your temperament a rather striking gravity and seriousness.

When you earnestly endeavor to exercise economy, patience, system and prudence, I feel that you will receive growing recognition for your penetrating mind and worldly wisdom, although persistence and practical ability will be paramount for your attainment of real success. I know a number of people born in this decan of Libra who incline to be highly impractical, austere and apt to go to extremes; their over-imaginativeness makes them thoroughly variable, while their extravagance continually depletes their resources. Because I have strong confidence in YOU, I trust that you make a better effort to hold a harmonious, beautiful attitude towards yourself; therefore, I know that you impress other people with your modesty and sense of humility. Surely you try to exercise both judgment and tact in the management of your personal affairs, although you will have phases, no doubt, when you tend to feel discontented or enveloped in gloomy forebodings. People of your decan who permit themselves to become "slaves" to moodiness instead of mastering it are often regarded by others as being overexacting or even self-righteous with respect to privileges and power they think they deserve as their "due", so to say. My very strong confidence in YOU brings me to a more encouraging outlook on your behalf, because I am sure that YOU turn from misgivings, centering your thoughts on constructive and optimistic concepts that earn for you most gratifying returns.

Individuals born in this second decan of Libra, as you were, ordinarily feel an effect upon their early childhood from the passing or absence of a parent or some other near relative. This and similar experiences may prompt you to show a more solemn regard for life than many people of your young age, or instill within your mind a slight fearfulness of close associations in the event that they, too, might respond to similar circumstances, although such happenings are highly improbable. Nevertheless, those years which are usually considered "school years" are apt to be quite restless, bringing "a sequence of changes" in your location, as well as your interests. Impressions you receive in this formative part of your life are likely to reflect vividly in your speech, actions and thinking when you reach maturity, and they may ingrain in your very "being" a certain offhandedness, carelessness and restiveness that will need your careful control always. Self indulgences almost always will take place in a particular area of the Libran's life.

Your intelligence may frequently seem remarkable to people who are closely involved in your rearing, while your alert, cheerful and sincere manner is almost certain to earn for you special favors or courtesies. You are apt to display an inspirational sense which is so keen as to seem almost prophetic at times, although you might focus so exactly the pictures presented to your mind that you tend to resent introduction of facts which are foreign to topics that hold your attention.

While siblings, cousins, or other children who share your upbringing more intimately than mere acquaintances, may be beneficial to many of your interests, you are likely to have estrangements or separations from them, upon occasion. It will probably seem to you that many of the influential people who come to touch your life at this time supply more of your mental and spiritual needs than what you think are your true emotional requirements.

The characteristic duplicity of situations that brings you through your "teens" will follow you on into early adulthood, in my estimation. At least one person with whom you become associated at this time is likely to enthuse some of your more intellectual leanings — but unless you determine that you will persist in your chosen undertakings, your lack of continuity will leave even your best efforts "up in the air", bringing expenditure of your fine energies without tangible accomplishment upon which you can pride yourself. I have friends born in this decan who dissipate their energies so thoroughly that they merely become argumentative, superficial and highly strung, but you surely recognize that your brilliant potential is responsive only to an absolute resolve that you will carry admirably through to conclusion that which you start. Therefore, I anticipate substantial progress for you, which will increase your eventual financial returns and give you many devoted followers, even though this cyclic period will almost certainly be accompanied by some stresses. This is a phase when additional precautions appear to me advisable against mishaps in travel, dissensions with relatives or "neighbors", and problems with the lungs, hands or arms. However, constructive outlets for your nervous energy should enable you to take strides forward that will later bring you to very satisfying achievements.

Although people who hold "important" positions will probably admire your superior memory; your intuitive, imaginative and impressionable approach may leave your sense of actuality somewhat sparse until you endeavor to develop it. Without simplification of your use of logic, your progress is sometimes likely to be delayed, probably because you absorb information almost too easily, automatically knowing answers without having foundation or reason behind your conclusions, or occasionally becoming so receptive that you easily "lose yourself" in thoughts people around you consider "idle fancies". Your position in your mutual activities will be greatly enhanced by an acceptance of opinions other than your own, there is little doubt. I am inclined to think that FIXITY is a keyword to which you should hold steadfastly in every situation, owing to a tendency so many people born in this decan have of feeling that they cannot endure "authority" when it is not their own to exercise; to seek perpetual change (more urgently in the face of long periods of stress that would, to anyone else, seem a normal occurrence in carrying out their daily routines), and a passivity that prompts them to be too impressionable, at times, "letting almost anything or anyone sway them in another direction" from that they originally intended to follow. In this respect, I conclude that you really care very little for the "hard work" which is essential for genuine success, yet are highly ambitious for the success itself. This is why I so adamantly encourage you to strive for greater stability.

Because I trust that you center your thoughts away from "self", I believe that your dignity and big heartedness wins many sincere and loyal friends who honestly wish to promote your better interests. You are apt to have "a keen, dramatic and artistic sense" that enables you to create quite easily a theatrical effect when you think it helpful to do so. People who come to touch your life are almost bound to appreciate your generosity toward them, and respond by providing whatever "services" they consider will be helpful to your efforts. I am sure you will not act overbearing, self-appraising, intolerant and impulsively extravagant, or give in to over-indulgence as some people in this decan will; therefore I feel that your acquaintances will long stand "at your side", giving their enduring and whole-hearted support to your favored interests.

Above all else, I believe that you wish for productivity from some of your more "creative ideas", as well as the loving affection of a particular relationship with one understanding individual, although you may be quite fastidious in your preferences. Individuals born in your decan of Libra often have romantic lives that are considered by many "unusual", owing to a tendency toward somewhat commonplace expression which is rather frequently unpredictably directed, or includes little "eccentricities" as compared with many people's tastes. Intellectual curiosity is apt to lead you into close associations more readily than sheer emotion, and friendship might be a basis for some of these, because of your inclination for having little partisan in any single area of opinion. You will often display a certain detachment from any strong involvement, in all likelihood. This might bring numerous changes into your courtships, about which you are almost sure to be rather secretive in some respect or another.

I think that you feel a strong need for relating yourself to other individuals in marital or business associations, and similar close alliances, although at least one of these will prove less pleasing than you would really like. One reason might be that you incline to select partners who display an enterprising spirit; singleness of purpose, boldness and assertiveness you think that you inwardly lack. While such people are often likely to be brilliant and powerful, giving extremely beneficial touches to your life, they may represent to you the "authority" from which you instinctively shrink, or sweep you up through your impressionability. These strong characteristics might make you feel impelled to call to the fore some of your more combative tendencies. I have observed that individuals born in your decan usually enter into close associations for financial reasons, frequently with a view to gaining through these greater recognition in circles of society where they are, or more easily fulfilling other hopes. When, on the other hand, they place sincere respect, esteem and emotional attachment at the foundation of any such undertakings, and they are faithful to responsibilities, they achieve more satisfying results, as you will, too, no doubt.

These close relationships and "partnerships" are ordinarily extremely beneficial to Librans of your decan from a material standpoint, almost invariably bringing solid and lasting returns that serve to increase your over-all position or "standing". At some time, people of your decan often "go overboard" in their spending for unusual wearing apparel. You probably think that you function at your best when you feel secure in your holdings, assets and possessions. In my judgment, you have almost a superhuman capacity for earning these favorable conditions, provided you apply yourself, but also, you will have additional help from other people or "corporations", receiving at least one endowment which will almost certainly include some sort of "property".

The older you grow, the more industrious, self-reliant, ambitious and authoritative you are likely to become, because I am confident that you will avert any tendencies toward disagreeableness, irritability, restlessness and maliciousness which some people display. With each passing year, you will tend to have more determination and will, I think, but it will therefore be beneficial for you to temper it with GENTLENESS. When you do this, you will be tremendously commanding and magnetic, gaining, I am sure, favorable recognition for your executive force and real diplomatic achievement. A "peaceful" domestic life is rarely found among people of your decan, although this is probably rather important to you. Your efforts to establish a favorable example your associates will wish to follow are almost bound to earn similar response, when you determine that you will let your inborn dignity and sweetness reign in all of your concerns.

I anticipate a very full, rich and happy life for you, because I have deep trust in your ability to FIND these gratifying rewards by facing up to problems instead of running from them, as some people would, and recognizing that you have a personal responsibility to MAKE the great "destiny" I know you seek. Once made it is destiny, but we made and may still "unmake" it. As you live each day to the BEST of your abilities, your future is bound to take care of itself, because, after all, when you conduct yourself NOW in a manner of which you can feel proud, and that will bring those around you to share your pride, by admiring your lofty actions, I am sure you will have as the foundation for your TOMORROW only those accomplishments upon which your TRUE fulfillment will stand, most securely.

Libra

October 14-October 23
Ruled by Jupiter

3rd decan

✧◝◈◝◈◝◈◝◈◝◈◝◈◝◈◝◈◝◈◝◈◝◈◝◈◝◈◝◈

Characteristic of your decan is a sympathetic, benevolent, sociable, lovable and kindly disposition, which I feel that you also display from day to day. Your generosity and amiability are likely to earn for you more than an ordinary degree of favorable recognition, winning others to you and bringing from them courtesies in appreciation of your charitable attitude toward them. You are apt to have a special fondness for everything that will serve to uplift Humanity and increase the beauty or artistry of the world in which you live. This may attract you to the fine arts, literature, music, history, science, medicine, law, and all intellectual and cultured pursuit.

I believe that you earnestly try to be hospitable toward people who come to touch your life, sometimes even denying yourself a few of the greater returns which you know you could gain when you think that by doing so you will improve conditions for someone else or add harmony to a situation. Having a sense of impartiality and justice, you probably tend to shrink from the superficial facts of life, giving Mankind the "benefit of the doubt", so to say, by looking always for the best and holding assurance that you will find it. Even when your confidence seems betrayed, you are likely to feel pity rather than condemnation for the weaknesses that brought the betrayal into being.

Putting to use your better judgment, you are probably adaptable to unexpected changes and flexible to alterations which are contrary to your original anticipation; you strive to build your undertakings upon foundations of simplicity and sensibility as well as inspiration, in all likelihood. I feel that you are optimistic, cheerful, generous and noble — qualities which prompt good health and make you well suited for authoritative positions, where your power and dignity will enhance your executive ability and enable you to be a leader in social or business affairs. You are almost certain to be popular with people who share your routines, because you are apt to make dispassionate judgments with phenomenal ease and display a great deal of mechanical and mathematical ability. I have friends in your decan of Libra who tend to be overindulgent, a characteristic that has brought to them serious difficulties in their closest associations, as well as loss of social prestige, but my confidence that YOU use the magnificent gifts of spirit, which are inherently yours, makes it seem to me unnecessary to comment further on the problems that result for those who choose to do otherwise. Yet, I'm sure there is an area in your personal life where you are over-indulgent.

The earlier lives of individuals who have birthdays in your decan are ordinarily exceptionally happy. This might be true of you, as well. Such youngsters are usually easier to rear than most, because of their cooperativeness and ready conformity to circumstances in which they find themselves. Obtaining an education is likely to be somewhat less easy for you. Owing to pressing issues that confront your parents, or other people who are influential in your "upbringing", you may have changes and restrictions that limit the freedom with which you might otherwise enjoy your original orientation to the world. This is a phase when you are likely to be somewhat too modest and retiring, because your ambition is apt to not be aggressive. Many of the responsibilities of brothers, sisters, cousins, or similar individuals who are closer than mere acquaintance may be placed upon you, prompting them to consider you too moralizing, from time to time, or putting you in a position where you think it necessary "to display" a selfishness and calmness which you do not always feel. You might be aware of any weaknesses you think you have, as compared to other people your age, to such an extent that you sometimes question whether you will be able to manage your interests with the degree of dependability you know you ought to have, or hold such optimistic ideals that your present limitations dim their achievement in your view, giving you a somewhat more pessimistic outlook, temporarily. A sense of duty toward religious concepts which you are taught may appear to you to restrain a few of your more expansive objectives, as well. Nevertheless, I feel that you will do whatever you think you can to prove that you are trustworthy, in such ways that your great practicality will stall some of your more altruistic inclinations, now and then. During this earlier cyclic period you are apt to develop a keen insight into human nature that will serve you well for all the remainder of your years. You might dream of becoming a great hero who will save nations, or work in a field where you will "save people". Evidence of this will probably take more definite shape in situations where you feel that someone else is being treated unfairly, at which times you may loyally show uncompromising and courageous concern for their welfare. There is apt to be at least one such occasion when your unselfish action brings upon you unwarranted punishment — but you would surely prefer this to the original injustice you felt was being done.

The approach of around "college age" will give you a sense of "coming into your own", in my estimation, enabling you to realize more easily your primary wishes, and bringing greater opportunities for personal expression. You might react to this new "freedom" by scattering your forces somewhat too widely and having less regard for "duty" than you really should. This is a time in your life when you will probably become intrigued with intellectual subjects, although your interests are frequently likely to be all too varied, giving you a strong inclination to "skim the surfaces" of many fields of endeavor without mastering many. This can be a rather critical phase, because it will be imperative for you to regain control over your more restless, diffusive tendencies in order to maintain the stability which will act as the mainspring for your major successes later on. You are almost bound to enjoy considerable popularity at this time, and win honors or similar recognition that will later prove helpful to many of your interests. I believe that you innately desire a higher education and realize that the fullest development of your true hopes will rest in this area. Nevertheless, it is very

- 223 -

unlikely that you will follow a single course in your efforts to reach this objective; there is almost certain to be some disruption and change involved near this time or even intermittent activity over long periods of time.

In your early adulthood, you may quite often have associates point out the vagueness with which you appear to be planning your goals, or that your actions are prescribed solely by "the mood" of the moment, bringing you to do things more because you are personally interested than with an idea of building up any important result for yourself. In view of your earlier, restrictive experiences, this short space of time in which you rather refuse to "keep your nose to the grindstone" will probably serve more of your interests than it will harm, provided, of course, you "come back down to earth" in really practical enterprises rather than mere "change of scene". Having had control over other people somewhat precociously, maturity might bring you into a stage where you will temporarily become depressed when things do not go your own way, but when you respond by putting your impressions into better perspective, as I trust you will, this trend should quickly pass, enabling you to react from then on with greater flexibility.

I think that you approach your interests with patience, often displaying a "maternal" or "paternal" quality in your management of other people as well as a keen receptivity and sensitivity to their needs. You are rarely inclined to take impulsive measures. Instead, you will gather facts, letting information that reaches you dissolve thoroughly in your mind before reaching more definite conclusions. This characteristic might prove misleading to individuals who mistake your placidity for "inactivity" — in reality, you are no doubt highly tenacious; when you finally decide that you want something, you will go after it with staunch determination which you keep carefully concealed under the suavity with which you are almost certain to accomplish your ends! Once your aims are established, you will probably pursue them with passionate intensity, but you will always temper this with breadth, balance and sympathy, in all likelihood, using warm persuasiveness rather than dictatorial methods.

Although you are apt to be singularly generous, there is little question that you hold in sight material advantages which you might gain. Should you feel "forced", you might surprise others with a certain obstinacy, or haughtiness of method, which you previously kept well masked. Under most circumstances, I am sure that you try to present yourself with grace and vigor, making shrewd discernments from "behind-the-scenes" and analyzing in private the most practical means of producing effects you seek.

The society of other people is occasionally likely to place some stresses upon a few of your preferred interests. This may be partially due to over-popularity that seems to make too many demands upon your time, energy and resources, and a "soft-heartedness" that will prompt you to make expenditures or investments in acquaintances, as well as "causes", which sometimes seem more costly than you feel you can really afford. I think that jealousy or envy on the part of another person will touch you at least once in a rather distressing way.

Your "closest" associations are apt to include people who receive more than an ordinary degree of public recognition, from time to time, although for the most part this area of your life will probably be somewhat unpredictable. You may have rather unconventional tastes in dress as well as with respect to the forms of entertainment and pleasure that appeal to you, while an affectionate nature might hide a certain detachment that makes you inwardly approach people whom you choose to "date" more in a spirit of friendship than deep or lasting affection. Surely those who know you well are impressed by your courtesies, and the imaginativeness you display in planning enjoyable activities, but they may come to find that emotionalism, sentimentality or rationalism have only a very small place in your over-all outlook. In circumstances that would seem "earthshaking" to someone else, another person might sometimes show "open surprise" over what they consider to be your "dispassionate" reactions.

You may be "pleased by sight and disappointed by touch" — or, in other words, enjoy the prospects of CONSIDERING an ideal romantic relationship more than the relationship itself. You might incline to place individuals you greatly admire upon a "pedestal" that requires their continual "perfection", if they are to give you a permanent feeling of contentment. On the other hand, I believe that you have exceptional contributions to make to close associations – because you will readily compromise differences and maintain a charming personality that substantially brightens daily routine. Many, many people who have birthdays in this third decan of Libra choose to marry or form business partnerships; for the majority of these people they prove highly successful. These are frequently entered into impetuously, however. Material considerations are often apt to bring you into such alliances, although the returns "you" receive from these will probably be relatively few; you will at least once assume responsibility for another person, in my estimation, yet, ironically, your major assets will come through your own ADVANCED IDEAS, WITH THE HELP OF ANOTHER PERSON OR A GROUP. Thus, I consider "partnerships" essential to your true success, provided you feel within them enough freedom of action and personal independence.

In the pursuit of your more gainful activities, you will probably be happiest when you are involved in several different enterprises at the same time. When your versatility may prompt you to enter into diversified undertakings, you no doubt prefer to feel that you are serving "the needs" of Mankind through your efforts, a trait that may frequently bring you to perform acts other people consider charitable in the execution of your regular "duties". You might even make substantial personal "sacrifices" when you think that betterment for others will result.

I feel that by accomplishing your purposes with steadiness, foresight, trustworthiness, fidelity and conscientiousness you will continue to realize more and more of your magnanimous childhood dreams. Like a great historical ruler, or a glorious leader, your vivid warmth, geniality and generosity will earn admiration from people who come to know of your efforts – and I am certain that you will be held in true exaltation!

Scorpio

October 24-November 2
Ruled by Mars

1st decan

The first decan of Scorpio gives an extremely powerful, ambitious and impulsive temperament, in my estimation, which endows you with an indomitable will and firm, resolute courage. Because your nature is no doubt strong, intense, forceful and energetic, you are probably capable of immense feats of prowess. I consider the most outstanding characteristic of your sign an almost "superhuman" capacity for accomplishment, and hard work over long periods of time which few people can equal. Although you will be mechanical and practical, your manners might tend to seem blunt, sometimes creating an initial impression that you are "hard-boiled" — but when people come to know you well, they are apt to more than like you as well as hold strong admiration for your sharp, acute, keen mind, and your superb proficiency for directing others. Having a serious disposition that impels you to produce effects out of definite objectives, you are likely to have little tolerance of "monkey business" when there are important details that require attention, but anyone who touches your life closely will surely recognize the great depths that lie beneath your "surfaces" which explain YOUR ABSORPTION with "tasks at hand".

I think that you are innately adept with sharp instruments, tools or the use of liquids, while you also have a knack for exercising dominant authority. This, in combination with a shrewd, penetrating and deductive mind, may be a reason why many people who have birthdays in your decan become successful surgeons, assayers, chemists or attorneys. You no doubt have the investigative powers of an "expert detective", which should give you a natural understanding of science. When this decan says, "I am going to sue you" — they mean it and shrewdly they often use their natural instinct to "detect flaws" in order to win.

You are apt to have definite opinions, which lead to strong likes and dislikes. While you will probably be one of the FINEST FRIENDS any person could have, at least one experience has surely cautioned you that you must earnestly endeavor to display grace and dignity toward those for whom you feel less regard. I observe that people who have birthdays similar to your own can become absolute masters of self-control. I consider it imperative to their true happiness that they use this outstanding characteristic to the fullest, as I trust YOU will — because a personality that holds such great force is rather like a vast sea: Magnificent when calm; raging in a storm.

Once you give yourself to an undertaking, the profundity of your devotion will be implacable and dauntless; scorning defeat and danger of reversal. You are likely to spare yourself nothing in your efforts to reach final results you envision, considering even the most trivial facts almost equally with those that seem more significant, and going without rest or food when it appears to you that these might divert you from your endeavor. You never ponder consequences as long as success in your achievement remains within your sights, I am certain.

When these qualities are directed to constructive channels, the energy supplied to people of this decan creates the power for boundless advancement on this "sea of life", but, like an automobile or an atom, such powerful forces out of control can be devastating. This is a reason why you will occasionally run across people born in this decan whose revengefulness is so great that they will trample mercilessly upon the finer sensibilities of other people, or appear quarrelsome, ungrateful, overbearing, and abusive of the otherwise fine creative energy — although YOU surely strive to be more adaptable, giving for the benefit of all of Mankind you can reach the strength of your remarkable abilities. Thus, I do not anticipate for you the "accidents" or mishaps that some people have.

The earlier lives of individuals of this first decan of Scorpio are quite frequently accompanied by some stresses, a few of which come about through health problems. Sometimes it appears that there are estrangements, or separations from, a parent or similar person influential in the rearing of these people, that brings one certain person into a rather dominant position where their personal interests are concerned. This might be true of you, as well, creating an impression that someone holds a colder, more critical, skeptical or fearful outlook toward your welfare than you would really like.

Nevertheless, the years that generally take one through high school will probably be exceptionally advantageous for you, bringing assistance from such people as siblings, cousins or youngsters and others who neighbor your day-to-day surroundings. You are quite likely to receive favorable recognition for your conscientiousness, productivity, resourcefulness and sense of responsibility at this time, being assisted materially, as well. Expansive ideas regarding your future security may prompt you to put your major energies into somewhat more serious activities than many people, but this does not mean that you will always be orthodox in your views. Sometimes you might appear to shift paradoxically from economy to extravagance in your attitude, although a few of your more ingenious, deliberative efforts may well bring lasting advancement in your financial affairs.

This is a phase of your life when some associates may consider you too austere, self-righteous, harsh or demanding, upon occasion, but these are the very people who are likely to enforce a "discipline" that will encourage the use of your more sterling characteristics, prompting you to employ organizational abilities, tact and diplomacy which will be fundamental in your greater successes later on.

Obtaining an education is rarely difficult for individuals born in this first decan of Scorpio. I notice that opportunities always seem to be available, from one source or another. Generally these come through scholarships and similar gifts or favors from other people; even when your preparations earn these favors, there is still strong likelihood that you will be able to attain a higher education when you wish to do so.

As you leave adolescence, you are apt to "take on" a more sensitive appearance than the one you held previously, occasionally concealing your true feelings or displaying a "moodiness" that makes it seem that you take some of your interests too seriously. Nevertheless, you are almost bound to enjoy a great deal of popularity and participate in pleasurable or entertaining activities with more frequency. You might have little disposition to seek love or companionship, but when these are offered you will gladly accept them – and you will forever hold a deep, quiet sentimentality for these years of your life, in all probability. You will need expression of your own tendencies, I feel, often finding it in secluded surroundings where you can cultivate newer appreciation of art, music and literature you are acquiring. This is a cyclic period when you may meet companions or associates who will come to play predominant roles in your life. In respect to your years of "growing up", I conclude that you will have some of your happier moments, although "a particular experience" occurring at this time, concerning another person, will forevermore remain your secret!

You are apt to be extremely discriminating and practical in selecting your goals, most of which will be directly related to the achievement of some of your more ambitious aims. There might be times when you tend to appear somewhat "fussy", worrisome, or even interfering, but on the whole you will probably endeavor to lay an efficient "plan" for yourself which you intend to follow explicitly. You are not likely to be overly-sympathetic of other people's problems, owing to your own determination that you will meet any obstacles squarely and work them out according to logical conclusions drawn from statistical facts. There is little likelihood of your applying these intentions to the letter, however, because you are apt to have strong intuition and a keen spirituality that will often enable you to draw upon "forces unseen", so to say, when you are on the threshold of realizing one of your hopes or wishes.

There will probably be a certain shyness in your disposition which will prevent you from showing yourself as you are, much of the time. While this might make it difficult for you to acquire the confidence of others, in some instances, you will no doubt have a distinct MAGNETISM that will win people to you and bring from them many gratifying returns. A certain instinct for "retirement" in your nature may prevent you from seeking numerous acquaintances, but you will surely value "true friendship", even though you might expect to receive from it quite definite returns in promotion of any position in mutual activities that you seek, having little regard for the society of people who do not serve your interests in this way.

In carrying out your daily routines you are apt to be quite self-willed, energetic and impulsive, often considering newer methods than those which have been previously used or pioneering "new territory". The majority of people born in your decan serve "the government" at some time, in a particular capacity or somehow partake in interests having to do with the military services. However, in all of your enterprises you will probably display a great power of execution, priding yourself on your mastery of technique. You surely realize that you have a tendency toward recklessness which you need to curb in order to gain the greatest advantages from the brilliancy with which you apply your energies. I believe that you have critical judgment that enables you to recognize the slightest flaw in any condition that comes before you — but because I trust that you also use discretion, prudently saving any assessments for pursuits that will be BENEFITED by them, I do not anticipate the dissensions and other stresses for you that many people have.

I think that you are foresighted, versatile and open-minded in matters concerning your assets and possessions, relating these directly to the interests of OTHER PEOPLE, group enterprises or "corporations", and bringing from them income from several different sources. Almost all of your major material attainments are likely to come through endowments or other very welcome returns you receive from particular individuals of importance to you. You might spend many happy hours examining your "bank book", and consider ways of turning to profitable account practically any information you receive. Although you may strike a balance somewhat less easily than many people, when it comes to weighing one alternative against another from a financial standpoint, "your wants" are almost certain to be provided.

I notice that the romantic lives of individuals born in this first decan of Scorpio are quite frequently linked to the ambitions, although your sympathies will sometimes bring you to form attachments with people you feel will benefit from your attention. You are apt to develop an interest in this area of your life somewhat later than some people, and realize from it less satisfying returns than you would really like. A sense of "responsibility" or "duty" toward another may sometimes lead you to feel that you are making personal sacrifices where your "date life" is concerned. You are apt to have some unusual and impulsive love affairs.

Business and marital partnerships into which you enter will be directly related to your material interests and major aspirations, in my estimation — but you will follow your "head" rather than your "heart" in forming such alliances, approaching these sensibly and realistically. Hesitation at the "last minute" might prevent you from making at least one permanent association, while the position you hold in "a mutual activity" is also likely to impose certain limitations. I believe that your closer relationships will be more favorable for you than otherwise, and when you give generously of your sympathetic understanding, kindness and cooperation, affection will strengthen with each passing year.

Individuals of your decan sometimes have a disappointment through at least one younger person, but others who come to touch your life are almost sure to compensate, amply.

I feel that tradition, heredity and custom give you a fondness for home and family life, although you will nevertheless retain a certain detachment from it. You are very likely to maintain "appearances" for the benefit of friends and acquaintances, at the same time preserving a less conventional "private life" about which few people know.

The only word of caution that appears necessary to me is

that you always evaluate very, very carefully your true aspirations, making sure that you establish these according to the highest principles in which you believe. Otherwise, you might incline to lose, instead of gain, the position you seek, just when you think you are nearing the summit of your accomplishments.

In my opinion, you have capabilities, strengths and assets with which you can lead a troubled world out of darkness and into the light, and when you place SPIRITUALITY at the foreground of all of your other efforts, your contributions to Mankind will earn, in return vast rewards!

Scorpio

November 3-November 12
Ruled by Sun

Few people have better prospects for commanding success and a singularly honorable reputation than those of you who are born under this second decan of Scorpio, because your temperament is no doubt replete with masterful and governing qualities. I believe that a proud and haughty spirit has already showed you that it needs very careful guidance from an early age; you are intense, enduring, fervent and secretive. A sunny disposition is likely to magnetically attract other people to you, while your personality is apt to shine with a sense of freedom and generosity that results from a somewhat rebellious spirit. Once you decide upon a course of action, you are rarely likely to give up until you have realized in full the accomplishments you originally envisioned. Although you will be outspoken, I feel that you surely curb any tendencies toward criticism, suspicion and skepticism, and therefore have confidence that your dignity is admired by other people, making you a leader in circles of society where you are.

Superficially, you probably give a light-hearted impression that occasionally masks the great depths that lie within your true nature, because you no doubt endeavor to brighten the lives of people around you, adding luminosity wherever you are and using your quick perception, stability and firmness as strength for those who are less favorably endowed with similar qualities. Although I think that you have a great deal of pride, you can create from it an almost majestic countenance which, blended with your subtlety, intellectuality and energy, will give you the "mark" of a true executive, fit for high rule.

Such a forceful and dominating personality as the one I usually associate with this decan has a wider range of potential than almost any other — from the lowest to the highest! One will occasionally meet people born under its influence who are capable of extreme cruelty, being tyrannical, cunning, crafty, highly revengeful, and intensely jealous. However, there is a transitionalism inherent to this birthday cycle that not infrequently prompts even those individuals who have gone to the depths of despair to awaken inwardly, emerge, and soar to the very greatest heights! While I feel that YOU endeavor to develop YOUR finest talents, abilities and capabilities at all times, I am sure that you realize that you, too, are gifted with somewhat more determination than many people, which brings you to follow through on resolutions you make to yourself or others, and prompts you to improve any condition within, or around, yourself that does not explicitly suit your present tastes.

Your inner seriousness may occasionally give some austerity to your appearance, or make you seem more formidable than you really are, but people who come to know you well will surely recognize that in actuality you have a kindly disposition. I think that you are capable of the greatest possible perseverence in any undertaking that attracts your attention; your tenacity will be inexhaustible. Self-centeredness, harshness and discontent may display themselves among people of your decan, from time to time — but because I trust that YOU direct the energies behind these to sympathy, efficiency and true generosity, your happiness is almost certain to increase, daily; while some people are stern in their sense of justice and integrity or uncontrollable in their desire for freedom, becoming cold and insensible to the sufferings of others, I have confidence that YOU are known for a self-sacrificing devotion to Mankind.

There is almost invariably an unpredictable quality in the earlier home surroundings of people born in this second decan of Scorpio, which ordinarily results from estrangement or separation from a parent, or another person with whom they are closely involved. This tends to place someone else in a "position" which is really too attentive. In early youth, ill-health or your winning personality might bring such profuse notice your way, as well, spurring rivalries with siblings or others in your environment, and otherwise prompting more than a few stresses. This is a phase when you are apt to be more self-reliant than most youngsters your age — and while your industriousness and ambition are almost bound to be admired, you will probably enter into disputes, now and then, that arise out of some of the more forceful, leaping methods that you employ as a result of not yet being thoroughly acquainted with ways and means of dealing with some of the more "sledge hammer" qualities of your disposition that will demand smoothness. While you will always tend to keep many of your true feelings to yourself, in my estimation, you will have a particular "secret" concerning your "childhood years".

As you grow older, I think that you will tend to become more and more impressionable, intuitive and imaginative, taking a keener interest in historical subjects, literature, music, art, and other cultural refinements; you might become a bibliophile, sometimes examining more closely your genealogy or acquiring collections of such things as antiques. Your efforts to break some of your stronger ties with the past may bring this to seem a rather emotional cycle for you, lessening your sense of actuality, and at times, leading you to appear unusually passive. The use of your better judgment in the selection of your surroundings and associates appears to me imperative, as you leave adolescence and enter adulthood, because your over-all outlook is often likely to reflect these.

I feel, however, that at least one "friendship" you form at this time will give deep and lasting meaning to your life.

I believe that one of your more intriguing characteristics, in view of the strength of your disposition, is a very keen receptivity to other people. You might be somewhat slow in forming your original impressions, gradually absorbing, weighing, deliberating, as you reach your conclusions — but your over-all reaction will be absolute and unbending with respect to your likes and dislikes. I am sure that you will have many, many acquaintances with whom you share mutual interests, sometimes materially as well as intellectually, and from whom you receive more than an ordinary number of invitations, courtesies and favors.

Among your closest associates, you will no doubt prefer those who seem uncritical, cautious and reserved, yet display integrity, stability, sympathy and affection. The gregariousness of "superficial" gatherings will appeal to you, in all probability, but intimate relationships with dilettante, cursory or shallow individuals are almost bound to bring displeasing results. Marital and business alliances into which you enter will frequently benefit your financial interests as well as many others, in my opinion, but you will earn these favorable returns through your efforts to be, yourself, a good partner. When close association with another proves disappointing, as it may upon occasion, you are apt to find it less easy to forget than many people — although I trust that you will forgive, and, through your constructive reaction, realize some pleasing compensation.

I observe that individuals born in your second decan of Scorpio have more opportunities for enjoying pursuits they consider pleasurable than almost anyone else — and it often appears to the onlooker that the supply of funds for sustaining these is inexhaustible! Some of the most lavish and perfect hosts and hostesses I have ever known have been friends who were born in this decan; a few send air line tickets to acquaintances who live in other parts of the world when they wish for them to come share an evening at the opera or ballet, or attend a similar occasion, for example. They will, themselves, arrange their activities in such ways as to benefit from pursuits they think entertaining, often in sequence, from place to place, where people they know can be seen along the way. Because this area of your life is likely to present few challenges, you will surely find it advantageous to take precautionary measures against excessive behavior of any kind — but provided you adhere to this policy, you are very apt to have an almost "theatrical" existence where your hobbies and more vital interests are concerned.

From what I have said, it might appear that there is a frivolity attached to some of your undertakings; quite the contrary, I consider that you rarely act without deliberation. Many of your more "speculative" undertakings will probably be successful, but I feel that you will first weigh them against the position in mutual activities you hope to attain, approaching these in a generous, big-hearted, expansive manner. People who hold "authoritative" places in circles of society where you are, are almost certain to have admiration for your more constructive endeavors and attitudes. They might sometimes claim that you are too tender hearted, even at the wrong time or place, but they will really hold great esteem for your gentleness and sincerity. This is probably a reason why people born in your decan of Scorpio ordinarily have changeable, but highly successful returns, materially. You are almost sure to have more than one source of income, or several possessions of the same kind.

When you become involved in mutual financial activities with other people, large enterprises, or groups, dissensions, disputes or differences are apt to arise, requiring an unusual degree of communicating back and forth or "transacting". Therefore, you may prefer to manage your own affairs when you can, rather than depending upon service provided for that purpose. At some time, you may participate in "the contesting of a Will" or similar legal matter, or take personal interest in a "claim" that proves problematical. The requirement of the services of a legal advisor invariably seems to mark the lives of those born in this decan. Nevertheless, I believe that your associations with others will enhance your more gainful efforts, for the most part, often by providing a stabilizing influence which you especially need at a certain time.

Younger people who come to touch your life will frequently prove fortunate for your better interests, in my estimation, just as the constructive "children of your imagination" will. Some such person or activity is apt to be directly responsible for attracting attention that will then lead to an honor or special courtesy.

In carrying out your daily routines, you will definitely prefer to be a participant rather than bystander, at least while you are getting newer undertakings "off the ground", so to say. Although you will probably be a master at handling detail, you will feel some aversion to tasks that place you under close supervision, or the management of "trivia" that could well be given over to someone else. Your instinct will surely be "TO EXCEL" in any field of activity you choose. It appears to me that you will enjoy greater achievements when you remain independent of neighbors and relatives such as brothers, sisters and cousins, yet an aunt, uncle or like person attendant in your childhood rearing may continue to exert a very helpful influence for many years.

You probably have rather unconventional ideas concerning your home surroundings, maintaining an almost meticulous sense of perfection with regard to social amenities and similar "appearances" — along with another type of existence which is strictly adherent to your personal wants and tastes. These, of course, might be quite different, indeed, from those to which your acquaintances are accustomed. I feel that this is a part of your personality which will exert itself more and more with each passing year: A confidence that will enable you to exercise a few little "eccentricities" that capture your fancy; a more inventive, original and inquisitive flair. Sexual urges are apt to require control in even early life.

People born in your decan usually have phenomenally strong constitutions that enable them to overcome even serious illnesses and otherwise enjoy good health, for the most part. I have noticed that when physical ailments arise, they generally evolve out of overindulgence, which makes it seem advisable to me that you maintain moderate habits. There are sometimes accidents affecting the knees, teeth, "one eye", bones, lungs, arms, chest or hands, or surgical operations are performed to correct certain conditions — but when you earnestly endeavor to cultivate peace of mind, your proneness to such afflictions should substantially diminish.

In summation, I consider yours one of the most POWER-FUL, CAPABLE, MAGNETIC natures that can be found; the whole key lies within a life lived on firm spiritual foundations. At some point, I feel that you will have a sense of AWAKEN-ING — a definite and indescribable experience — through which you will KNOW, with little question, what your purpose is and must be. By devoting yourself to these higher "forces" you feel within, I am certain that the pride of your accomplishments will be not only well earned, but over- extraordinary achievements!

Scorpio

November 13-November 22
Ruled by Venus

 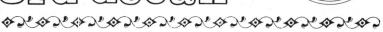

At the root of your very "being" is a great, great intensity of emotion and feeling, I believe, which radiates forth in a powerful magnetism that irresistibly draws other people to you and often enables you to gain what you seek through sheer charm. Having a "fascination" of this magnitude will be one of YOUR finest assets, because I feel that you will use it for the BENEFIT of loved ones, but for many people born in this decan it presents too few of those challenges that prompt them to turn the fervency of their extreme ardor toward constructive pursuits. This is surely a reason why large numbers of people born in this third decan of Scorpio act in an overly intense, even hurtful, jealous and hateful manner that invariably seems to leave behind them a path of total destruction.

These disharmonies also bring back enmity and disfavor, or react upon their health, denying them the brilliant accomplishments which are innately theirs to have, and I trust that *you* will earn, for I am sure *you* will control yourself when you meet conditions that could result in such behavior by others who would face the same situations.

Generally there is little altruism in this nature. Being straightforward, in addition, individuals of your decan always find it advantageous to pursue their plans scrupulously, weigh carefully all considerations, and modify their actions; otherwise they frequently tend to "frighten the birds which they intend to ensnare", so to say. There is no doubt of a keen, dramatic flair in your approach. I think that you have large ambitions and display a fiery enthusiasm for realizing these, frequently displaying persuasiveness and warmth in your efforts to give breath and balance to your major objectives. You are often apt to impress other people as being arrogant or dominating, owing to a confidence with which you present yourself, but those who come to know you well will no doubt recognize that there is "a generosity" behind your exuberance, as well as a dignity or vigor around which you endeavor to model your achievements. You are likely to be interested in many things besides the "business of the moment", yet when you are moved by a certain idea, you probably persevere on its behalf, showing an indomitable courage in your efforts to "promote" it, regardless of the reception it originally receives.

Many of the finest hosts and hostesses one will ever meet have birthdays in this cycle, owing to a fondness for luxury, sensation and pleasure. Your performance in any undertaking in which you participate will be superb, in my opinion, provided that you hold your mind firmly on your highest goals, living and acting in a manner befitting of these lofty aims. I cannot honestly discuss this birthday period, however, without mentioning that it needs more control than almost any other — because this decan's emotions are pinions on which the personality may descend into the lowest states of debauchery or rise to a true throne of grace.

It usually seems that individuals of your decan are separated from at least one parent during their childhood, sometimes merely through emotional detachment or public recognition that takes "a toll in personal and domestic affairs". Similar circumstances might be evident in your life, as well. This, or temporary health conditions, may bring another person into dominance, who is very often employed for household duties or an "aunt", "uncle", or grandparent. I strongly feel that a particular individual will have outstanding influence over your earlier environment, and that your relationship with this person will be accompanied by some stresses or clashes of will.

During this earlier phase of your life, you are likely to display a rather reserved, calculating, responsible and practical attitude. From time to time you might tend to become worrisome, selfish, slow or inhibited in your outlook, especially when you have reason to feel that you do not excel intellectually or otherwise, although you are almost bound to display a strong capacity for hard work and attention to detail. I think that you will have tremendous power of initiative for improving yourself mentally as well as materially, using more than an ordinary degree of prudence, thrift and caution in your efforts to realize this ambition. A real sense of humor is apt to be startlingly absent; you will take matters seriously, in all probability, giving a devoted attention to "duty", and reaching always for a position above siblings, neighbors and others around you. You may very well set a "shining example" associates will wish to follow, occasionally winning awards and similar "honors" as a result of your conscientiousness.

As you grow older, you are likely to become more sensitive, sometimes overly so. Impressions might reach you in advance of events, upon at least one occasion, bringing a recognition of forces beyond those many people ordinarily accredit and leading you to cover a few of your stronger sensibilities with a protective shell that conceals many of the more powerful emotions you feel "within". Maturity will bring with it a growing desire for security; home and family life, in my estimation, and you will sympathetically take a greater interest in your own heredity or genealogy, history; country. In all likelihood, you will go through temporary phases when your reactions seem uncertain and slow, not because your mind is idle, but rather because it is meditative, reflecting upon impressions it receives more readily than stimulating your interest in acting upon them. An experience you have with a female person during these years of "growing up" will probably be vividly mirrored in your later years, while you may well visit a place that will later become for you a more permanent home. You will make at least one major change as you leave adolescence and enter maturity, in my estimation, and implant within your memory facts, figures, information and statistics which will never again escape you.

It is imperative that people who are born in this decan of Scorpio remain realistic, at all times, with respect to the forms of entertainment they pursue, seeking only those which are wholesome and will lead to over-all personal improvement. When they do otherwise, they are inclined to excessive behavior that frequently results in serious difficulties, because their passions are apt to be quick and volatile. I have confidence that YOU direct YOUR energies to charitable enterprises that will advance the interests of children or better conditions for people whose circumstances are less fortunate than many others — or that you give pleasure to Mankind by selflessly using your brilliant talents to create something worthwhile on their behalf. Any use of alcoholic beverages, narcotics and similar means of artificially taking flight from actualities, ordinarily serves to increase the violence of feeling within individuals of this birth phase, frequently leading to almost demoniac results. Upon occasion, your sympathies might prompt you to action you will later regret, until you determine that you will hold in control those emotions that can bring you to reverse yourself almost instantaneously "mid-stream", so to say. There are individuals born in this decan who always take a compliment as a tribute to their own superiority — as surrender — and there are some who are gross and coarse; who let a trifling disappointment turn love to hate, or twist into jealousy a passion far more consuming than the love which has given birth to it . . . SOME OF THE GREATEST SPIRITUAL GIANTS, and SOME OF THE MOST DEEPLY ADMIRED, GENUINELY LOVED people in all the world have also had birthdays in your decan. I FEEL THAT YOU ARE CAPABLE OF ABSOLUTE SELF-MASTERY!

I observe that this birthday cycle often gives a feeling of responsibility toward marriage and business partnerships, or brings people born under its influence to feel that they have a "duty" to enter into these. In these close associations, you are apt to select individuals who are older than you, or who seem so because of their stable, enduring, methodical and constructive approach. Some delays are likely before you will form a strong alliance; owing to a "childhood experience" you might forestall them indefinitely. I believe, however, that you intend to give your deepest devotion to relationships of this kind, and, provided you hold this within sensible limits, you should have few troubles. Material considerations are very often likely to be closely linked with associations you form, which might sometimes give you an impression of being limited or restricted by people to whom you are closest, or a tendency to place weighty requirements on these individuals, yourself.

Yours is a decan that seems to have a desire for children more intensely than many others. Even when one or more disappointments arise from relationships with younger people you know, or in having them, as may sometimes occur, a realistic attitude toward their welfare which you maintain should earn favorable results, on the whole, substantially diminishing the number of stresses that would almost certainly result otherwise.

I think that you prefer to establish a home life, although you will remain somewhat independent of it, having little real sentimentality on its behalf. Individuals of your decan seem to settle in locations distant from the one in which they were born rather frequently, although I know one individual who has lived all his life in the house where he was born — however, this is rare. Many incorporate antiquity or interior designs traditional to another country in their decoration, as you may, too.

Some of the finest stylists hail from this third decan of Scorpio, although I consider individuals born under its influence to be well suited for almost any field of endeavor that appeals to them, provided, of course, it is constructive. Ordinarily, you should be happiest when you are in a somewhat "executive" capacity, free from close supervision and able to command matters as you think best. Owing to a certain impulsiveness you are apt to display in your day-to-day undertakings, there may be a fitful brilliancy to your efforts, now and then, although when you give graciousness and floridity to your manner, you will surely earn cooperation from individuals who share your usual activities — and you might increase your reputation by creating a new design of some sort! I have noticed that my friends who are born in this decan often participate in the occupations of their marriage partners.

You are likely to be quite secretive about many of your interests; your financial affairs among these. For one thing, you will probably have somewhat larger resources than most people who know you suppose — and these will no doubt come from more than one place — but regardless of your circumstances, you are apt to have a few problems in this area of your life and consider that you rarely attain the degree of financial freedom you would really prefer. At some time you may take responsibility for the assets of a neighbor or relative. Basically, you should have a thrifty disposition, although the use of your better judgment will be imperative in speculative enterprises that attract your attention, because reversals of fortune are probable through some of these.

Inheritances and other very welcome gifts will reinforce your income, in my estimation, while "partnerships" and similar alliances with other people, corporations or groups will also serve to increase your holdings, sometimes just when you most hope to fulfill a certain wish! Thus, I conclude in this respect that you will receive more gratifying returns from your relationships with other people than your more singular efforts.

Friendships and acquaintances you have will most often

result from mental rapport, in my opinion, and you will prefer among them individuals who approach life analytically rather than emotionally, and show an interest in facts, statistics, hygiene or intellectual subjects. Coldness of perception will usually attract you, although you are almost certain to have fascinating contributions which you will make to these relationships, as well. Human silliness will appeal to you very little, in selecting your companions, because I think that you will have strong preferences for people who are tasteful and conservative in their manner; intelligent in their outlook. I trust that you have tolerance with people you like less well than some others, judging by a genuine liking and rapport rather than the size of a bank book; therefore, you will often receive advantages from individuals who touch your life.

I have the greatest admiration for your third decan of Scorpio; it is endowed with abundant strength, magnetism, intuition and depth — and it has within it a SPIRITUAL INTENSITY that can lift the values of the world to boundless heights. With each passing year, you ought to develop instinctively a "universality" in your emotions that will enable you to react quite effortlessly according to the true needs of Humanity. It usually seems that people of your decan are long remembered for something they do, or that they leave something to posterity. When you earnestly seek to find means for improving conditions around you, and because I have the utmost confidence that you will endeavor always to make BETTERMENT your first interest, I feel that your name will act as an inspiration for others.

Sagittarius

November 23-December 2
Ruled by Mercury

Foresightedness and restlessness are likely to be two of your stronger characteristics, giving you such resilience to life that at least in some degree you feel free from the shackles of convention. I believe that the versatility of your interests brings people who know you to regard you as openminded and a hard worker. You are apt to have a fondness for travel, and give a great deal of thought to religious and philosophical subjects; law, education and politics. As a general rule, individuals born under this first decan of Sagittarius display good judgment in the management of their interests; they have sober minds and a quick intellect — but these powers sometimes seem to run into profusion and disorder through richness of reason or understanding and lack of method. Surely you endeavor to coordinate your efforts in such ways as to realize the fullest advantages from your capabilities, although many people who have birthdays in this cycle tend to be unstable, nervous and unconcentrated. I trust that you absolutely adhere to HONESTY and INTEGRITY, observing yourself regulations or rules you think that other people ought to obey; therefore, I anticipate that you will develop a greater intelligence than many individuals, which will enable you to steadily rise in life.

There is likely to be something fleeting and temporary about your manner, making you appear illusory as well as quick. You may prefer to evade serious matters, maintaining an appearance which will be simple, sincere and honest. Nevertheless, you are apt to say whatever comes to your mind. The discontinuous nature of your thoughts might bring you to seem too direct and forthright, upon occasion, your bluntness striking wounding blows or misunderstandings that result from an absence of prior reflection rather than mal-intention. It often appears that people of this decan are incapable of weighing one thought against another and finding a balance between them, but you no doubt consider carefully in advance the response your remarks and actions will earn, allowing these to ripen beforehand and repenting with the same haste in which you speak or conduct yourself. PATIENCE is the key to doors that will lead you to success, in my opinion. Individuals born in this decan who make a practice of carrying out undertakings according to their promises, or ideas they conceive, invariably enjoy growing happiness; any tendencies toward interrupting conversations also diminish. Because I have confidence that you make a practice of formulating a judgment, I am sure that you are deeper and more genuine than many people.

You probably approach your interests with an air of efficiency, striving for the most practical course; analyzing, criticizing and discriminating until you feel that you arrive at the most logical conclusions. A keen INTUITION is no doubt helpful to many of your interests, although you are more likely to occupy yourself with everyday facts than explorations into the "unseen". As you reach for your preferred attainments, you are apt to be just, but not overly sympathetic, which may sometimes give people around you an impression that you are, at heart, unapproachable. An acute awareness of yourself, combined with a keen interest in serving as a powerful example for other individuals who come to touch your life may prompt you to react to stresses by losing a sense of equilibrium, your emotional balance often being delicately poised upon the realization of any current hopes or wishes, admiration and praise.

You are almost certain to have more than an ordinary number of clever, dexterous and ingenious qualities to draw upon in carrying out your day-to-day routines, which might prompt you to seek a somewhat "executive" position in circumstances around you, to the extent that you will have control over matters which concern you without close supervision or direction by other individuals. Generally, however, people of your decan accomplish more easily what they set out to do when they methodically direct their energies toward a definite objective that will serve practical purposes. By making few pretensions and attending to any tasks at hand quietly, amiably and sometimes even unobserved, deserved credit for your "effectiveness" is almost bound to come in abundance, bringing automatically honors or the favorable reputation you no doubt seek.

I believe that you have a superb capacity for developing sensible, realistic and thorough plans that will be useful to groups, individuals or corporations with which you become associated, although you probably find it advantageous to display responsiveness rather than resistance to newer ideas which are not your own. Otherwise, it may occasionally appear to others who know you that concepts which you might gain for your personal recognition or benefit can bring you to "lightning-like" action which is frequently premature, while you tend to hesitate over another person's suggestions or even consider obstinate rejection of their decisions. I feel sure that you are motivated by a desire for these to be correct choices, but because you will often attract broad-minded and highly intelligent associates, your flexibility will prove that they are often singularly helpful to your interests.

From an early age, you will probably seem especially communicative; talking, asking questions, changing about and carrying messages, always preferring to be busy. The subtle, wary and scientific characteristics which are, I think, inherent to your nature will make you especially adept at use of the spoken or written word. So many super-salespeople or those who "sway others" through writings are born in this decan. You are apt to have a special fondness for travel, frequently making friendly visits to neighborhood areas. Owing to weighty problems within your family life, or "denials" which you consider restrictive to some of your personal wishes, you are likely to have moods during your "growing up" when you tend to be worrisome, fussy, untidy or selfpitying, although any seeming limitations will no doubt prove favorable in many ways, by attracting you to pursuits and where knowledge is imparted to others and encouraging you to develop companionable relationships with certain relatives or people who comprise the society of your daily interests.

In all probability, you will be somewhat more self-sufficient than many youngsters your age, holding a coolly-affectionate attitude toward close associates and an idealistic outlook for your future. This is a period of your life when I believe that you will need to learn to make compromises and adjust to rules, regulations and customs which will later enable you to form deeper attachments without feeling that you are "fettered" by them. There might be some ill-health at this time, originating from nervous conditions, but on the whole, the phase that will carry you from childhood through your teen years should be filled with happy remembrances. You will no doubt enjoy the majority of your experiences, like most of the people you meet, and will gain many favors.

As you enter adulthood, you might encounter temporary obstacles, sometimes feeling "hampered" financially and having dampened spirits as a result of fewer doors opening for you than you originally anticipated. In reality, individuals you come to know at this time may not accept your authority as readily as many of those you have known in the past. The "right of kingship", or "queenship", might be questioned in these newer circles, causing a few of your previous concepts to crumble and your sense of humility to be "put to the test", so to say. When you face any apparent duties responsibly, practicing HONESTY and generosity in your intentions, you should have fewer difficulties than many people, although I must conclude in this respect that you will be impelled to learn strong lessons in this cycle. Sometimes one of these disappointments arises from a particular love affair or early marriage. Emergence into maturity may prompt you to hold more skeptical, cold or critical views that reduce your inherent "faith", but I trust that you will turn from these in an earnest endeavor to cultivate your more aesthetic, humane perceptions.

Duplicities of various kinds will almost certainly stamp both your conduct and interests, multiplying your experiences, possessions and activities. The underlying temperament of many people born in this decan of Sagittarius is aggressive, revengeful when cheated and crafty when hurt — but I have the greatest confidence in you; therefore, courage will be the background setting you establish for yourself — brilliant research, constructive investigations or studies, and creative achievements will enable you to emerge from "behind-the-scenes" victorious in praiseworthy accomplishments.

Hobbies that require the handling of weapons, tools, driving of vehicles, usually seem attractive to individuals of this birthday cycle. I believe that you have strong preferences for "the freedom of the outdoors" and enjoy "pioneering" either new areas or ideas. You no doubt have a great power of execution that will enable you to master techniques in artistic design, music or literature, while you should have ample energy for refining vital interests.

You are apt to look upon your material interests with a great deal of seriousness, weighing the majority of your actions and alliances upon their promise of gainful return. Although you will probably be productive, resourceful and responsible in "the management of enterprises" that concern you, long phases of budgeting will probably be followed by substantial expenditures, or you might tend to save with the utmost conservatism in some areas and spend lavishly in others. I usually associate your decan with successful acquisitions, however, considering it more fortunate than otherwise. I think that you will acquire many of those possessions and assets you most wish to have, and that even when your financial affairs seem less hopeful than you would really like, providence will always appear to come to your rescue, bringing at least one very welcome advantage that serves to "tide you over". Gifts, estates and "benefits" are very apt to increase some of your holdings. You might have a tendency to feel more sensitive to reversals or material limitations than many people — but when you judge others by human kindness, they will accordingly accept you on your own merit, in all likelihood. Therefore, I feel that by seeking orthodox means of income, you will earn gratifying returns in measure to your constructive efforts.

Romantic relationships among individuals born in this first decan of Sagittarius often occur quite impulsively, some being of short duration but long remembered. I believe that this area of life will present rather intriguing challenges for you that will require the use of your better judgment. You may incline to be aggressive, impatient, quick-tempered and reckless. Order in affectional attachments you have might become unsettled, upon occasion, but when you have patience, you should enjoy several deep love affairs.

Business and marital partnerships are almost bound to

attract you, although troubles and bickerings may accompany some of these. I think that you will often enter into associations with individuals who serve your better interests and improve conditions for you materially, although you will be aware of certain impositions that result from differences of opinion or relationships with a few of "the relatives" of these people. Some degree of craftiness, diffusion, indiscretion or scattered effort is likely to enter into at least one alliance you have — but because I have confidence that you will contribute all the happiness that you can, giving sympathy, benevolence and genuine concern to those to whom you are nearest, I feel that you will usually develop strong rapport that gives more depth to your associations and enables you to have greater control over them.

Children and younger people sometimes bring a few additional stresses into the lives of individuals born in this decan, or a disappointment may occur in this area. When you have reason to concern yourself with the interests of youngsters, a display of compassion, understanding and gentleness is likely to earn satisfying returns, while you might realize substantial benefits by endeavoring to let them dominate their own activities, within reasonable limits, of course.

You are likely to consider that your home surroundings are more of a responsibility than pleasure, although aside from your usual daily routines you are very apt to use these for gainful purposes. You might sometimes remain "secretive" with regard to activities in your immediate environment. With each passing year, you may have increasing preference for seclusion, retiring more and more often to a private place with few distractions.

I feel that your talents are remarkable and your personality delightful. When you devote yourself to constructive purposes you will have fewer opponents and more gratifying conquests, in my opinion — and because you center your life on other people rather than your personal wants, your great ideas will become satisfying realities and other people will respond to your integrity and kindness by reflecting your wishes!

Sagittarius

December 3-December 12
Ruled by Moon

2nd decan

Enthusiasm is the first word that comes to my mind when I think of this second decan of Sagittarius, because it always seems that people born under its influence have true "sporting blood". They usually adore taking chances, hit or miss — but of course they hope to hit. I have often observed, however, that these characteristics incline to be more "mental" among individuals born between December 3rd and December 7th, and more "physical" among those born between December 8th and December 12th. The former group frequently tends to cultivate the mind at the expense of the body (getting insufficient rest, little time in the open air, or inadequate diet and exercise), while the latter often tries to perfect the body through arduous exercise and similar methods. With these somewhat contradictory means of expression in mind, I consider that all of these people have strong imaginative faculties; they love traveling and thinking of foreign lands, and they often lead quite romantic lives. You may, too.

It seems that there are rather vivid traces of a "superconscious" mind to be found among people born in your decan. You no doubt have a cold, clear intelligence that permits you to focus impressions you receive to an almost preternaturally acute point. Effects produced upon your mind will be blurred only rarely, ordinarily occurring to you in sharp and well-defined perfection, in my opinion. You are probably optimistic, sincere, alert and cheerful in your outlook, while a quest for variation may keep you continuously on the move. People of this decan who do not have clearly established objectives often develop this inherent quality to a fault, appearing restless without aim, or careless and offhanded in their manner, but, even so, they might still enjoy more than an ordinary number of opportunities for acquiring polish and knowledge through their experiences. These are "born Bohemians", who happily hang their hats wherever they happen to be, continually looking forward for new fields to conquer. Provided they exercise sufficient forethought in such matters, as I am sure you do, they bring themselves to high renown and steadily improve their assets, but in almost any circumstances, an unsettled life should be expected.

People who come to know you well will probably notice that you have an inexhaustible energy, displaying continual, or, certainly tireless, activity. You are apt to accomplish everything you do in a hurry, tending to think quickly, speak out too impatiently, and be quick to make changes in response to your curiosity. In all likelihood, you have greater pride of achievement in singular undertakings to which you can devote your full attention, one at a time, without confusion of issues, or introduction of facts that have little relationship to matters at hand. At the same time, you like to hold in mind the next goal you will pursue when you complete the one that presently occupies your attention, I feel. Because I have confidence that you are motivated by a desire for betterment, I anticipate that you will realize substantial accomplishments and earn valuable assistance from certain individuals who hold esteemed positions. Having a tendency to react upon impressions from within and without, you will be philosophical in your outlook, no doubt.

Every sign and every decan has its strengths and weaknesses, too. I cannot honestly discuss some without mentioning others — and I must say, in this respect, that the most serious difficulties encountered by individuals of this second decan of Sagittarius are usually caused by a temper which is largely undecided, bringing habitual and sometimes unpredictable explosions. Surely you endeavor to master YOUR personality, so that you substantially reduce any such inclinations, but nevertheless, you are apt to have a good deal of impetuosity within your nature that will often prompt you to go off on "tangents", or, at least, act without sufficient forethought. Eccentricities in either manner, attitude, speech or choice of automobiles are often characteristic of this birthday cycle.

Your earlier environment is likely to be exceptionally happy, even changes that might occur among individuals influential in your rearing proving beneficial for your interests. For some people of this decan there is too little discipline, however, which leads acquaintances or other associates to appear imposing later on. You are apt to seem independent from a young age, acting with such inquisitiveness that others consider you a perpetual question mark, or thinking so far in advance of your ability to speak that your utterances momentarily turn to hesitating speech, giving little understanding to a hearer. Your tendencies toward science and humanitarianism might be strong, making you a quick observer and giving you a fondness for people of all ages and from every walk of life. You will easily gain control over situations in which you become involved, in my estimation, frequently understanding several sides to the same question, but being partisan to none. The restless activity of your mind, combined with a rich creative power, should develop with each passing year, while your interpretive faculties; far-seeing, original, sharp and dissecting instincts will enable you to learn with relative ease. You might master several different languages or the use of words to put over your ideas in the advertising or selling fields with seemingly little effort. I believe that you will have a keen intuition and accurate perception, but you will often debate old venerated ideas or ways of achieving particular objectives.

You are really likely to "come into your own", so to say, as you approach the "twenties". I feel that you will make most of your own opportunities, but abundant good fortune will appear to be at your side as you endeavor to realize a goal. I feel certain you will be able to obtain a higher education or will increase your knowledge when you have a desire to do so. I know that people you meet at this time will be especially responsive to your warm sense of humor, bighearted disposition and sincere generosity. At least one deep affectional attachment which will be influential in your later years is likely to occur at this time. Now and then people of this decan are considered intolerant, extravagant, over-bearing and self-appraising — but I trust that YOUR full, frank, expansive nature will materialize in a strong religious quality that will enable you to bring to the fore your more gentle and beautiful qualities. You will no doubt have a fondness for power, but people around you should willingly follow your lead in this cyclic phase, often in admiration of the sense of drama you display in promoting your purposes.

I think that you will have an interest in forming romantic alliances, some of which will be impulsively entered and charged with a desire for immediate results, once you set your sights on a person as your objective. Sagittarius is called "The Sign of the Bachelor", owing to a wish for freedom from control which is usually found within it, but people of this decan who do have a preference for marriage are rarely satisfied with long courtships. Being aggressive by nature, they are apt to take strong initiative in their more sentimental activities, showing the most clever and persevering manner of acquiring the attentions of another — because any challenges which are encountered will probably seem all the more intriguing. Having more confidence than almost any other people, individuals of your decan benefit by magnanimously receding when there are indications that their pursuance is unwelcome, but provided they thoughtfully respond to such intimations, their directness frequently makes them victorious over opponents who hold admiration similar to their own.

Such a spiritual nature as this decan of Sagittarius signifies might necessitate a few adjustments in close relationships. Thriving on adventure and having great zest for life, you may be impersonal in your emotional outlook; often quixotic. You are apt to cherish an almost incorrigible romantic ideal which you weave out of fancy, rather than a particular individual who is almost bound to prove only human. At least "one" of your associates may consider that you are less steadfast or dependable than they anticipated, because in all likelihood you will first be whatever you most want to be and a partner after that. I believe that you will be unusually capable, companionable and interesting, but you will prefer to take over the management of most mutual concerns. Financial and other material matters will probably seem especially important to you, frequently being your reason for forming alliances. While you are very apt to increase these substantially, you may tend to appear to another person quite forceful, now and then. An inclination "to express your exact thoughts" may occasionally wound, even though any outspoken remarks might, indeed be perfectly accurate. The tendency is to desire to impart knowledge or to "teach" others. Individuals born in this decan of Sagittarius who find too little active expression for their variable natures become inclined to take opposing viewpoints which results in heated arguments — but a pursuit of hobbies and similar vital interests will bring rapid solutions, in my opinion. My point in mentioning all of these probabilities is that you should be somewhat more discriminating than many people, in your selection of "a partner", so that you will find the degree of happiness I know you want and richly deserve. Because I trust that you will strive to give patience, sympathetic understanding and warm appreciation, I feel that you will be a generous and superbly loyal contributor to partnerships you enter into, although I am sure that disappointments, or one, especially, will touch this area of your life. People born in the sign Taurus almost always play a strong role in the affairs of those born in this sign.

When you observe constructive policies, particularly those most advantageous for you in partnerships, you ought to enjoy quite gratifying relationships.

I think that you will take pride in your home environment, having a fondness for spacious surroundings and artistic or unique effects that will provide a feeling of comfort and privacy. At some time you are very likely to dwell near water, and possibly will have more than one location you consider your residence; you might live in a dwelling which is shared with other inhabitants, such as an apartment, or have a fondness for mobile homes, or a houseboat. Multiplicities and transposal conveniences may be quite evident in your life. One of the more intriguing observations I have made, regarding friends of mine who have birthdays in this phase, is that a place to live always seems to be supplied at times when such possibilities appear dim. A number of these people become active in real estate, I notice, and bring from such enterprises outstanding success, or some particular piece of property.

You are apt to have shrewd business acumen as well as rich creative power, approaching "deals" with an obstinacy which is equal only to your fervor. Ways of "serving" the better interests of individuals with whom you transact will no doubt occur to you, yet you ought to be able to conduct yourself with a cool efficiency that brings practical results.

Although your closest personal relationships will probably present some of your greatest challenges, I feel that you will receive strong advantages from people in high positions or those who are placed so they can favor them. You are almost certain to receive a legacy or inheritance — probably more than one! I believe that you will tend to attract individuals who will tend to deplete some of your resources, even taking responsibility for another person from time to time, yet in spite of minor disillusionment, there will be those who will improve your reputation and "standing" in circles of society where you are, or will be influential in bringing benefits your way.

Individuals born in this decan ordinarily have strong, sturdy constitutions which, combined with a cheerful attitude, insures generally good health. When any ailments do occur, they are often of emotional, rather than physical origin and of longer duration than it seems they might be. I feel that by practicing thoughts of peace, patience, harmony and poise you will substantially reduce the probability of accidents and other "mishaps" which might otherwise result from impetuous moods or actions. Almost all Sagittarians have scars resulting from accidents or operations. Restraint in every area of your life seems to me advisable, because by taking precautions against extremes you will be assured of a more providential, productive and satisfying future.

I consider this second decan of Sagittarius brilliantly promising of favorable distinction, "wealth" and good fortune. I am absolutely certain the boundaries to your successes are contained "within your thoughts" — and when you center these firmly on only the highest aims, directing your energies accordingly, the ultimate borders your life can reach will hold the prospects of fulfillment, at least as great as the gratifying outcomes you conscientiously seek. There is no need for you to create better conditions, because these will always be ALL around you in abundance. You need only to recognize that you have a personal responsibility to aim your wonderful talents toward a constructive mark which you will then swiftly reach, I feel certain!

Sagittarius

December 13-December 21
Ruled by Saturn

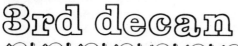 

There is little doubt that you have a sober and philosophical temperament, and because this is combined with pronounced mental ability as well as an inclination for abstract thought, you might have more than ordinary capabilities for writing or teaching. It will probably be instinctive for you to notice ways in which you can direct and guide the lives of people you know. While your judgments may be perfectly correct, this might occasionally lead people you know to consider that you are moralizing. One quite often meets individuals born under the influence of this third decan of Sagittarius who are blunt in speech and tactless — but I have confidence that YOU carefully weigh your words before speaking them and anticipate in advance the result your actions will create; therefore, I know that people who make your acquaintance consider you trustworthy, and favorably respond to your fearless, frank, humanitarian and obliging manner. A strong duplicity is likely to be evident in your nature that makes you optimistic and pessimistic all at the same time, or brings you to blend swift and transient qualities with some which are more heavy and slow, a mixture of varieties that lead you to seem many-sided. There are apt to be times when it appears that your spendthrift and active characteristics serve to accelerate those which are less quick, prompting a kind of thrift which is not at all incompatible with real altruism. You are very likely to have a keen, retrospective mind. Sometimes it might even seem that you are genuinely prophetic, when you turn your "insight" to future welfare. Owing to these fine qualities, I think that you generally display a disposition that earns trust, honor and respect from other individuals, and makes you well suited for activity in industrial, social or philosophical circles.

Although you are apt to be extremely ambitious for material security and personal prominence, there is also likely to be a retiring and modest streak in your nature. I trust that you earnestly endeavor to earn YOUR own way through life instead of expecting that accomplishment is your inherent "right", as some people of this decan do, and that you overcome any tendencies toward coldness and self-centeredness by giving warmth and joviality to individuals around you, projecting your own feelings to their sensibilities and those of Humanity as a whole. For this reason, I anticipate that you will acquire growing success, in measure to that which you seek, although numerous people within this birthday phase will sometimes forfeit these marvelous promises through weakness and irresponsibility; sarcasm, cynicism, resentment of opposition or reproof, and "impulsive actions" preventing their elevation to honor. You have probably discovered, as they may, too, that "rapid solutions" to almost any stalls in your progress lie in participation in knowledge; learning, philosophical, scientific, legal and religious subjects being especially responsive to their talents, as well as your own. Having a fondness for travel, you might find that voyaging or shipping may afford scope for some of your capabilities. I mention this, because I feel that individuals born under this third decan of Sagittarius ordinarily possess a remarkable capacity for "piercing the illusions" many others might have and thus soaring to some of the highest states of achievement.

I think that weighty problems during the earliest part of your life, owing to difficulties with physical well-being, possibly of another person, or similar limitations, will leave an imprint upon your future, bringing you to view your interests more seriously than many individuals your age, and cautioning you prematurely that adversity is a part of the completeness of "the grand scheme of things". This might give you occasional moods when you consider that your life is an "uphill" struggle, or feel that you are filled with discontent and gloom, although instead of becoming overexacting as many people will, I know that you will turn your thoughts to more cheerful concepts in thankfulness for all that you DO have. Thus, you will surely use patience, method, steadfastness and persistence until goals which you have set become tangible realities in your life, even at times when someone else would permit an "impetuous thought" to strike, and with lightning-like speed lead to action that might later be regretted, or even accidents and similar mishaps.

Many changes within a somewhat fixed environment are likely to occur during your years of "growing up", the influence of a certain female being particularly strong. At this time, you are apt to react somewhat dispassionately to situations in which you find yourself, responding admirably to your natural senses by developing out of these human interest combined with a scientific attitude. For the most part, I believe that you will tend to be courteous, detached and imaginative, although erratic, aloof or unpredictable behavior will be noticeable when you feel that your independence is being challenged by another person. This is a phase of your life when you are likely to have more than an ordinary degree of material aid from benefactors, or one, especially. While I think that you will often display a loyalty which will always be evident in your nature, neither sentimentality, rationalism nor emotionalism will predominate, enabling you to measure your over-all reflexes more easily than many of your contemporaries. You are apt to take a rather devout approach to any religious teachings that come to your attention, although there is little likelihood of your leaning to extremes in any direction. Your seriousness of mind when a child may bring you to seem in advance of many other children, making you appear somewhat futuristic in your outlook; an avid student and friend to many without devotion or intense satisfaction from any particular chum, because your sympathies will move in many different channels. Actually, these are years when your finest responses will be drawn by people who are not too indulgent or unselfish in their attitude toward you, in my opinion.

More aggressive qualities are likely to come to the surface as you leave adolescence and enter adulthood, prompting you to challenge many of your previous beliefs and to question religious, philosophical or educational concepts you previously held. While you are apt to alter your original estimation very little regarding these, you are almost certain to debate them with some vehemence. I feel that you will tend to be ambitious, enthusiastic, intense and dramatic; sometimes melodramatic, dominating and arrogant in your methods, plunging whole-heartedly into enterprises that have appeal for you and holding wider sympathies on a personal level. Your desire for travel may be keen, while a newly-found romantic spirit will encompass almost everything you do, in all probability. Although your generosity, warmth and persuasiveness will no doubt hold you in good stead, you will need to direct your energies into constructive channels in order to sidestep accidents, dissensions and similar stresses which are almost bound to occur otherwise, proving disruptive to some of your prospects for receiving a higher education. I believe that you will participate quite actively in such things as sports and cultural or creative pursuits, although your interests will be abundant possibly because of your need to replenish your source of financial supply — or it will seem that way.

Ideals you hold "within" are now likely to create an image of love that will prompt you to seek a person who matches perfection you envision. Dreams, however, are often more beautiful than stark realities, which might lead you to "love by sight and be disappointed by touch", so to say — or to place a cherished person on a pedestal "too shaky" for one who is, after all, only a human being. Like Don Quixote, many people of this decan tend to conduct a life-long pursuit of a perfect love, as it has grown in their imagination, that yet proves upon actual contact to be but a "windmill". In all honesty, I must say that you are apt to enjoy the "chase" more than the "catch", your true spirit finding its forte in the challenge of conquest. The very soul of this decan is likely to be independent, free and strongwilled, which is often better suited to single life — yet you are almost certain to feel that your security, material and otherwise, lies within close relationships.

My indepth description, is meant to show a few reasons why individuals of this third decan of Sagittarius usually marry, but often do so several times — and, also, why they should be especially careful in their selections of either business or marriage partners. I think that their true happiness most often rests in their standing ready to give as much of themselves, spiritually and emotionally as they expect to receive. Obtaining in advance practical experience that will fulfill any desire for travel, pursuits and enterprises that might not easily adapt to established routines will also prove helpful, I feel. I trust that YOU take pride in another person's achievements instead of holding jealousy, suspicion and distrust as some individuals will, and that YOU keep YOUR temper within control, holding in check some of your more trifling inclinations and sportive tendencies. Therefore, I anticipate more pleasing returns for YOU than many people.

You might wish for children. As in your other interests, your associations with younger people are likely to be happiest when you place THEIR needs and wishes before your own, persuasively guiding their activities without enforcing them — but by observing these policies, you should enjoy many gratifying returns, favors and courtesies from those who come to touch your life.

I feel that you will find it beneficial to seek, above all else, a sense of "inner" satisfaction, although earnest effort will be necessary before you find it in your more "domestic" interests. It appears to me that stresses will frequently be noticeable in your home surroundings and that you will have at least "one" secret regarding circumstances in these, which may involve a younger person. I think that you will have a preference for spacious quarters which are both artistically designed and facilitating for your many hobbies and interests. You might like to have water nearby, and to maintain places you consider residences in more than one area, each of which will be different from the other. Regardless of conditions around you, you are apt to have moods when you feel a "stranger in your own home", so to say, or are aware of some loneliness there — yet you may sometimes seek a cloistered life voluntarily. When it seems to you that "pressures" are building within your immediate environment, as it probably will from time to time, I urge you to direct your energies to constructive outlets that will give favorable vent to them.

There is sometimes a phase that brings difficulties with the legs, or one at least, while I also notice that individuals who have birthdays within your cycle almost invariably have a taste for lofty speculations and deep researches. I believe that you have plasticity and receptiveness in your over-all approach, although this will bring you to be sharply critical of seeming defects you discover in enterprises that concern you, and analytical with respect to their solution. You might sometimes appear intolerant towards stupidity in other people, but you have surely realized that it is necessary to accept the world as it actually is instead of as it ought to be. You are likely to wish for position and standing, although you may prefer to gain these through other people rather than personal effort and strangely this sign frequently does benefit through the efforts of others. Services you perform on behalf of other individuals, business endeavors or "groups" may seem especially burdensome and laborious, although "self-enterprise" is not apt to be instinctive to you, either, requiring that you exert somewhat more initiative in order to achieve success in undertakings you pursue individually. Nevertheless, your close association with at least one person will probably bring gratifying returns just as some of your more "speculative" ventures will undoubtedly prove fortunate with steady application. I am certain that you will enjoy more than an ordinary degree of gain, even when it originally appears that your assets accumulate less quickly than you would really like.

The society of other people is almost bound to respond to your sympathetic, just, charitable and hospitable outlook, earning for you many valuable acquaintances. In my opinion, your most outstanding qualities are "loyalty and illumination". When you give generously of these, I know that you will make strong contributions to a better world, and that you will be rewarded by steadfast friendships among a few individuals who truly have your best interests at heart.

The older you grow, the more you should strive for constructive, external expression of your brilliant talents and abilities, I believe. Creative effort, appealing athletic pursuits, cultural activities, and frequent associations with the quietude of nature should provide very worthwhile flights from some of the harsher realities of day-to-day routine.

Cooperation and tranquility will become enduring conditions in your life when you cultivate modest habits and devote yourself to the benefit of people whose circumstances will be aided by your magnanimous behind-the-scenes effort, there is little doubt. I am absolutely certain that by relishing each moment which is yours to enjoy in this wonderful world, peace, joyousness and devotion returned will take a larger place in your affairs, from this moment forward.

Capricorn

December 22-December 31
Ruled by Jupiter

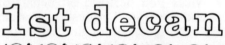

Self-control and self-reliance are probably two of the most dominant characteristics you tend to display, creating upon people who meet you an impression that you are economical, careful and trustworthy, which might lead them to think you able for dictating wisely and well, therefore, deserving of some degree of popularity, esteem and power. One will occasionally find individuals who have birthdays in this first decan of Capricorn who seem cold, overly thrifty in money matters, austere or self-righteous, but I have confidence that you earnestly endeavor to show that you are conscientious, responsible, resourceful and productive, expressing practically your enterprising ability, with essential restraint, and assuredly proving yourself worthy of the favorable opinion your original appearance earns.

Some of the most solid intellectuals in the world hail from your decan. You, too, may have a seriousness of mind that makes you less hopeful in your outlook than many people, but gives you great powers for contemplative learning. While concepts you accept might not always be entirely orthodox, you are almost bound to give deep consideration to philosophical, religious, legal and educational subjects, sometimes analyzing, criticizing, assimilating these with a view of devoting your life on their behalf. When you place at the summit of your life, the highest of these principles in which you believe and steadfastly conduct yourself in accordance with them, I am certain that you will realize extremely substantial returns, as well as favorable recognition you richly deserve.

There is likely to be a strong contradiction within your personality which some people might consider absurd, but nevertheless it is apt to be very true in fact. This will be a tendency you have for showing the most extreme frugality in certain areas, and going beyond the limits of reason or moderation in others. You might budget, scrimp and save, on one hand, and on the other spend lavishly in order to maintain certain appearances. Traces of extremes may be noticeable, occasionally, in moods that swing from diplomacy and pleasantness to despondency, suspicion and cold judgment of others although I trust that you will never give vent to the least favorable of these inward feelings. In view of this rather paradoxical combination, I think it to be of first importance that you continually endeavor to maintain your life upon an even BALANCE, because the outcome of your whole approach will frequently be reliant upon such effort.

You, no doubt, have shrewd judgment that enables you to observe introspectively situations in which you participate, acquire from them extraordinary stores of knowledge, and build from these great ideas. While your mind is almost bound to be masterful and ambitious, there may be times when it tends to be filled with doubts, many of which result from an ideal too firmly planted within material realms. This might bring you to take a somewhat fatalistic outlook, now and then, or lead you to be ever questioning your destiny, yet will carry onward, nevertheless, by a prevailing self-confidence and high ambition. I am certain you have learned that when you widen your sympathies and broaden your viewpoints your spiritual understanding steadily increases, giving growing brightness to areas of your life which were previously darkened, and happiness in replacement of prior vacancies.

I have observed that the earliest environments of individuals born in this first decan of Capricorn are ordinarily dominated by one particular person, owing to a more passive role taken by another as a result of absences or other circumstances. This frequently leads to "regimented routines", at one time or another, that discourages spontaneity, an awareness of personal responsibility, or initiative, and substantially "limits the degree of pleasure" that might otherwise be received during the years of "growing up", and instead imbeds deeply a feeling of "aloneness". I believe that for you, too, this cyclic phase will seem somewhat less easy than many of those later on, owing, partially, to a feeling of responsibility you will tend to have toward at least one sibling or relative, or someone who "neighbors" your day-to-day surroundings, which will appear to require of you certain sacrifices and ultimately lead you to be more retiring in your manner than many children of your age. Regardless of circumstances, you are apt to be aware of loneliness during this period of your life, and this sense of "confinement" will no doubt stall your learning. Many, many children of this decan repeat a grade in school, I notice. I think that you will wish for approval, yet question whether you really have it, while "over-sensitivity" is likely to give you a tendency toward brooding contemplation, worry, untidiness and occasional self-pity, habits which I am confident you have now overcome. During these earlier trends, you may have impressions, such as "premonitions" of a sinister nature, that forewarn of problems, or one problem, that will then manifest in the precise manner you originally imagined; a similar happening might give you glimpses of possibilities within the "here and hereafter" that will sometimes weigh heavily on your mind. Possessions will probably seem tremendously important to you, those you are "without" appearing to offer good reason for declining certain invitations or occasions you might otherwise attend — or at least giving these less appeal — and although your needs may be provided, you are likely to feel that the returns you receive from other people are less adequate than you would really prefer, a characteristic which you will surely need to suppress throughout your lifetime.

As you emerge into adulthood, your more practical instincts should come to the fore, enabling you to better communicate the real intricacies of your mind for the development of some of the efficient, discriminating methods with which you can organize future undertakings. You are apt to gain better control over your powers of logic at this time, reasoning matters out in minute detail and applying more of your vitality on mental planes. These are years of your life when your true self may "shine" at its best; by seizing opportunities that come to you now and then endeavoring to maintain the success you realize from these, you will substantially improve your future outlook, in my opinion — although I have known individuals born in this decan of Capricorn who frittered away endowments supplied for a higher education and similarly neglected interests that held for them great promise, each of whom have continually appeared to bring more than the usual number of problems upon themselves later on.

You are apt to develop a desire for romantic attachments at a relatively early age, approaching most of these deliberately and somewhat cautiously in the hope that a thorough, realistic and sensible attitude will bring solid and constructive results. You will, I am sure, tend to be rather secretive about a few of your more impulsive attachments, or you may conceal certain facts concerning a particular alliance or as to a purchase. It is quite unlikely that you will form serious associations without first considering the effect these will have upon your position and standing in mutual activities, but when it appears that a person will prove favorable for your purposes you are almost bound to seek permanency, being tenacious in your pursuit and patient in your efforts to weave circumstances to your own advantage. There is little doubt that you will have more than ample magnetism for attracting attentions you hope to gain!

In business as well as marital partnerships, you will probably have a fondness for "domesticated" types of individuals who show an interest in home and family life and have harmonious, sensitive, gentle, amiable dispositions that will reflect, rather than challenge, your wishes. In your selection of close associates, I think that you especially admire those who have a keen intellect combined with an attractive nature that will earn many friends and observe social amenities. Such people are almost certain to be helpful to many of your interests, and you are likely to react with tenacity, seldom seeking to dissolve alliances you have formed. Nevertheless, you are apt to have a few problems in this area of your life. A reason might be that it is an effort for you to let yourself go emotionally, and because you may turn your feelings "inward" upon yourself, there is a strong probability that you will rarely exhibit the affection you feel, to the extent that another person expects. I trust that you endeavor to be forgiving, tolerant and trusting — and when you thoughtfully perform courteous gestures that will show you place your loved ones above "practical considerations of the moment", sentimentally as well as materially, you will substantially increase your prospects of finding truly harmonious conditions.

Your home and family life will frequently seem stressful to you, in my opinion, although when you make your immediate surroundings a center for constructive activity, having patience with people who share your routines, your enthusiasm is apt to be contagious, heightening both the pleasure you will give and that which you will receive in return.

I believe that you are especially "aware of the impression" you make upon people who come to touch your life from day to day. You probably try to show balanced judgment in your approach, evaluating facts with great acumen. The older you grow, the more energetic, strong-willed and impetuous you are apt to become. When you direct your energies to worthwhile pursuits, you will surely attract favorable notice for your organizing and executive abilities; having keen regard for mastery of technique, you will wish to execute quickly enterprises you start, so that you can investigate newer areas of endeavor that have appeal. Because I have confidence that you will modify your zeal with kindness, looking always for a means of improving circumstances for people around you, even when this requires that you concede to opinions which are different from your own or make compromises on behalf of others that slightly lessen gains you might otherwise receive, I feel that you will earn many, many gratifying rewards which are spiritual, emotional and material. Sooner or later, women born in this decan enter the business world and show amazing shrewdness.

I believe that you are less creative than methodical, thorough and capable, which gives you a preference for activities and pursuits you can perfect from an original idea. Such things as "sound equipment" or audio fields, frequently appeal to individuals born in your decan of Capricorn, because these enable them to combine their superb and concentrated mental powers with their more mechanical aptitudes. They are rarely likely to involve themselves in "trivia" or participate in endeavors for the sheer purpose of pleasure, owing to a desire to realize profitable returns from their efforts. Upon occasion this can be overdone, leading associates to think them a "wet blanket" when more frivolous entertainment is on their agenda, although I trust that YOU earnestly try to be a "good sport" when your efforts to do so will promote happiness among individuals around you.

Younger people with whom you become associated are frequently likely to prove helpful to your interests, especially when you strive to be a pleasing companion as well as a disciplinarian. There are individuals born in this decan who tend to be diffuse, indiscreet, crafty and scattered in the conduct of their daily routines, being firm "upholders of law and order" according to strict rules they establish for other people in actuality or in their own judgment of others — but you are surely more broad-minded, constructively directing your varied talents and high intelligence in such ways as to honestly EARN favorable notice from the "public" around you, through your INTEGRITY, TENDERHEARTEDNESS and GENEROSITY, on a constant rather than sporadic level.

The inherent qualities which are ordinarily characteristic of your sign and decan are usually admirably suited for productivity, which generally brings people born under its influence to be happiest when they are active in the "business", governmental fields, or "political" world — although a real sense of SATISFACTION and JOYOUSNESS is sometimes less easy to attain, making this one of the more temperamentally depressed of the various personalities. When you make it an absolute policy to cultivate feelings of trust, peace, humanitarianism and benevolence, considering another person's sensibilities as if they were your own in every situation, you are almost bound to achieve greater balance in ALL of the areas of your life that concern you most.

You may be somewhat more aware of the degree of "competition" which is a natural part of the grand "scheme of things", but I know that you will never permit this to slant your attitudes toward an attitude of "taking advantage of other people before they can do so with you", as many individuals do. An ability to view material matters more abstractly than personally may be one of your strongest assets, provided that you always keep sight of a high spiritual ideal, following the promptings of your "heart" as well as your "head", so to say. I sincerely think that by adopting these constructive concepts as a permanent part of your daily living, opportunities for advancement will grow in abundance, to lift you steadily higher, toward the degree of success you most hope to achieve! This is the sign that will climb to reach the top!

Capricorn

January 1-January 10
Ruled by Mars

2nd decan

This second decan of Capricorn represents to me the acme of intense ambition, forceful self-assertion and red-hot enthusiasm, because people who are born under its influence almost invariably display a strong taste for conquest, as you may. I believe that you will be blessed with opportunities to devote your remarkable intelligence to some very useful pursuits, and when you seize these in an effort to improve conditions for all of Mankind you can reach, as well as your own interests, abundant success is certain to be your reward. You are apt to have an air of dignity about you that creates an impression of solemnity upon people who come to touch your life, bringing some of those who feel overpowered by your formidability to "shy away" from you until they know you better. At least to some degree, this is probably because you resent anyone prying into your affairs, so that you automatically take precautionary measures against their taking liberties with you or seeking to approach you upon too intimate terms, finding it preferable to first learn about their concerns.

You are likely to be exceptionally self-reliant, industrious and ambitious, your authoritativeness manifesting in a blended personality of fiery energy tempered to obstinacy, but there will no doubt be additional power and vigor to your activity. Confidence, together with skillfulness, may give you tremendous magnetism, as well as a spirit of command, dourness and tenacity also being evident in your disposition. Therefore, I feel that you have the executive force which is necessary for real diplomatic achievement, provided that you guide these marvelous qualities to constructive channels.

- 271 -

I think that you like to have a sense of freedom and independence in your personal enterprises, expressing a courageous, pioneering, fearless nature toward large objectives that will lift you even higher than the environment into which you were born. You should be a tireless worker who is willing to assume responsibilities and capable in managing these, good organizing ability being one of your strongest assets. The intensity with which you apply yourself to "tasks at hand" may bring associates to consider that some of your methods are overly-forceful, now and then, yet in the end you may very well prove triumphant in these, even when they appear to others to demand more smoothness than you have originally given them. Impatience might occasionally give you a tendency to seem somewhat blunt or curt in your manner of action or speech, although I trust that you make an effort to use tact and diplomacy, which invites courtesies that would not otherwise be extended to some people.

Power, especially financial power, is almost bound to appeal to you, although you will find it highly beneficial to select your goals very conservatively, basing these on solid, lofty ideals, so that you can enjoy to the fullest the returns you receive from their realization. I mention this because I have observed that some individuals who have birthdays in this second decan of Capricorn tend to "climb too high", burning bridges behind them, so to say, and it seems that these people on occasion will then lose the position they gained at the height of their "glory" for reasons that could have been avoided. Because I have confidence that you will persistently balance your major aims with your better judgment, I think that you will have substantial promise of finding LASTING exaltation in any position you attain.

Until you develop it, docility is not likely to be one of your stronger characteristics, so that dissensions and stresses may occasionally arise. These should, however, lessen with each passing year, when you earnestly endeavor to promote harmony in your surroundings. I have noticed that there are sometimes circumstances in the earlier lives of people born in your decan that seem rather pressing, but at least some compensation may be found through brothers and sisters, or other relatives and "neighbors". You, too, may find that close ties will frequently prove helpful to your interests, even when you grow older. Among your childhood experiences might be an impression that an "authoritative" person maintains a less fair attitude than you would really like or appears to limit in some way a few of your associations with other people. Nevertheless, you are apt to find that any discipline which is thus enforced by circumstances in your youth will later become valuable, when you use lessons it teaches, as a worthwhile example for your future.

You might have a tendency toward recklessness while you are becoming acquainted with the energetic nature you will wear through life. In this respect, I might mention that individuals born in this decan of Capricorn sometimes have a cyclic phase when a mishap occurs to a limb, or limbs, or a momentary act of rashness leads to an accident affecting a similar part of the body. For the most part, you will probably display many compassionate, genial, numerous and benevolent qualities, occasionally leaning toward over-imaginativeness, extravagance and reliability, and nearly always showing a keen interest in artistic pursuits; music and poetry. From an early age, you are apt to display great generosity, even to such a degree that it will be necessary for you to learn that one should only give away one's own things. There will probably be a few repetitious cycles during this period of your life, or one, in particular, while you might be aware of brief phases of loneliness. I think that you will display some duplicity in your attitudes, following a distinct line of endeavor for a while; then turning and pursuing its exact opposite, or otherwise directing your attention to undertakings which are entirely different from those that previously appeared to have the greatest appeal. "Prophetic" dreams may occur, now and then, illuminating events which are yet to come — and, owing to this "intuitive" faculty, you might well draw upon "unseen forces" in forming many of your later conclusions.

Early adulthood is likely to give you strong awareness of some of your practical instincts, inclining you to seem more refined, cool, modest and neat than you were before;

occasionally you may appear such a perfectionist as to be "fussy". You are now apt to feel quite self-conscious, or even shy, sometimes, which may bring a few of your acquaintances to think that you are cold and indifferent. Opportunities for obtaining a higher education are almost bound to reach you, some of which may be in the form of gifts, or endowments, supplied by a person you once considered restrictive toward your better interests. Being fastidious about people, you will probably tend to have "more acquaintances" than deep friendships, holding yourself somewhat aloof from certain circles of society. Your intellectual progress is likely to advance very rapidly now, indicating that you will realize the greatest advantages by cultivating emotional warmth, sympathy and understanding.

I feel that you will be rather slow to react to the advances another person makes toward you, romantically, during this earlier stage of your life — but that you will then respond with surprising intensity, forming an unusually enduring relationship. Many individuals who have birthdays in this particular cyclic period attract at this time in their lives, business or marriage partners who will have powerful influence over their interests for many years which are to follow.

I believe that you find the greatest contentment in close associations that develop out of mental rapport. While there might be some changes in this area of your life, you will, nevertheless, hold tenaciously to your alliances, usually preferring the companionship of individuals who seem intuitive, imaginative and impressionable, and yet display a good memory and regard for history or antiquity. A passive disposition is likely to seem most suitable to your own, while you are quite apt to consider that similarities in spiritual, political, educational and philosophical outlooks are highly important. Even though additional responsibilities or problems might bring disappointments into a few of your closer relationships, I think that you will generally have powerful friends, from whom you will receive substantial favors.

This second decan of Capricorn ordinarily indicates a

nature which is capable of extreme energy — but any kind of energy needs direction and control. Although individuals born under its influence frequently achieve exceptionally high honors, they sometimes tend to "overstep" the limits of prudence, which threatens them with a speedy downfall; a few among them become overly cold emotionally and with a strong desire to "rule". In such instances, it usually seems that there are many and constant rivals who threaten the fame or position of these people. I know a number of others who are pillars of society, their sterling qualities of tact, diplomacy and ability earning deep admiration! I am sure that you, too, moderate your personality with proper feeling and sensitivity. It is rather remarkable how many people who have birthdays in this particular cycle become active in political and governmental circles, either locally or nationally, regardless of their other interests. I must conclude, in this regard, that your decan holds greater promise than almost any other for securing very high honors and wide fame.

You are likely to take special pride in your "home", preferring surroundings that indicate "elegance" and provide you with opportunities for incorporating newer ideas. I think that when you consider it possible to do so, you will tend to use available services for "routine tasks" instead of attending to these yourself. People who have previously met you only casually are apt to develop a warmer impression of you after they see you in this environment; knowing this, you might often entertain acquaintances you make, or open your dwelling as a meeting place for some of your "outside endeavors". I feel that at some time you will also use your home base as a center of activity for accomplishing a few of your more vital interests.

Younger people who enjoy more than an ordinary degree of "recognition" are likely to touch your life quite strongly — or "one will", especially, I am certain. You will probably have a fondness for youngsters and an inherent "know-how" for patiently imposing strong discipline while showing that this is still combined with affection, so that you will easily earn respect and favorable rapport when you are in their association.

I believe that you will have little regard for hobbies or entertaining pursuits which are not productive. Those that require physical activity will frequently prove to be satisfying outlets for "day-to-day pressures", in my opinion, particularly when you feel that through these you are accomplishing something worthwhile and somewhat creative. You are often likely to "bottle up" your true emotions, or to react inwardly to situations without showing outwardly that you are doing so. Similarly, you may often tend to exert your most "restless" energies "behind-the-scenes", so to say, regaining an appearance of dignity and composure before other people. Traces of this quality might occasionally be seen in a subtle humor you will display, while you are frequently apt to enjoy other people's clever actions or remarks more than they realize.

With each passing year, you may tend to show more and more impetuous, confident and assertive tendencies. Because I have strong confidence that you will direct these to constructive channels, they will serve to increase your overall effectiveness, I feel sure. It might, however, be advisable for you to take precautionary measures against overstrain.

You will probably "think and talk" about financial matters more than many people, and while your own returns are likely to be somewhat temporarily unsteady from time to time, undergoing many unpredictable changes during your lifetime, your progress should, on the whole, be favorable. People who have reason to "deal" with you may sometimes consider you a dangerous opponent, because you are apt to have keen insight into their weaknesses or strengths, combined with shrewd ability for applying ingeniousness, resourcefulness, concentration and logic toward your own advantage. Speculative undertakings, some of which may have to do with "properties" or real estate, will no doubt appeal to you. Your success in enterprises of this kind may very well be substantial, with the likelihood that other people or a close associate will be involved. When you have reason to manage the interests of "corporations", groups or individuals, as you may upon occasion, you are likely to display superb skill, while your most gainful returns will come from such sources, in all probability. I feel that you will receive at least one gratifying inheritance or bequest that will increase your assets and possessions, while in some measure endowments or "favors" will always seem to come your way when you think that you need them the most!

In summation, I earnestly think that "seeds of kindness", selflessness and good will which you implant in your daily interests will blossom forth, flowering profusely in growing happiness for you!

Capricorn

January 11-January 20
Ruled by Sun

3rd decan

Your decan of Capricorn is likely to confer excellent mental powers of a type well directed to science and similar fields that require in depth intellectual understanding without affectional involvement. Although you might tend to be notably suspicious on occasion, particularly if someone is trying to take advantage of you, and skeptical about "far out" new ideas so this may at times incline you toward timidity, you no doubt have a great many responsible, practical, reserved and calculating qualities within your personality which result in a solid type of energy that you can apply to HIGHLY constructive achievement. Individuals who have birthdays within this third decan generally have a tremendous power of initiative for attaining material success, as well as a capacity for hard work. Your nature may tend to be somewhat melancholy, or to view life's problems with an overly serious outlook. I trust that you make a special effort to develop a cheerful attitude, sympathy and grace, so that YOU appear less austere than some people, although you no doubt display a certain proud, cold reserve. I believe that you have quick perception, combined with a firm ambition, which enables you to cultivate worthwhile undertakings in an assortment

of areas.   Individuals of your decan have lives that continually IMPROVE, when they generously place other people's feelings, wants and needs before their own and look
optimistically FORWARD, as I am confident YOU do, although those who lose sight of the many, many wonderful
blessings they enjoy daily, centering their lives on "self",
invariably have a hard struggle.   You probably have a quiet,
thoughtful, serious disposition, while you may be, at the
same time, practical and economical in your outlook.   Being
able to silently "observe" and absorb that which is around
you, you might be an apt "detective", while you will no
doubt have a strong determination to persist in your endeavors until you triumph over even the most difficult circumstances.

I think that you intensely dislike being "obligated" to
anyone; thus you are happiest when you do not feel that you
are under restrictions, or impelled to take orders from other
people.   For these reasons, you are apt to be a born leader
and organizer.   You can no doubt "ferret out" practical
means by which results you seek can be obtained, and otherwise show splendid executive ability.   In all likelihood, you
instinctively concentrate upon the successful pursuit of any
"business in hand", automatically "sensing" the proper
methods of procedure you should follow, as well as how
best to use the talents of people at your disposal.   The independent spirit of the "free-lance" is apt to seem less attractive
to you than more routine undertakings, in commercial
pursuits.

A flexible attitude will always serve you well, in my
opinion, because emotional rigidity, if you permit yourself to
follow this tendency, will result in too set a viewpoint toward
life.   People who are born in this decan of Capricorn often
become leaders in the social and cultural life of their community when they similarly take steps to radiate warm appreciation and tolerance, as I am sure you do, so that their
natures will not become crystallized and arid.   You have
probably noticed that your accomplishments diminish, too,
when you permit yourself to worry.   Conversely, when you
earnestly endeavor to make all things right and orderly in

your life, your interests, and all that concerns you, your mind and heart will become filled with peace — because you will be confident that a Universal Power is at work in your life, and that BETTERMENT will be the outcome of every situation.

In your over-all approach, I feel that you frequently endeavor to expand from "behind-the-scenes", so to say, gaining balance through a display of charitability, sympathy and justice. You might impartially weigh one point against another in an effort to gain a broader picture of the whole of a situation. People who hold "authoritative positions" will often be impressed by a display of good judgment that inspires a gentle spirit in people around you; they will frequently consider your enterprises sensible and simple, as well as inspired, owing to your superb capacity for constructing. You might show especially fine ability for managing assets belonging to other people, corporations or groups, although occasional stresses or dissensions are likely to result in such undertakings. I think that you will become involved in at least one controversy over "an estate" or a similar mutual financial matter.

I believe that you will display different reactions in different circumstances: when your personal and material interests come into the foreground, you will probably often give an impression of cold detachment, dispassionately showing courtesy and imaginativeness without being influenced by either sentimentality or emotionalism. Individuals who "deal" with you might occasionally consider that your methods are erratic, unpredictable or coldly aloof, in these respects. In your close relationships, however, you will probably incline to be somewhat more sensitive and receptive in your outlook. I feel that other people will be extremely influential in your financial affairs, their tenacity sometimes being the key to your success!

You are seldom apt to be content when you are involved in singular enterprises, having preference, instead, for several varied undertakings that will provide outlets on a wider scale of knowledge and give you frequent "changes of scene"

- 279 -

which will, in themselves, be your relaxation from extreme "routine". Because appearances will probably be especially important to you, you might instinctively wish to impress other people in carrying out your daily activities, sometimes tending to become depressed when matters do not go the way you expect that they should – but when you settle down to a fixed set of objectives and hold as your "keywords" tact and diplomacy, you are almost certain to earn growing admiration which will often bring others to ask for your opinions.

I have observed that individuals who have birthdays within this particular planetary phase generally have exceptionally strong constitutions. When ailments do arise, they are ordinarily a result of nervous conditions or excessive behavior. Attention to your physical well-being might be especially advisable as you leave adolescence and enter adulthood, or during the late "teens" and early "twenties", because temporary trends at this time may incline to place a few additional stresses upon you emotionally, leading to physical reactions. It will also be beneficial for you to observe safety and precautionary measures when you are visiting in distant places or foreign countries, I feel. Ordinarily, I anticipate that you will enjoy good health and excellent recuperative powers, frequently finding rapid improvement in planned schedules which include sufficient rest, a moderate diet of food and drink, and ample fresh air. When you seek peaceful surroundings that remind you of serene and tranquil conditions, and you hold your thoughts on optimistic concepts which are filled with true joyousness, harmony and happiness, you are almost certain to establish a practice that will bring very gratifying results, indeed.

There is apt to be a large discrepancy in your mental outlook that leads you to swing from moods which are intensely emotional, generous and temperamental to others which are purely analytical, factual and informative. Your earliest environment might be almost too favorable for practical purposes, prompting you to enter the "outside world" with expectations which are somewhat unrealistic or too idealistic. This might lead to dissensions and controversies among siblings or other youngsters who share your day-to-day routines, and bring you to perform at least one "deed of valor" in defense of some of your cherished principles. Children of this decan almost invariably go through a phase when they tend to be rather scheming and mentally combative — although I have confidence that in *your* life this has been only a *very* transitory cycle. Sometimes an incident concerning a brother, sister, cousin or "neighbor" leaves a particularly strong impression upon children of this decan, while these little individuals should take precautionary measures against "mishaps", particularly in traffic, or when they are around water and large animals. It will surely be necessary for you to cultivate "peace of mind" from an early age, directing your energies to music and other artistic pursuits, because you are apt to be more keenly aware of any vacancies in your life than most people. I know a number of people born in this decan who conduct a lifelong battle against "loneliness", even when they are surrounded by other individuals.

As you grow older, you will probably tend to develop a colder type of perception which will stimulate your interest in intellectual subjects and enable you to look upon religious, philosophical, educational, legal and political concepts with rather critical acumen. A higher education will no doubt seem exceptionally important to you — and even though its attainment will probably depend largely upon your own resources, you are almost sure to accomplish this goal when you earnestly wish to do so. At this time, as in the remainder of your lifetime, you are apt to realize substantial gains by recognizing opinions which are different from your own and displaying genuine kindness toward "opponents".

Individuals who are born under this third decan of Capricorn usually develop the somewhat more "romantic" areas of their lives less quickly than many people, and they almost always feel some disappointment in this respect. You, too, might tend to prefer the companionship of people who are older in their attitudes and less "frivolous" in their outlooks, finding little pleasure in entertaining pursuits that will make small contributions to your material assets. You might participate in "lighthearted" activities because you feel a duty or responsibility to do so, but you are rarely likely to achieve from them a strong sense of satisfaction. Athletic and creative pursuits seldom appeal very greatly to individuals of your decan, I notice.

You are likely to have extremely definite convictions regarding people you meet. Because I have confidence that you are magnanimous toward individuals for whom you feel less regard than others, I think that your acquaintances will often serve to promote your position and standing in life, and that you will earn high esteem for offerings of true friendships. I know that YOU will never "use" friends, as some people do, or let cynicism bring you to consider their kindness a surrender to your personal wants; therefore, YOU will not alienate individuals who come to touch YOUR life, enjoying, instead, honors, favors and pleasing recognition which they will create in YOUR behalf.

I might mention that many, many people who have birthdays in this cycle think that their true success in life is often hampered by enmity and opposition — but in every instance that has ever come to my attention, such individuals have been responsible for their own adversities. I anticipate much happier outcomes from YOUR efforts, because I have complete trust that YOU unfailingly use your better judgment and act in a manner that will IMPROVE conditions in YOUR life.

Close associations you form will probably be related to your material aspirations, at least to some degree. I believe that you will seek relationships with individuals who have high regard for "domestic amenities"; tradition, heredity and custom. There are frequently likely to be changes in these "partnerships", but in all probability you will hold to these tenaciously, responding most readily to people who reflect your own attitudes and opinions. You are often likely to attract individuals who enjoy more than an ordinary degree of "public" recognition, and while there are almost bound to be some differences concerning possessions, assets or holdings, other people will be more helpful than otherwise toward your material gains, in all likelihood.

I believe that you will display a fondness for "luxurious" surroundings, often viewing your home environment as a means for furthering many of your "outside interests". Although you might not always be an active participant, in endeavors within this immediate atmosphere, you will probably have high regard for its existence and contribute considerably to measures you think will make it more harmonious. Individuals of your decan often shine as hosts and hostesses, as you may, too, and they frequently display some of their greatest creative talents in the improvement of their dwelling place.

While you are apt to feel a responsibility toward younger people who come to touch your life, you are likely to have at least one disappointment or hurtful experience concerning such a person. I have noticed many, many times, however, that the older people of your decan grow, the more happiness they appear to enjoy. I feel certain that this will be true of your life as well, bringing you — through your constructive efforts — to your most satisfying relationships and warmest emotional experiences.

In summation, I believe that your rewards in life will be rich and abundant, provided that you continue to constructively look forward to your highest aims, optimistically viewing these as the ultimate goal you WILL SUCCESSFULLY reach. A conservative, rather than speculative, approach will enable you to realize substantial benefits, in my opinion — while I know that your lofty outlook will enable you to find greater happiness with each passing year.

Aquarius

January 21-January 30
Ruled by Venus

I often consider that people who have birthdays in this

first decan of Aquarius are the "social chairmen" of the world, because they are less inclined toward domesticity than spreading a spirit of "friendship" around the earth. I doubt that you are ever really happy unless you feel that you are making some contribution toward better conditions for Mankind — and, even in your smallest effort, this will be your first objective. Although there is likely to be great intensity in your feelings of affection, your intentions are apt to be idealistic and detached, bringing you to express these more easily toward the whole of Humankind than upon a personal level. You may have an acutely accurate power of judgment, which indicates to you at the merest glance another person's inherent character traits. This, combined with a genial personality, probably enables you to form immediate acquaintances with strangers and win friends most readily — although it might be advisable for you to reserve your opinions regarding people your closest associates know, discerning them with the same uncritical acceptance which you use in your own relationships. Yours is likely to be an unusually independent nature; quiet, peace-loving, friendly, coolly-affectionate, and desirous for originality. Although you may be loyal and faithful in many of your actions, there is strong likelihood that you will refuse to be bound by restrictions, rules or regulations. This might manifest in hundreds of different ways — but, mostly, it will bring you to act in the most unexpected manner with such startling suddenness that neither you nor anyone else will be able to foresee what you may say or do next! You will add your own unique touches to almost everything you do, I am certain, often improvising, or even inventing newer methods altogether. It usually seems that people of this decan are incapable of conforming exactly to any consistent practice, unless it might be a practice of inconsistency; they will follow "to the letter" neither directions, a recipe nor driving rules. Their "saving grace" is that they are absolute masters at TACT and DIPLOMACY! Appearing agreeable and amiable in their manner, these people readily listen to suggestions, or even seek these openly; they amicably show a willingness to follow instructions and comply with standards which are laid out for them . . . then they go ahead and do exactly what they please, anyway. For this reason, it sometimes appears that they are less honest than they might be, but because they are so sincere and kind in their convictions, their associates rarely fail them. One will occasionally meet people who have birthdays within this cycle who carry these tendencies to a point of being touchy, uncompromising, and unconventional to eccentricity, although I trust that YOU make better use of your inherent potential. Every person of your decan whom I have ever known has displayed a fondness of and ability for the fine arts and all educational and intellectual pursuits, as you may, too. You are apt to have a special affinity for nature, often finding great solace when you are in touch with isolated places in scenic settings, while a liking of such things as animals, birds, trees and flowers may lead you to have an almost uncanny knowledge of their various names.

A calm countenance which is characteristic of individuals born in your decan often conceals great "inner" nervousness. Faith rather than "excesses" of food, drink and other "tranquilizers" will be your solution, I feel. You might tend to appear more assured than you really are until you are approached with a new idea, when you will then almost invariably "hem and haw" before making a definite commitment, usually thrusting your lower lip forward and "frowning" as you do so. Provided that you have sufficient time to think matters through in your own way, you will probably make every effort to agree to changes in your previous plans. This lack of confidence in your future may prompt negative reactions, from time to time, that bring you to doubt the permanency of almost any situation in which you find yourself; regardless of how stable it might seem to another person, you are apt to make elaborate plans as to what you will do when this condition no longer touches your life. Inwardly, you are always saying "goodbye" to something.

A pleasing disposition is one of the most outstanding traits you are likely to display, and even though you might sometimes incline to appear forceful, only strong promptings are apt to arouse you to anger. Should you lose your temper, however, your instinct might be to retaliate by hitting, slamming or, preferably kicking whatever or whomever happens to be nearest (such as a cabinet) and to say things you really do not mean. I have confidence, however, that you withhold responses of this kind and offer sincere apologies to compromise any little dissensions that do arise. I doubt that you can bear to witness mistreatment of a child, or animal, an act which may bring to the fore surprising ferocity.

Individuals who are born in this first decan of Aquarius ordinarily spread sunshine and happiness in their earliest environments, which earns quite favorable results; courtesies and popularity. I have noticed that one extraordinarily dominant and strong-willing person frequently has powerful influence in their rearing, and that there are often little rivalries with siblings or other youngsters "nearby", such as cousins or neighbors. During your years of "growing up" you are likely to have an alert, bright, keen mind, your resourcefulness often displaying itself in ingenious, inventive ideas and quick repartee. You might, during these years, tend to be somewhat impatient, a characteristic that may bring you into occasional dissensions. When they are very small youngsters, many people of this decan seem to have at least one "mishap" while they are on their way somewhere or preparing to go somewhere, which leaves a mark or scar upon their head or face. There will probably be some stresses in this cyclic phase, a few of which will be due to the excitability of your mind, in all likelihood — but when you have enough to do, and are given the means for finding new "avenues" you can explore that will enable you to learn as rapidly as you would like, these should be years when you will make substantial accomplishments — and, besides your brilliancy and energy, you will no doubt enjoy a great deal of popularity, being a "leader" among your associates.

A more harmonious phase will follow as you reach maturity, in my opinion. You will make important changes at this time, but adulthood will be accompanied by a stronger capacity for forming "correct judgments", I feel, enabling you to make better use of your reasoning powers, although you are apt to allow others to over-rule your decisions. While you will surely have a fondness for music, art and intellectual pursuits, a kind, sympathetic and agreeable manner is likely to earn for you a large circle of friends, your popularity bringing more than an ordinary degree of recognition. For these reasons, I anticipate that your interest in social pleasures will balance your enthusiasm for intellectual attainment. This will be an admirable trend which will serve you well throughout your lifetime, provided that you concentrate on DEFINITE GOALS, and then take measures to fulfill these, immediately setting newer ones as you do, because you may have an immense capacity for procrastination. I have noticed that any failures individuals of your decan have almost always result from a tendency to say, "I am not sure whether I can" instead of, "I WILL".

The majority of the acquaintances you make will probably be among knowledgeable and fascinating people who are entertaining conversationalists and display a variety of interests. An ability to be a good listener is likely to be one of your finest assets. You are apt to be generous with compliments, often building other people's confidence, although some might occasionally think that you are insincere, because one of the ironies of your disposition is that you are likely to cultivate an exceptionally active social life without forming "confiding" relationships or fast friendships. You are almost certain to maintain an impartiality which holds others at a "comfortable distance", yet you will no doubt leave an impression that your heartfelt aid is as near as a request — and there is little question that your conduct will bear this out.

There may be an "airy" quality about your "romantic" life that prompts you to place "friendly good times" and pleasurable activities before deep emotional attachments. This might create a certain "diffuseness" that will prevent you from singling out any particular individual, yet you are apt to feel inwardly that you have a duty toward marriage and a secure future in mutual financial endeavors. At some time, you are almost bound to form an alliance, in either business or marriage, that has primary significance in your material affairs and is closely attached to your sense of responsibility toward the other person.

The intricacies involved in your closest associations are likely to be many, primarily due to an instinctive desire to rise to the "top" of circles of society where you are. I think that your approach will frequently be ambitious and enthusiastic, and that you will have a surprising degree of energy upon which to draw. This may also lead to a masterful nature with good executive ability, bringing you to feel well qualified to direct and command other people rather than perform tasks yourself which another person can carry through. This might bring you to use available "services" more readily than most people — although I have confidence that you will regard the rights of others, abandoning an autocratic attitude and self-assertion that would otherwise give people around you an impression that they can never quite "live up" to your expectations. Having a keen, sharp and forceful mentality, you might recognize more easily than many individuals inherent faults and talents that exist within people who share your personal life, and you may feel impelled to channel these as best you can. I believe you will earnestly endeavor to be faithful and loyal to obligations you consider to be yours — but, at the same time, you will wish to exercise your independence and establish your own "code" as to what these incumbencies are.

Your feelings, too, are apt to be intensely sincere, as well as your sense of devotion toward people who touch your life affectionally, but at the same time, you will display an air of detachment devoid of partiality. There is apt to be little you would do for a close partner or associate which you would not do for an acquaintance; you will probably distribute your courtesies and kindnesses equally among all of the people you know, a characteristic which is both extremely admirable and easily misunderstood. When you make a special effort to give attention to those closest, reserving certain little "private notices" which are just for them, you should enjoy extremely gratifying responses.

Individuals who have birthdays in this first decan of Aquarius usually feel somewhat "bound" by strong attachments, although they have more ability than almost anyone else for forming those which might be considered "better-than-average". When they adopt a similar policy of allowing for differences between their own thinking and that of younger people with whom they associate, these relationships are also likely to be extraordinarily gratifying.

Regardless of your circumstances, you will probably have frequent phases when you are less satisfied with your possessions, assets and financial concerns than you would like. There are apt to be times when you will be aware of a strong sense of "aloneness" in this area, occasionally due to what you consider as a "lack of cooperation" on the part of your closest associates. Nevertheless, I believe that you will realize substantial benefits through your attachments with organizations, group enterprises or "corporations", receiving at least one very welcome "legacy" — and, in spite of a few "personal sacrifices" which you will feel it is necessary to make concerning your resources, you will enjoy some favorable returns from enterprises you consider "speculative" or from "private" returns about which few people know. Any association you might have with fields of communications or "commuting" to and from nearby areas should also prove more profitable than otherwise for you.

In carrying out your daily routines, your own kindness is almost bound to earn a pleasing response from people around you, your sensitivity to their needs bringing back in kind devoted servitude. While your very closest alliances are sometimes likely to be marked by a critical coldness and skepticism that appears to limit some of your better efforts, these more "superficial" relationships will probably bring substantial favors your way, your charitable outlook promoting among those around you, an opinion that you are generally adored, admired and respected. You might have a real knack for "salesmanship" that enables "you to get ideas across" or win approval when few other people could.

I think that you will become more deliberate, thorough, sensible and realistic with each passing year, basing the majority of your decisions or plans upon thought and reason. Therefore, a more reliable atmosphere should prevail where abundant changes once created greater uncertainty. You will probably be more assured of your real wishes — and when you hold your thoughts upon constructive concepts, you should realize these in abundance, often through the help of other people.

Your decan generally has an exceptionally devout spiritual outlook. Although you are apt to change your philosophical and religious opinions during your lifetime, you are likely to have the greatest regard for other people's beliefs, even when these are not identical to your own, because you will easily see "both sides" to most conceptions, finding for yourself a balance somewhere in between. When you practice the highest of that in which you believe, seeking as your first interest self-improvement and improved conditions for Mankind, betterment is certain to result. Beyond the boundaries of your immediate environment lies a world in need of your wonderful talents, abilities . . . your understanding . . . and when you endeavor to develop these on its behalf, I know that you will enjoy increasing happiness and satisfaction, at the same time, lifting values of Humankind to greater heights!

Aquarius

January 31-February 8
Ruled by Mercury

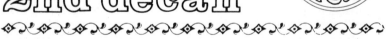

Yours is likely to be a progressive temperament which is filled with independence and originality, prompting you to repudiate some of the social conventions of present "times" and live according to highly idealistic conceptions. You are apt to have a keen understanding of science and humanitarianism, although your "mind and habits" may not be stubbornly fixed. This might make you better suited for research into subtler matters of the soul, and for practical invention, than purely artistic enterprises, because you are probably an accurate observer, easily judging human nature and deriving your conclusions both from intuition and experience. Conformity may appeal to you little, bringing you to dress in a style entirely your own rather than strict adherence to current fashions.

I believe that you are inquisitive, inventive and original; often unpredictable. You may manifest traits or advocate ideas on social subjects which seem hundreds of years ahead of the present age, having a special liking for "the unknown", undiscovered and undetected, and being particularly adept in your understanding of the "whys and wherefores" of human behavior. This might enable you to grasp almost automatically the mechanics of such fields as psychology, occultism, handwriting analysis or astrology. One will occasionally meet individuals born under the influence of this second decan of Aquarius who are contrary, eccentric and abrupt; many are disloyal and ready to prey upon their friends by using them to further their own selfish ends, or criticizing and demanding in their attitude toward them. I trust that YOU endeavor to rise above inclinations of this kind, and therefore I anticipate that YOU will display keen, intellectual ability, being kind, sociable and fond of friends. I feel certain that you are quick-witted and alert in your manner; talkative and expressive at times. You no doubt have a strong faculty of concentration, often showing surprising logic and resourcefulness. When you do not appear to comply with established social codes, it is very likely because you are not really violently partisan on either side of a particular question; you will understand both positions and lean heavily to neither. Associates might occasionally think that your statements are misleading, owing to a tendency to "exercise your wits" by making assertions in an argument which you do not seriously believe but are "testing" others. In instances where your perception and your acquaintance with certain facts appear to conflict, you are apt to feel at a loss.

Although your visualization may be extraordinarily great, there might be something "commonplace" in its expression, the reason being that pure artistic impulse is probably one of your less strong characteristics. While you should be a devoted student in the "school of life", and exceedingly attentive, you are likely to be "in want" of imagination in its highest sense.

Your approach to interests that concern you will be single-purposed, intent, sharp and forceful, in my opinion, but you will need to make a special effort to have regard for the finer sensibilities of other people, due to a tendency upon occasion to appear somewhat blunt. Once your interest in an undertaking is sufficiently aroused, I think that you will have indomitable courage and inexhaustible energy to carry you over all obstacles to whatever goal you set for yourself. There have no doubt been times in the past when you have had to overcome an inclination toward a biting tongue or quarrelsomeness, which is apt to result from your relationship early in life with a person who displayed these distinguishing traits and whom you consider responsible for stalling your efforts to seem more "grown up". Nevertheless, there probably has been another person who acted as "a steadying" force in your life, compensating at least in some measure, and enabling you to adapt better to the various changes which are almost inevitable during these phases. I believe that you often go to great depth in your thought, weighing and balancing philosophical subjects, values, customs and traditions; frequently theosophizing in your outlook. While you are likely to seem a dangerous opponent in argument and perfectly capable of "standing up for your rights" when a principle appears to be at stake, for the most part you will have a patient disposition, which you will exercise more and more with each passing year. You might have a strong power of assimilation, your penetrating mind easily adapting itself to the basic elements of mathematics, science or astronomy — and at some time you are very likely to take a special interest in medicine or hygiene, as well as "art" in some form or become involved with people who give these rapt attention. I have little doubt that you will have a magnetic quality which enables you to bend even the most stubborn thinking and persuade large groups of people, yet you will be "a lover of solitude and of learned society", often displaying at least some degree of "clannishness".

Until you reach your late "teens", you might be somewhat more impulsive than you will be later on, having a knack for expressing your ideas while attempting to show people around you newer or better ways of managing problems. Being observant and eager to investigate conditions and things, you are almost bound to excel among siblings, "neighbors" and companions, and win favorable recognition from people who hold "authoritative" positions. Proper direction of your vital forces will be imperative during these earlier years, in my opinion, because you will have a wonderful fund of energy that can later promote great successes, provided that you learn to use this constructively. Procrastination and lack of initiative are faults against which you should guard throughout your lifetime.

The cycle that brings you from adolescence into adulthood is apt to be somewhat less satisfying than the one preceding, bringing certain limitations, restrictions and obstacles that will RESTRAIN YOUR EFFORTS to easily obtain a higher education and occasionally depress your viewpoints in general. Some sort of confinement − or feeling of limitation − is almost certain to be evident now. Among my friends who have birthdays in this decan, I notice that a few encounter the animosity of an influential individual or find it necessary to have a surgical operation. Something or someone may leave your life. Regardless of circumstances, I feel that you will become aware of occurrences, or one, in particular, which you will forevermore conceal from even people you know well.

You may consider this "initiation into maturity" a "period of testing", because you are apt to learn some of your greatest and most important lessons in this trend. Lacking self-confidence, some Aquarians forsake their previous convictions, developing an austerity, impracticality and changeability that will color their values permanently − and these individuals always seem to then live a turbulent, disturbed existence. I trust that you will respond more favorably to the promptings of events, using these happenings as stepping-stones toward a better future and developing out of them your finer talents, abilities, and personal resources. You will probably doubt many of your previous beliefs at a certain stage in your life approaching these more cautiously and seriously than you once did, and then mellowing them. In all likelihood, you will select newer concepts within the framework of those you held before, many of these imposing stronger discipline and containing somewhat more "ceremony" . . . and I believe that you will then have lasting devotion to these, gaining from them some of your greatest tranquility and happiness!

People who have birthdays within this second decan of Aquarius ordinarily have strong constitutions and powerful recuperative strength, but they are amazingly impressionable and imaginative where their health is concerned. For this reason, I consider a harmonious environment imperative to your physical well-being. You might tend to worry more than many people, or react more strongly to circles of society in which you are, reading into your own interests "conditions" that come to your attention in conversations and feeling alarmed that events of which you learn will affect your own circumstances. When problems do arise, they are ordinarily likely to be of emotional origin. I believe that a practice of holding your thoughts on confidence, faith, harmony and favorable outcomes will bring increasing peace of mind and strength of body. "Tranquilizing" strolls in quiet, natural settings should often prove helpful when your "nerves" seem on edge — and I strongly urge you to seek these as your outlets, rather than assuaging your anxieties through excessive intakes of such things as food and drink. Individuals who have birthdays in your decan usually have a rather strong aversion to strenuous exercise. Additionally, they generally acquire a habit of asking other people to perform for them "little details" another person would attend to personally, which prevents them from obtaining even the ordinary degree of exercise one would receive in carrying out their customary routines. This is no doubt a reason why many people born under the influence of your sign develop arthritic conditions and stiffening of the limbs and joints, much of which might be allayed by limbering activity.

I think that you take a very optimistic, pleasing, good-humored approach toward people you meet, showing interested receptivity to their accounts of travels and other experiences which enable you to enjoy vicariously pursuits that match your own true wishes and encourages them to feel at ease. This is almost certain to earn favorable response, giving you an extraordinary degree of popularity. In your closer affectional relationships, however, you are likely to have greater stresses, preferring the company of a number of different people who have varying interests to settlement upon one particular individual. A "steady" quality is quite likely to be absent from this area of your life, intermittent intervals which are "on" and "off again" giving little continuity, sometimes owing to your overly-high ideals. While you are apt to attract attentions from people whom you find mentally uplifting, few are likely to be "staid" in their outlook.

I feel that you have a truly refined gift for tact and diplomacy. When you form business or marital partnerships with individuals you consider "friends" and place your material interests in the foreground of purposes for entering into these, as you no doubt will, you will probably realize exceptionally gratifying results. I have noticed that such associations almost invariably serve to increase the "public positions" of people born in your decan, proving, over-all, far more helpful than otherwise.

In your relationships with younger people, you may incline to give exceptionally close guidance along intellectual and cultural lines, prompting their use of abilities in a number of different directions. There are apt to be conflicts between these associations and "obligations" you feel toward certain "outside interests", which might make it advisable that you make a special effort to avert little "rivalries" that can result from your participation in undertakings that will seem difficult for a youngster to match. I must conclude, in this respect, that you will have at least one disappointment concerning a person younger than yourself, but this will be compensated by another who will prove exceptionally helpful to the realization of some of your more cherished hopes.

The older you grow, the more effective your personal efforts will become, when you direct these constructively; I know that you will become aware of less and less changeability in your endeavors, being able to better control modifications in your undertakings which occur. People around you are almost bound to feel impressed by your gentle, self-reliant, determined manner, because you should easily combine kindness with perseverance and forethought. These are likely to be characteristics that will earn from other people many, many special favors, courtesies and benefits. I think you will be remembered in at least one person's Will, and that other "endowments" of cherished items which are both attractive and serviceable will often become your inheritance from individuals who trust that you will hold for these the same high regard they, themselves, have enjoyed. Acquisition of houses and real estate I am confident will improve your circumstances, at some time.

Individuals born in your decan of Aquarius generally appear to derive from their efforts unusually gratifying financial increases, ordinarily receiving income from more than one source. I anticipate that over your lifetime there will be "changes of fortune", so to say, or varying circumstances that will follow thoroughly opposing directions — but it will seem that you have a "special protection" that always supplies your greatest needs or brings an apportunity at the very moment when you most wish for its welcome introduction.

Having a charitable, sympathetic and hospitable nature, I feel certain that you will often be recognized for your philanthropic deeds — but because I am equally certain that whatever you do will come back to you in kind, I anticipate for you a very prosperous, joyous, opportune life blessedly rewarding in return for your personal efforts.

Aquarius

February 9-February 19
Ruled by Moon

You probably appear to other people a keenly intuitive

individual who has little need for depending upon the faculty of reason, because it will seem to them that you express a very vivid imagination and have the power of calling images up before your mind's eye in such a manner that these will present themselves as almost tangible. Although there is apt to be a certain "reserve" in your manner, people who come to touch your life will no doubt be impressed by your sociability, kindliness and courtesy. The result will be that you attract many friends and are very popular in your environment, in my opinion, your more generous efforts coming back to you through the ready help of your friends. I believe that you tend to be somewhat overly melancholy at intervals, often displaying a fondness for solitude and nocturnal life, and having a liking for the strange and curious. Unusual, original and eccentric subjects are apt to appeal to you quite strongly, although I have confidence that you will endeavor to maintain an even emotional balance that will prevent you from carrying any of these to extremes.

The minds of people born in this decan occasionally incline to be somewhat erratic, and unless they devote themselves to constructive and worthwhile undertakings, as I trust YOU will, their fancies become changeful; they are attracted to the lugubrious and usually to a feigned or tending toward a ridiculous degree. This can have serious implications, giving them feelings of inner fears and at times even "weird" experiences, which often occur through not well balanced imaginings or "visions" of unhappy outcomes. These particular individuals have a tendency to wander from place to place, or job to job, seeking a means of escape — but of course they finally discover that neither roaming nor their peculiar and fantastic appetites provide the freedom they seek — because, after all, there is no escape from one's self.

I feel that within your own interests you will be aware of this potential for persistent difficulties, coupled to bitter disappointments — but because I am confident that you will RESPOND by seizing opportunities as they come to you — holding to a positive mental outlook — and conscientious toward duties dependent upon true depth of affection, I anticipate for you a life RICH IN FULFILLMENT of your highest aspirations, through a whole-souled cooperation with other people.

When you earnestly endeavor to reach out to individuals around you in a true humanitarian spirit, I am certain that you will earn favorable recognition for your "sympathetic understanding", which will often renew confidence and restore faith, bringing back in kind to you courtesies, favors and "honors". Your acquaintances are often likely to turn to you for advice, because experience will show them that you always react by giving practical assistance, using your natural "insight" to reach to the depths of their problems and find worthwhile solutions. In moments when you tend to worry over trifles or react to apparent stresses less conventionally than you ordinarily would, you might "seek your own advice", so to say, asking questions of yourself which you think another person would put to you under like circumstances, and by having such a "heart-to-heart" talk with yourself, you might more logically arrive at the correct solutions. Even though you will surely be independent in your views and attitudes, you are apt to have an inherent desire for showing tolerance, diplomacy, reasonableness and discretion. Still, you might have occasional moods when less hopeful feelings lead you to fidgety efforts in which you will forget yourself through continued action.

You will probably tend to approach interests that arouse your enthusiasm with such vehemence that you sometimes tend to sap your vitality, a characteristic you will surely hold in check. As a general rule, individuals born under this third decan of Aquarius enjoy excellent health. I notice that indications to the contrary are often a result of an over-active imagination, being emotional rather than physical in origin, although it will be advisable to take special precautions to protect your vision. I think that in selecting your over-all objectives, you will prefer those which provide "special benefits" that will make your life more pleasurable and satiate, insofar as possible, your emotions. I believe that you have an intense magnetism which enables you to sway "public opinion" and move groups of people. When you direct your energies to spiritual betterment, your devotion is almost certain to earn the sense of satisfaction you seek, and there is little doubt that you will often serve as a great inspiration to other people, becoming a leader of higher thought among circles of society where you are. I know that these constructive efforts will earn an esteemed reputation which you will richly deserve.

There are apt to be more than an ordinary number of changes in your earliest environment, some of which will probably occur within a fixed atmosphere. Your relationship with individuals responsible for your rearing may create a few challenges to your personal interests, owing to "one person" whom you consider overly-strict and a sway this person holds over someone else, whose reactions might not always seem to serve your better interests. This may lead to a lifelong distaste for "domesticity", making your home surroundings appear to you more of a responsibility, restriction or "discipline" than comfort.

In childhood, you will probably have a cheerful, optimistic outlook that enables you to look upon the bright side of life and enthusiastically anticipate all of the exciting "new worlds" you will one day pioneer or conquer. You might excel in, or at least have a fondness for, music, the arts, literature and everything that has a refining influence. In all likelihood, you will display an unusual facility for expressing yourself in an appropriate, happy manner, aspiring in the theatre and other "mass communications". You should be an avid little visitor around neighboring areas, becoming known by people "near and far" who warmly respond to your friendliness. Such visits, or trips you take in this phase, may hold lifelong advantages for you, leaving in your memory some of the happier times you will recall from then on. I believe that you will be an affectionate child, highly dependent upon praise, respect and admiration. The amount of this which you receive will seriously mark your future course, in my estimation — because it will become the measure by which you will tend to judge yourself. You are almost sure to be an idealistic youngster; often tremendously impulsive. Your sympathies may prompt you to act rashly, upon occasion, sometimes bringing you to help unworthy causes.

During these earlier years, you are apt to have a liking for "expensive possessions", but you may be aware of some sparsity in this area, sometimes feeling that your dreams are greater than your tangible attainments. Nevertheless, I think you will be popular among siblings and other associates, often leading their behavior by virtue of your towering sense of romanticism. Happenings that occur during these years of "growing up" might be more important where your interests are concerned than for almost anyone else — because these are likely to determine the ultimate values to which you will incline to subscribe, as well as the goals that will assume in your mind the greatest significance.

As you begin to grow into adulthood, you are apt to replace a good deal of your previous impetuosity with balance. While you might give more credence to material assets than you did previously, you should primarily expand your basic impressions, rather than make many substantial changes in these. Other people are almost certain to show ready response to your conscientiousness, sociability and benevolence. Your REACTION to attention you receive throughout your lifetime will be the key to "unhappiness or beatitude" surrounding conditions which concern you, I feel. Individuals who accept it graciously, showing their gratitude through their lofty actions lead some of the most enriching lives of which I know; those who choose to give way to a less favorable side of their nature or tend toward "over-indulgences" invariably go from one trouble to another, eventually meeting with public scandal and consequent "loss" of popularity, prestige, position and even possessions.

You should realize more easily than most people a wish to obtain a college education. Among my various friends born in this decan, however, I notice a decided tendency to forego this privilege, supplementing it instead with travel and similar "practical" experience. Many of these acquaintances enter into very unsuitable — and often hasty — marriages that thrust them into other interests instead. It appears to me, however, that a formal, higher education will be imperative to your true feelings of success, owing to a consideration, otherwise, that neither your hopes nor your material aspirations ever really reach the degree of fulfillment you think they could without the knowledge an educational background would have provided.

With each passing year, you will need to make more and more effort to maintain equilibrium, inwardly, I believe, by making a practice of moderate habits in food, drink and your selection of entertaining pursuits, at the root of which will be a buoyant outlook that holds unwavering faith in a bright future. A flexible attitude will also serve you well, in my opinion, because your foregiveness, tolerance and charitable deeds will earn abundant and MOST gratifying returns.

I definitely feel that there have been some stresses with respect to your possessions and other assets. You are likely to be free and generous with your belongings and have a splendid earning capacity. Although money might come fast and easily, it may also go quickly; you are rarely apt to accumulate wealth very rapidly, owing to a fondness of comfort and pleasure. I know that you have had some stresses in the financial areas of your life, yet you have no doubt met any reversals with newer approaches that replenished your "supply" for the time being. I trust that you are thoroughly honest with yourself as well as other people in all of your dealings; therefore, I need not mention the extreme adversities that befall individuals of this decan who are not. In all probability, you will generally have more than one source of income, and certain matters concerning your assets may well be attached to interests involving partners in business or marriage, from time to time, although I doubt that these will always be free from dissensions.

I strongly believe that your most gainful returns will result from associations you have with other people, groups or corporations. Such things as insurance, trusts, legacies or land holdings are likely to touch your life favorably at least once. Speculative investments or "get-rich-quick" schemes are apt to appeal to you strongly, but your judgment in enterprises of this kind may be less accurate than another person's or company association who manages endeavors of this kind on your behalf. Thus, I conclude in this regard that you will better consolidate your holdings when you seek and follow the counsel of knowledgeable people who will gladly provide such services.

When you reach to the heart of that which you most hope to gain from your life, I think that you will find a desire to work for the public good according to your ability and "station". This is frequently likely to attract you to acquaintances who have charitable and philanthropic dispositions and aspire to elevate humanity by self-help under just laws and true spiritual impulse. You might know a number of people who show qualities of value in social, industrial or spiritual circles, although you are occasionally likely to meet some who seem insincere, cynical and sarcastic, and are ambitious to fill positions of trust or honor for selfish purposes. During your lifetime, women, or one woman in particular may be responsible for some of your more pressing "problems". I am inclined to judge that you will often consider your friends more of a "burden" than enjoyment, especially where attitudes concerning "values" incline to touch.

In reality, I believe that you expect a great deal from other people, often thinking your true "life-force" rests within your close relationships with them. Provided that you also accept the RESPONSIBILITIES such associations require on a "give-and-take" basis, contributing steadfastly the happiness you like to receive and remaining always sensitive to the other person's needs, I anticipate for you exceptionally gratifying alliances. You are almost bound to select individuals who appear industrious and aggressive, but you will probably also admire those whose natures are fearless, independent and honorable. There may be a disappointment in this area of your life, but through a constructive approach you are very likely to promote almost "ideal" conditions. It often seems that people born under your decan learn less quickly than many that close relationships necessarily involve association during times of stress, problems or difficulties as well as those which are more pleasing. Before you form close alliances, you ought to feel inwardly assured that you are ready to meet these COOPERATIVELY, giving generously of your understanding, compassion, loyalty and aid, "through thick and through thin", so to say.

Even in your relationships with younger people, you may tend to seem an entertaining "companion" and excellent promoter of surface knowledge in cultural lines, but you are still likely to maintain something of a "non-entanglement policy" or neutrality of attitude that, while excellent for a scholar or professional person is apt to become a burden in closer personal connections.

I feel that it will be to your advantage to continually make a very special effort to increase your ability, to narrow your interests to a purely personal sphere, or, in other words, become wholly concerned with one individual in a manner that will earn the degree of devotion, in return, which I am sure you basically seek. An effort to be more "confiding" might also be helpful, because you are often likely to be secretive.

Yours is a fine, brilliant and exceptionally talented decan, in my opinion — and because I have confidence that you will constructively direct your many illustrious qualities toward a peaceful, happy and productive life, rather than a solitary one, I know that you will realize even your loftiest ambitions.

Pisces

February 20-February 28
Ruled by Saturn

1st decan

When you set your sights on an objective, you are likely to approach it by scorning shackles of conventions that might interfere with your freedom of thought and speech, yet you are rarely apt to carry this characteristic to a point of eccentricity by entering paths that are contrary to the commonly accepted standards of usage and conduct practiced by circles of society in which you are active. I think that you strive for respect in your community and to earn admiration from individuals who hold "authoritative" positions. People who come to touch your life, in the conduct of your outside daily routines, will probably be impressed by your display of a quick wit, versatility, foresight and frankness. Sometimes, you are likely to decide upon an accomplishment you wish to achieve without first formulating a judgment, aiming directly at your "mark" free from fetters of previous reflection. You might occasionally promise with sincerity or conceive an undertaking with earnestness . . . and then as suddenly turn with equal veracity to another, entirely different, enterprise that interrupts your first intentions. I feel, however, that the "flashing" quality with which you will tend to push yourself forward on the "sea of life" will prove to be a distinct asset, provided that you place patience, honesty, stability and concentration at the forefront of your motives, as I have confidence that you will.

At the root of your nature, I believe that there is a strong conservatism which has brought some people to regard you as "retiring" and restrained, from time to time, although you will incline to shed this appearance more and more with each passing year. It results from certain experiences in your earliest childhood, in all probability, that led you to think that the realization of your true wishes was, somehow, linked to a complete sacrificing of "self". Owing to these inward impressions which you are still likely to retain, at least to some degree, you may have had phases when you tended to be worrisome, untidy, or even self-pitying — but I trust that you now view your interests in a different perspective, recognizing that the spirit of "giving" is in no way connected with "surrender", and that your devotions generously placed, can earn in return loving affection from other people rather than personal loss. I have noticed that individuals who have birthdays in this first decan of Pisces frequently become separated from someone "to whom they feel especially close". Because this ordinarily occurs when they are still at a "young age", so to say, the effect it has upon their lives seems to be particularly deep and lasting. You might recall a similar event — but I trust that you use "the favorable impression" this person left upon you as a constructive guide for managing your interests. This response is surely productive of a patient, persistent, self-controlled disposition, instead of the self-pity, timidity, secretiveness, melancholy, and aversion to undertaking responsibility with which some people react, or a tendency to covet money or possessions.

Relatives, or people you consider as relatives are apt to be quite influential in your earliest environment, bringing you to feel that individuals other than those to whom you were actually born also fill a parental role in your life. Although, I believe you will receive a great deal of sympathy, benevolence and charitability from people who are directly attached to your rearing, you will have moments when you think that a "certain person" receives attention which is rightfully yours, a condition that will prompt moods of inner dissatisfaction or unhappiness, or give you a tendency to "change directions mid-stream" in an attempt to gain the notice you seek. Children of this decan are very sensitive, imaginative little individuals, and I have often observed that they quickly discover openings that will enable them to "play one person against another", as the saying goes, or obtain sympathetic understanding through "illness". You may remember times when you tried some of these "tactics", or showed one "face" to one person and the complete opposite to another — but with maturity, you have no doubt learned to direct your energies to pursuits which are centered on other people's happiness rather than your own. Nevertheless, in this respect, I conclude that during your earliest years of "growing up" you found that you were often able to get "your own way" without arousing opposition, and that this created certain obstacles later which you have had to overcome.

Through your "teens", or what is generally considered "high school age", I am inclined to think that you will often have a tendency to "mimic" many of the habits and mannerisms of the very person I mentioned previously, for whose attention you sometimes vie, although basically you will be less restless, frequently seeming amazingly sensible, thorough, deliberate and realistic for a youngster. You will have an ardent desire to learn, in all likelihood, showing a special fondness for singing, dancing and music, even though you may not partake in these activities, and while it might take you a bit longer than some children to grasp knowledge that comes to your attention, you may retain what you learn better, carrying it with you forevermore. You are seldom likely to act on impulse at this time, preferring to "sleep on problems" and give matters careful thought before placing them permanently into your mind's "computer". This characteristic "stalling" may occasionally bring you to hesitate at times when you ought "to act" or lead you to resent "new situations", preferring familiar circumstances with few major alterations, because these are the ones in which you therefore feel most secure. Owing to this tendency, associates may accuse you of being "stodgy", prejudiced or brooding, now and then, but in actuality, you will simply hope to "work things out" in your own way without jumping to conclusions, in all probability. You should enjoy solid and pleasing relationships with siblings and other companions during these years, while trips you take are almost bound to leave a favorable impression that will substantially increase your perception, just as visits in "nearby areas" and little excursions will.

As you make your transition into adulthood, you will probably show marked aggressiveness that was previously latent, reacting so energetically to your endeavors that you frequently leave associates lagging breathlessly behind. During this emotionally-charged phase, you are apt to challenge spiritual and philosophical concepts, an effort that may destroy some of your previous values and lead you to develop out of these newer ones which you consider more pertinent, with respect to your own role in the "grand scheme of things". You might give considerable thought to the "here and hereafter", or taking up some cause having for its object the social or spiritual upliftment of Mankind. It appears to me that these years will seem quite stressful, in relationship to your financial affairs, especially. I am sure that other people will often be impressed by your sharp, keen, forceful mentality at this time, although there will be moments when you will tend to display a somewhat blunt manner or seeming indifference to the finer sensibilities of others. Consequently, you might encounter a few dissensions among people you know, until they come to know you better and you, in turn, learn to modify both your stronger feelings and any tendencies toward excessive behavior. There are individuals who have birthdays in this decan who now discover within themselves an inclination toward jealousy and revengefulness which it is imperative that they learn to control, or they will have moods when they incline to be cruelly fault-finding and critical — although I have confidence that YOU will endeavor to bridle any emotions which seem this intense, channeling them into worthwhile outlets. Thus, I believe that tensions of which you are aware in your initiation to being "grown up" will prompt you to sever unfavorable bonds you have with your past, explicating higher beliefs from these. Even disappointments which are almost sure to occur, now and then, can serve to assist you in making a most gratifying transition into a whole new way of life. While adulthood necessarily implies change, I consider that this will be far greater for you than most people, being a cycle which you will later look upon as a major "turning point". Because I trust that you will found your activities on lofty principles that improve conditions in your life and for Humankind, as well, I am sure that this transmutation will be favorable.

Affectionally, I have observed that individuals born under the influence of this first decan of Pisces either have strong feelings of devotion induced by sympathetic understanding, or are too shy to feel comfortable in the company of people whose admiration they would like to gain. Your sentiments are apt to be changeable and nostalgic, your preferences generally leaning toward individuals who seem "domesticated", sensitive and gentle. While you might have little inclination to go in quest of deep personal attachments, you are likely to show little resistance to another person's advances when they are offered. You will probably hold tenaciously to relationships you form, responding especially to continual attention. Underlying your outward appearance, there may be a strong streak of independence, impatience of restraint and disregard of convention that will prompt you to disregard other people's opinions — but when you know you are going against these, you will no doubt try to do so with discretion. Although you might appear to take your more "romantic" interests too seriously, you will actually recover very quickly from disappointments, in all probability, in spite of the likelihood that love is apt to mark your life by two marriages or a serious love affair and marriage.

You are almost certain to seek partnerships in marriage, as well as business, because these are the only circumstances in which you are likely to feel that your "true self" can really function. It appears to me that there will be a very definite "service-link" joining your feelings in this area with distinct advantages which you will think that you ought to receive, the other person acting as "go-between", so to say. In all likelihood, you will admire a person who appears quick to find favorable financial opportunities, yet has a pleasant, sociable and agreeable disposition, displaying, above all else, a sense of servitude toward you. Measures that will prevent "rivalries" or dissensions with the relatives of your closest associates should be taken, in my estimation. I think that mutual happiness can be yours when you earnestly strive for a sense of satisfaction with what you have, counting your blessings regularly!

Possessions and material assets will always be extremely important for they represent security to you, I feel, although there will be some stresses in this area of your life I know, owing to impetuous expenditures or "sudden shifts" in your affairs that accutely affect your "pocketbook". You should have an exceptionally large earning capacity, because in all probability you will tend to direct the majority of your energies toward gainful pursuits. You are apt to find it difficult to balance "income" with "outgo", yet I am confident you will "squeeze" expenditures till you do balance your finances. Other people's influence upon your material security may tend to be changeable, rather than assured, although at least one other person's management of a "speculative venture" is very likely to bring gratifying returns. Female persons, or one in particular, are sometimes likely to be influential in increases which you will realize. I believe you will need to make a special effort to overcome any tendencies toward being fearful of loss or suspecting "the worst" in matters that concern you, both of which are characteristic of people born in your decan.

Throughout your lifetime, you are apt to consider that "you give much more than you receive", but the reason will probably be that you expect to receive much more than you are really ready to give. When you place spiritual, rather than material, aspirations at the forefront of your objectives and determine that you will hold your thoughts to cheerful and optimistic concepts, more and more of your true wishes will become realities, I know!

I think that you will have a fondness for younger people and children, your tenderness toward them earning, in return, favors, courtesies and admiration. You might sometimes incline to cater too much to their wants, owing to an "inner" desire to encourage continued reliance upon you – but when you place their best interests first, they are apt to become even more endeared to you, gaining a growing appreciation of your needs. I have noticed that "foster" children, "step" children and adopted children frequently prove to create a highly fortunate influence in the affairs of individuals who have birthdays near your own.

The older you grow, the more gregarious you are likely to become, owing, primarily, to a dislike of being by yourself. People who come to touch your life are almost bound to respond to your genial manner and kindly disposition, so that you will surely have large circles of friends and acquaintances, often among people who neighbor your usual surroundings or those you consider as "relatives".

I think that you will prefer comfortable living quarters, which will sometimes be in either a large multiple dwelling or "home" locations you will maintain without too much cost. Travel is apt to appeal to you greatly, bringing you to take an exceptional number of little "bouts" from place to place, or plan interesting excursions.

I feel that you will be unusually aware of the "position" you hold in circles of society where you are – but because you will surely use your finest talents, abilities and capabilities, always, your outlook will become more optimistic each year! I am certain that either conditions or people whom you know will see that your needs are provided, in time yet to come, and that a particular matter which you once feared was far beyond your reach will become a tangible realization.

Pisces

February 29, March 1-March 10
Ruled by Jupiter

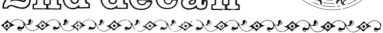

I feel that you have a genial nature, warm, kind disposition, and very sympathetic, philanthropic outlook, sometimes regarding yourself as an "angel of mercy" to all who suffer in soul, spirit or body. People from every walk of life are likely to look upon your charitable deeds and hospitable manner with extremely high regard, so that you can enjoy the prospect of reaching high positions in circles of society where you are, coupled to much success. You have considerable executive ability, I am confident, as well as cordiality, while you no doubt love pleasure, particularly out-of-doors, and are fond of traveling. People who have birthdays in your sign, and in this decan, especially, are frequently unusually intuitive; many seem gifted with "extra sensory perception". Certainly, I consider that you are more acutely sensitive to conditions or people around you than many individuals, sometimes having "impressions of events" in advance of their occurrence or which you cannot easily explain.

With so many, many wonderful characteristics upon which to draw, the lives of people of your decan ought to be filled to the brim with opportunity, its realization being dependent only upon their willingness to avail themselves of it through honest effort. It sometimes seems that individuals who have birthdays within this particular cycle acquire "affluence" so naturally that there are too few challenges to encourage their use of many of the brilliant talents with which they are gifted, which another person might apply toward gainful pursuits in a hope of "making ends meet" or as a means for hurdling some similar obstacle. Therefore, I think it imperative that you hold to thoughts of MODERATION as a daily practice — because you are rarely likely to UNDERDO. If a little bit of something works well, more should prove even better, in your estimation; you may be overly-generous, even when you or people close to you must temporarily "do without" as a result of your lavish actions; you might sometimes tend to be too funny, or too talkative, or to think too big for practical purposes. There are almost bound to be times when you incline to be overly-emotional. For this reason, the greatest fault to which you are vulnerable is that of OVERINDULGENCE. When people of this decan let their tastes get out of control, they generally treat these as being insatiable, their marvelous capabilities quickly deteriorating to vacillation, nervelessness, inconstancy and untruthfulness. I trust YOU endeavor to contribute your ableness for the betterment of all of Mankind you can reach — and, therefore, I know that YOURS will be a life of elevation . . . HONOR!

One of the most notable features of your decan is a love of music, the arts and literature. I feel sure you have considerable ability as a performer; whether you apply this trait professionally or merely in the conduct of your day-to-day routines, you are likely to make "a production" out of many situations. You probably have a tendency to see the world as "a stage", sometimes dreaming, scheming, formulating, in anticipation of performances you will "see" upon its floor; you may even think of its people as your "puppets", visualizing in advance of an undertaking the specific roles each will come to play — and then anxiously awaiting the "grand premiere" when the curtains will lift, vividly revealing that which you originally pictured in your imagination. From time to time, you are apt to have associates who consider that you are indolent, owing to the fact that they cannot peer into the stereoscope of your mind as witness to some of your major activity. Another idiosyncrasy that might occasionally give someone cause for remark may be a tendency for you to fill your life with restrictions which you will take on voluntarily, in an assumption that this is the price exacted by the world for the privilege of living.

While children of your decan usually enjoy a happy beginning to their "earthly stay", that basically supplies the majority of their needs and improves their future prospects, there are ordinarily multiplicities in their earliest surroundings which place them in the care of several different people and prompt them to make more than a "reasonable" number of adjustments to new situations and conditions. In your own childhood, there are likely to be times when it will seem necessary for you to act as the "stabilizing force" behind adults who closely touch your interests, owing to dissensions among them, argumentativeness or a decided lack of continuity on the part of one individual creating restlessness in at least one other person, or because of demands made by someone's "outside interests" that hinder prospects of having a concordant household.

During your years of "growing up", you will probably be slow-reacting, patient, self-reliant, gentle and determined, yet fixed in your habits and stubborn when pushed. Music, dancing, singing, and other artistic pursuits, will give you some of your greatest pleasure, in my opinion. Your aptitude for these sometimes earning for you a wide reputation in comparison to that which youngsters of the same age would ordinarily gain. Although your education may take unusual forms rather often, it will no doubt be versatile, providing ample exposure to intellectuality, as well as the customs, traditions and practices of many places. Your RESPONSE to people and experiences in these formative years will determine the course your life will take, I believe, because this will not only be the time when you will inwardly find the aims you intend to fulfill, but also when you will absorb the information and knowledge that will have the greatest bearing of all in years to come. Throughout your lifetime, I think you can more easily resolve current problems by reflecting upon this chapter of your life and following an example set for you by a person who left in your memory the most favorable impression.

When you begin to leave the teens, your efforts are likely to become increasingly intense. I feel that this will be a cycle in which you really "come into your own", so to say — and there will be times when the magnetism, upon which you can draw, at will, will frequently surprise even YOU! Other people will incline to hang upon your every word, when it is your desire for them to do so; you will know how to move audiences and "gain the ends" you seek. Because I have complete confidence that you will use this power for the benefit of all of Humankind, I need not dwell on the obstinacy, and troublesome characteristics which some people of this decan tend to display at this time in their lives. You will surely take an interest in such things as science, philosophy, education, law and matters pertaining to the "spirit". You may go through phases when you will tend to explore the depths of various subjects, taking measures to destroy certain concepts which have previously come to your attention and advocating "causes" you think will correct conditions that displease you. Health, finances and acts you perform, on behalf of other people, will predominate in this cycle, I believe. Unfavorable, as well as favorable, occurrences will serve to trigger your sensibilities, in all probability, placing before you every necessary opportunity for penetrating realms "unseen". You are apt to encounter everything from the most grossly imaginable happenings to the HIGHEST states of being . . . the reason being that you are now to take a "choice" as to which you will select as your own. People of your decan who determine that they will lead their fellowmen to great ideals develop out of their genius principles that will serve as an archetype for history! I feel that this will also be YOUR preference, and that your LOFTY actions, in whatever field of endeavor you pursue, will earn for you eminent friends as well as a standing held in admiration by people who learn of your undertakings.

It will be imperative that you give careful consideration to your GOALS, in my opinion, being positive that these are clearly defined in your mind and then determining that you

WILL ACHIEVE them. In spite of the good humor and optimism which is ordinarily found among people who have birthdays in your decan of Pisces, a true sense of SATISFACTION is sometimes surprisingly absent. Unless you set your sights on definite aims, you, too, are likely to have a growing sensation that whatever you have is not what you actually want. There will be an underlying agility in your disposition that will prompt you to disperse your vital forces or become excitable and irritable when there is not enough activity to keep your vigorous mind constructively occupied. For this reason, I recommend that you make it a policy to pursue several enterprises which are dissimilar in nature, relaying your energies from one to another of these as often as you like, until you have brought them all to completion. For the greatest sense of gratification, you must then immediately establish newer "projects" that can again hold your interest, I believe.

Consistency will be an important key to your happiness, in all likelihood, and you should not enter into either business or marital partnerships until you have mastered it completely. Love undoubtedly will leave its mark more than once, however.

It usually seems that individuals born in your birthday cycle are able to adjust themselves to the opinions and ideas of other people with seemingly little effort; therefore, their affections are frequently superlatively adaptable. As they require praise and flattery, it is ordinarily advisable for them to be especially careful not to do anything whereby they may forfeit the good opinion of others. I feel certain that you recognize any tendencies you have toward over-impressionability, and will set for yourself limitations that will insure the preservation of your true dignity in all situations – and I anticipate that you will be known for your interesting and charming companionship.

You are apt to think and talk about "domesticity", children and younger people more often than many individuals, although the sociability and companionship these will provide will probably mean more to you than the idea of giving deep devotion or realizing great romantic fancies. In all probability you will have a strong dislike of being alone. I believe that you will tend to lack discipline in your management of youngsters, your generosity sometimes being more detrimental than helpful to their interests. While I think that you will want people around you to be dependent upon you, it might be advantageous for you to encourage a moderate degree of independence on their part, by letting them assume certain responsibilities and solve some of their own problems. This practice will then enable them to do so in the event of a time when they might need to make immediate decisions, should this seem inevitable without first availing themselves of your advice or material aid. I feel certain that someone will always take care of you, when you wish for assistance.

A somewhat "avant-garde" home environment may appeal to you, which you think will leave a favorable impression upon your friends and acquaintances. In all areas of your life, you will be inclined to duplications. This might bring you to have more than one location which you consider a "dwelling place" or to live at some time in a building that is intended to house a number of different people who are unrelated to one another. I think that it will be beneficial for you to take sensible precautions against such things as careless actions among people who are in your surroundings, in order to prevent breakage and similar "mishaps", because at least one incident of this kind is probable. I believe that your immediate surroundings will frequently be a center of activity for you, although there will probably be occasional contentions over people you think of as "relatives" or "neighbors". It is seldom likely to seem that true tranquility reigns in your dwellings.

I have little doubt that your personal aspirations will be highly ambitious, which will bring you to feel happiest when you receive wide attention and public recognition. At some time, you are almost bound to consider taking an active part in politics at some level. Individuals you know may occasionally interpret advice you give or some of your actions as being quite "authoritative" — but when you endeavor to be a good LISTENER, and to show a genuine interest in other people's activities without taking such active participation that it seems you are "meddling", more and more of your acquaintances should prove pleasing and helpful to the high position I am sure you hope to hold.

It appears to me that you will have "a knack" for finding favor with people in a position to further your material prosperity and will by their help gain a comfortable living. You might have a fondness for newer endeavors that will prompt income from unusual sources, or for placing your interests into enterprises that appear to "pioneer" fresh ideas or areas that can be explored. Your very closest associates may occasionally appear to impose restrictions upon your possessions which are not entirely to your liking, but any such discipline will probably curb certain tendencies which you may have toward financial stringency that result from overly lavish expenditures. You have surely learned to recognize which of your dreams can earn gainful returns and which are idle fantasies, although it might sometimes seem to you that the demands made by taxation, groups or organizations are outrageously steep, while "collections" are almost impossibly slow in coming.

I earnestly believe that you will receive the greatest fulfillment from life when you devote yourself to alleviating the distress of others. When you FOCUS your thoughts and activities on constructive, tangible concepts, I know you will find that your greatest dreams CAN come true!

Pisces

March 11-March 19
Ruled by Mars

It almost always seems that individuals having birthdays in this third decan of Pisces, as you do, lead eventful lives, because they are inclined to live them in a succession from one thing to another, alternating their activities so completely that many different fields of endeavor become open to them. I believe that you are absolutely FILLED with ambition for success. During infancy a phase that seems somewhat "critical" is occasionally reached by people born under this influence, but, even then, there is strong likelihood that determination will supply sufficient energy to bring them through apparent debilities, enabling them to then successfully overcome the difficulties posed. Although you are likely to give considerable thought to your health, frequently regarding it as a reason for omitting from your routines activities which seem distasteful to you, you are apt to have growing strength for carrying out undertakings over which you are enthusiastic. When you "set your sights" on a definite objective, you are likely to let neither consequences nor supposed "principles" stand in your way. Should difficulties arise, they are likely to result from some of your more "headstrong" tendencies which might bring you to place a few additional stresses upon your constitution, through continued rashness and impulsiveness which prompts you to neglect ordinary precautions to safeguard your health or hold your weight at a level suitable for your height and age. Throughout your lifetime, you will need to control an inclination to act before you think; in my opinion, one of the more pronounced characteristics of your sign.

I think that you have a charming personality that immediately attracts people to you and earns their trust. Being a born "performer", you will have a special talent for knowing exactly what you should say and do around whom — and an exceptionally keen intuition might give you immediate awareness of another person's strengths and weaknesses that fortifies your position even further.

You are likely to consider your abilities well suited for an "executive" capacity in undertakings which concern you, although there is less probability of your successfully "setting out" entirely on your own than performing similar responsibilities within the framework of groups or organizations that can provide freedom of expression, at least to some degree, but might still require that you carry your endeavors through in cooperation with other people. While a "limelight" manner of living will probably appeal to you strongly, your abilities are apt to be better suited for activities which do not place you in direct contact with the public, but, rather, make you a "power" from behind-the-scenes, so to say, exercising authority that will bring large enterprises to gratifying accomplishments. Professionally, many, many individuals of this decan discover a great sense of fulfillment as detectives, surgeons, or wardens of large establishments, such as institutions and even prisons. A sizeable number choose a cloistered life.

I have never known a person born in your decan who was not absolutely BRILLIANTLY TALENTED, usually in many different directions. I feel, however, that they are sometimes torn by extreme "inner" conflicts, owing to a sensation that there are several underlying personalities, all of which have demanding requirements wholly different from one another. Being intensely passive AND active, all at the same time, it might seem to you that "forces" are sometimes pulling you toward opposite poles with the most colossal strength, giving you a desire for recognition, and, at the same time an enormous wish for privacy and seclusion. Such contradictory promptings will probably make it appear less easy to find your true place than for many people, because endeavors that satisfy one of these segments of your disposition might seem stifling to another, and vice versa. Eighteenth Century composers wrote a music entitled, "The Sacred and Profane" that might describe chords which seem to be stuck within your nature, now and then, by shedding upon your very soul a feeling of "Divine Light" that prompts the deepest spiritual devotion, while its counterpart urges you to destruction. A vivid imagination is almost certain to make a differentiation between fact and fantasy seem almost out of the question for you. I must conclude, in this regard, that you will often be aware of a paradox between utterly dissimilar emotions, even when you have exactly what you want within your reach. I think that your first step toward a happier, more harmonious life will begin with TRUTHFULNESS — with yourself, as well as other people — and a continual effort to keep yourself CONSTRUCTIVELY OC-CUPIED.

While you will tend to be extremely aggressive, I feel that you will be at the same time quite unsure of yourself, inwardly, contrasting qualities that will give you a fondness for phases of solitude; yet you will know times when you will wish to have people around you every instant. Individuals born in your sign nearly always have a "double life". You might also have a tendency to seek the society of others rather adamantly, leaving within your arrangements a provision for finding another, entirely different, existence that enables you to retreat when it is your desire to do so.

During the earliest part of your life, you may feel aware of certain limitations or restrictions that somewhat dampen the degree of freedom you would like to have. You will probably think that a person who has charge of your care expects too much of you, or that this person's "outside activities" or "beliefs" make demands that necessarily deprive you of attention you consider that you ought to receive. At the same time, there is apt to be someone else who is responsible for your well-being causing you to be shifted too often from "relative-to-relative", "neighborhood-to-neighborhood" or "situation-to-situation". This might lead you into occasional moods which are filled with gloomy forebodings and general despondency — habits which I am confident that you have now overcome — that may give you a dislike of means taken to promote your "education", and otherwise stall your efforts to learn. You are almost bound to be a serious, sober and thoughtful child, capable of concentration and well able to understand the most profound sciences and other serious subjects in life. When you use tact, diplomacy, honesty and justice, you will surely attract a circle of friends and acquaintances that holds for you admiration, although you will no doubt need to make more effort than many children to get along with youngsters around you and to find a sense of satisfaction in the number of siblings which you have, or the absence of these. While you will probably be fond of music and dancing, you are apt to be self-conscious of your voice, as well as other attributes. Because you will have a quiet disposition, slow to decide, in all likelihood your speech may seem delayed or problematical — but once you take a position, there is little question that you will be stubborn in maintaining it.

The intensity of your emotions will grow vehemently as you approach adulthood, in my opinion, bringing you into a cycle which is charged with mental agitations that place before the image of your mind every possible alternative in life and "life hereafter". Being inwardly like a "sea in storm", it is apt to be particularly important that you guard against misalliances or a tendency for the extreme ferocity of your feelings to react upon your health. While moderation in food, drink and other habits is advisable for everyone, I consider it absolutely IMPERATIVE for individuals born in your sign and decan. This initiation into adulthood will create within you a need for making substantial choices, in my estimation, and the outcome of decisions you make with regard to your moral values, beliefs and objectives will strenuously influence the remainder of your life — for bad or for good. Because I trust that YOUR choice will prompt you to place your total energies into betterment for all of Humankind you can reach, the transition you now make will lift you to truly great spiritual heights that will make you a beneficent leader of your associates, held in esteem, honor and respect, and enable you to be looked upon as an inspiration to people whose lives come to touch your own.

In matters of affection, you are apt to be extremely self-possessive. When you care for another person, it might seem less easy for you to await a display of mutual response than for many people. Your instinct will probably be to launch a full-scale pursuit, precipitating encounters whenever possible, even though your methods might seem brash by ordinary standards. I have observed that individuals born in this third decan of Pisces ordinarily have an undefinable sense of guilt that prompts them to place their greatest determination into impossible situations, or those which they really know are detrimental to their better interests, because these will invariably bring disappointments that administer punishment of the imagined deeds for which they think they must be admonished. Strifes and rivalries frequently mark this area of their lives, therefore, and they very often have at least one unconventional love affair which they keep a secret. You may notice that you also have an occasional tendency to receive the most enjoyment from relationships that either give you a feeling that you are "putting something over on another person" or seem to show the greatest resistance to your advances, because these display the least likely prospects for placing upon you responsibilities which you might not be able to fulfill, while they supply the excitement of "challenge".

You may find people who appear "domesticated" and familial most attractive in courtship, but mental companionship and a rather vestal association will no doubt have stronger appeal for partnerships in marriage or business. I think that you will often rely on other people to solve your problems, although it will be necessary for you to keep some of your more critical opinions to yourself, as intolerance towards stupidity in those with whom your closest efforts are allied will be one of your stronger tendencies. Marital difficulties or changes and separations within family life are often a signature of this decan, but because I have the greatest confidence in YOU, I know that you will base your life on lofty ideals that will prevent many, many thwarted expectations such as some people have.

Individuals of this decan often have larger-than-average families. In your associations with younger people, you are likely to be aware of numerous changes, but your own attitude toward them will probably be receptive, placid, and somewhat inclined to withhold action upon impressions you receive concerning their welfare. You will probably dislike interferences with your methods of managing the interests of youngsters who closely touch your own interests. While you may give an impression of being dependent upon other people and flexible to trends around you, there might be an underlying "exemption from arbitrary control" which will often prompt you to attend in your own way to matters which concern you, regardless of previous promises or commitments. I believe that consistency along these lines will often prove helpful with youngsters in your "care", while your disciplinary practices should not be overly-severe. It might also be advisable for you to make sure that you distribute fairly the delegation of duties and responsibilities, as you might have a tendency to place more stringent rules upon some "children" than others.

Such an ambitious temperament as you are likely to have needs always to be combined with altruism, owing to an inclination to try to "climb so high" as to risk "toppling", or to have reversals at the summit of large achievements — but because you will surely hold your goals in reasonable perspective, I feel that your brilliant qualities will win friends among people in esteemed positions and earn from them most welcome assistance. It might sometimes appear to you that your progress is less rapid than you would really like, although with patience and the utmost care that each step forward is solidly placed in a foothold toward a constructive and enduring future, you are almost certain to insure a prosperous outcome for all of your activities.

The contest between material and spiritual concepts will often be a strong one in affairs that most greatly concern you, in my opinion, but by finding a sound "middle-ground" that gives expression to both, your life should rapidly grow into balance.

You are apt to have somewhat "luxurious" tastes, liking possessions that give comfort and are also "pleasing to the eye", so to say. Your tendency might be toward "impulse" spending, or investments into enterprises that will pioneer newer ideas and bring you into territory previously unexplored which will enhance the appearance of an item or endeavor, as well. Although you are often likely to feel hampered from the degree of spending you would prefer, or to reach phases that require especially careful management, you are apt to have an uncanny "knack" for making acquisitions or receiving gifts at unusually appropriate times. Other people will be extremely helpful to your financial interests, I think, being responsible for at least one inheritance or endowment which you will receive, and providing you with income or advantages that will serve your interests well in almost any circumstances. Such things as "credit", "benefits" and insurance might often prove helpful to your resources, giving you a means of reaching more easily some of your major aspirations.

I am deeply and sincerely interested in your happiness, and I have a strong feeling of assurance that it will continue to grow with each passing year, bringing your efforts more and more into the "limelight" where they can earn deserved appreciation and admiration — because I trust that you will devote yourself, every moment, to improved conditions for other people. You are, I know, capable of reaching the highest pinnacle of success!

The Truth About Hidden
Cycles Affecting All Life

Notice it must be borne in mind that while your Sun sign will be sensitive to these cyclic patterns, "the year" of your birth may give so much strength to powerful planets that were placed in another area of your personal chart that even though these cycles are very much in evidence "the pull" from other strong planetary configurations may "lessen the impact" of the natural rhythm of the cycles I have pointed out. This can only be determined, of course, by your individual birth chart, although 90% will be strongly influenced, I have found, by the rise and fall of the cycles I have designated.

Small cycles move within larger cycles. For example: those who respond to a 6-1/3 year rhythm and the longer 19 year cycle will tend to follow the pattern shown at top of next page.

All cycles are not permanent or lasting but are points to a peak or a low   point where a termination is reached, bringing a new condition. They point to "the ebb and flow" of life to which your birthdate is sensitive. Also, two birthsigns may have a similar cyclic rhythm but the years of impact will not be alike!

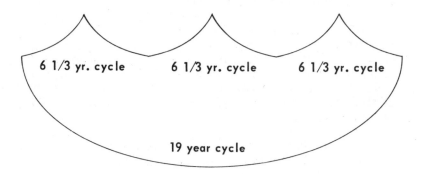

Note: The "beginning and ending" dates of each birthsign may be altered by the year of birth, sometimes one to two days. I have taken the most popular changing dates as starting and closing days.

Cycles in Nature
A startling disclosure of little-known facts

It was many years ago that I first felt the need for investigating the mysteries of life, and the resultant desire to seek the sources of information — information that was and is not only valid but vital. Information that had been expounded centuries ago and then allowed to fall into the discard to some extent.

The travels I have outlined were of inestimable value, not only for the beauty and individual points of interest each locality held and still holds, but also because they enable me to pass on to you direct from the original site those verities that are so essential to the well-being of Mankind.

It is, I feel, most regrettable that in the past we witnessed an attitude of cynicism; an attitude which, happily, is now being dispelled by recognition of the validity of knowledge held millenia ago. Today there is an increasing light of hope and awareness as scientists examine and proclaim anew many of those ancient truths; and not only the scientists but the "man on the street".

Truth may be buried for a time by skepticism, but like the Phoenix, it will rise again at the proper time — and this it is doing today!

In the chapter to follow we will summarize some of the findings of this "new breed" of scientists, and consider how the effects they have noticed involve us in our daily lives — how we can turn these effects to our best advantage.

It is, of course, not possible in a volume this size to report on all findings; but we will offer I am sure, a sufficient number to prove the thesis that we are affected by forces outside our own personal beings — forces that do guide us advantageously if we will but follow their beneficent inclinations.

When I first commenced my studies of planetary phenomena and their relation to not only our personal lives, but also those circumstances affecting all existence, I was immediately impressed by the various "cyclic theories" that were and are so prevalent. Additional study has not only confirmed but strengthened my original belief that all life is governed in varying lengths and degrees by cycles.

I am, of course, not the only person to believe this. Actually it can be traced back with very little difficulty to the writings of the ancients; Herodotus, Lucretius, Plato, and Virgil, to name only four. In addition, there is increasing evidence that the idea of influential cyclic patterns is being noted and accepted by men and women who pursue what is customarily called "pure science".

There are so many cycles involved in this study that it is truly impossible to discuss them in detail here. Innumerable books have been written about them, and there will undoubtedly be many more. Then, too, in considering words, we come to the point of deciding where "cycle" ends, and "rhythm" begins. In this connection, dictionaries agree that a cycle is "A series that repeats itself"; while rhythm is "Movement characterized by regular measured or harmonious recurrence of stress, beat, sound, or motion".

Under these conditions, cannot we safely say that "rhythm" develops from "cycle"? At the least, I feel we can assume this; and consequently the words will be used more or less interchangeably throughout this chapter.

Examining briefly some of the many cycles which have been studied and outlined, we find the "Dionysian Period" — 532 years in length; the "Metonic Cycle" of 19 years; the "Cycle of 432"; and the "Great Zodiacal or Precessional Year" of 25,920 years!

In addition we have, of course, the various cycles of the planets which play a more recognizable part in our individual lives; but here again we must consider the length of time involved for each planet to make its accustomed round.

The Moon is the most readily recognizable body that exerts an effect on everyone; recognizable not only because of its nearness to us, but the frequently recurring effects — approximately every 28 days. Who of us has not experienced "the ups and downs" of emotion — those days of unexplainable depression, balanced by days of equally unexplainable optimism and knowledge that "everything is going to be just fine"? Anyone who has observed the tides of the oceans has witnessed the effects of the Moon; and it has been shown that even the crust of our Earth is subject to similar tides, although to lesser degrees.

The Sun and Mercury return to their original places in one year, give or take a day or so; while Venus completes her transit in approximately one year and two plus months, on an average. Consequently, along with the Moon, these bodies must be considered as having the greatest immediacy.

The complete transit of Mars is only slightly less than 2 years, while Jupiter takes about 12 years. Saturn's transit is 29½ years, and we then arrive at those planets which few of us will ever experience having a full return — Uranus (about 84 years); and no one can anticipate the return of Neptune (about 165 years).

These cycles (with the exception of Uranus, Neptune, and Pluto) have comparatively recently been under serious consideration in connection with many events that can and do affect our daily lives — weather prediction, construction probabilities, the death of prominent personages, the stock market's probable activities and the like.

As a matter of fact, in a recent national publication a scientific analysis was given top priority as the result of medical research being focused on what is now called man's "biological time cycles", or "inner clocks". To quote the authorities, "Man's days — his nights — his diseases — troubled times — periods of confusion — and moments of clarity may well be determined and balanced by a delicate and vastly complex intermeshing of biological time cycles".

The recognition of the "inner clock's" existence is nothing new, but understanding of this situation is only now being clearer on an almost daily basis.

Man's bodily temperature is apparently controlled by a hidden "clock", which causes it to rise during the day. There is impressive evidence that "cycles" and "rhythms" may well be the cause of one's body being more vulnerable to ill health or disease at certain times. It has even been noted that in some way body rhythms contribute to the death pattern. It is fairly common knowledge, for example, that heart attacks and strokes tend to occur most often in the early morning hours.

A member of my family who was a well-known physician mentioned this quite frequently. It was, incidentally, his encouragement that was to a great extent responsible for my following the career which seemed to choose me, rather than my choosing it! His was not a small practice, but extended around the world through correspondence as well as personal visits. I have, in my judgments, been guided by many of the things he said which have been proved accurate.

It was his stand that age does not kill — but the "MENTAL OUTLOOK DOES", and that every living thing (including man) is affected by cyclic rhythms emanating from the Moon. Today it is generally agreed that the mentally disturbed become increasingly disturbed, in many cases to the point of unmanageability at the time of the full Moon. Police blotters show an increase in crime at this same time, according to several sources.

Is it logical to assume that only those who are least in control of their urges should be the only ones affected, and not everyone to some extent? We know that plant life responds to the Moon — the tides rise and fall by the dictates of the Moon. Why should Man be uninvolved?

- 329 -

This basis of logic is the very foundation upon which the scientific theory of Astrology lies. Anyone with scientific bent cannot overlook these facts:

1. Evolution is theory — accepted but not proven fact;

2. Einstein's theory of relativity is theory — not proven fact;

3. The atomic theory — accepted but not completely proven fact;

4. The cell theory — not proven fact.

Yet the above are taught in our schools as facts: so why should not the theory that mankind is influenced by phenomena beyond his control at certain cyclic periods also be given serious consideration in our places of higher learning?

In one of our leading scientific journals it has been stated that electro-magnetic occurrences have been observed which are associated with the biological processes, and subject to variations induced by certain influences in our solar system. Findings of recent date have related geomagnetic variations to Lunar phases. Rainfall and the number of hurricanes are said to have their peak during or just following a full Moon, and before or after a new Moon — with the first and third quarters being the lowest in incidence!

We know that the Earth is constantly bombarded by solar streams, so our magnetic field is altered in intensity — flattened on the side facing the Sun, lengthened on the dark side. Surely such tremendous force would have effect on life here on Earth!

Disturbances caused by the planets are being given serious consideration, and particularly the Jupiter-Sun-Saturn angle of 180 degrees every eleven years — approximately a major solar cycle!

The pigeon is said to navigate and find its way through a

sensitivity to the magnetic field. Is Man's nervous system less subject to such influences? If we believe this we must say that Man's nervous system is not as sensitive as that of the pigeon!

Now, let us turn from these generalized statements, and examine the proof.

At Northwestern University Dr. Frank A. Brown, Jr., undertook a series of experiments in an attempt to discover what it was beyond the influence of ordinary laboratory procedures and conditions that affected animals and their reactions. This in turn led to vegetable matter, and a study of lunar and solar periods developed theories of rhythm which became (as he puts it) "more fascinating than our former problems".

The results of this research and experimentation were first published in an article entitled LIFE'S MYSTERIOUS CLOCKS.

While habit patterns of various organisms had been noticed for centuries, Dr. Brown set out to find why these patterns were existent, and how they developed. Why, for example, would oysters from Connecticut continue for a period of about two weeks TO TIME THEIR LIVES according to "tidal" movements occurring 800 miles away after they had been transferred to the Midwest? Why do seeds in a laboratory, removed from their normal outside temperature and humidity, maintain the same sprouting cycle that they would have if planted in the earth under ordinary conditions? Why do fiddler crabs maintain their schedule of darkening by day and paling by night — even though they are under controlled laboratory conditions of maintained light levels?

Turning first to what may be truly termed now "the famous oyster experiment", quantities of the mollusks were collected at New Haven, Conn. and transported to Evanston, Ill., where they were placed in pans of sea water in a darkened room. It is an accepted fact, of course, that "the tides" of the ocean are governed by the Moon primarily. Indeed, all bodies of water experience tides to some extent, although in some this may be so slight as to be unnoticeable except by accurate instrument measuring; while at the Bay of Fundy in Nova Scotia they may be as high as 53 feet. For two weeks the oysters opened and closed their shells for feeding at the periods of high tides in New Haven; then, they adapted to the zenith and nadir positions of the Moon at Evanston! These two Moon positions are when that body's maximum gravitational effect is present on the atmospheric tides, and if Evanston were a coastal city it would experience ocean tides just as New Haven does! It is obvious the oyster responded to this influence!

The fiddler crabs, when deprived of obvious cues such as light, continued to darken their shells by day, and lighten them by night to accord with the lunar zenith and nadir; resetting their inner tables of activity after being brought to Evanston from various localities of different tide times.

Turning from animal to vegetable organisms, Dr. Brown found that potatoes are subject to solar-day and lunar-day rhythms in their own particular metabolism — while under constant laboratory conditions. As a matter of fact, even while contained in hermetically sealed containers, the tubers were able to predict atmosphere pressure trends two days in advance!

What, though, of those subjects exposed to outside stimulus? Was it possible to "reset" their time clocks? Taking for one subject the ordinary bean plant, Dr. Brown found that it is possible, in the dark, to expose the plant to a bright flash of light, and thereafter the bean will follow a regular "sleep rhythm" based on the time it was exposed to that light IF it is kept in the same environment. In case the "sleep rhythm" phase is new to you, beans do follow such a pattern, with the leaves rising and falling.

Apparently there is valid reason to assume that living organisms, animal and vegetable, are subject to "cyclic forces". The effects of these forces can in some cases be altered gradually, in others almost instantaneously. In either case, however, the forces themselves remain, although in a somewhat different relationship as to time.

Now, how can that last paragraph apply to us? In these days of jet travel, to take one instance, one can fly from California to England — upon arrival find that his "inner clock" is still set for California, some eight or nine hours difference. It may take as much as 10 days in some cases for the ordinary aspects of life such as waking, body temperature, blood-cell count, and hormone secretion to readjust to what can be called the "normal condition" for that individual.

Even such a seasoned traveller as Lowell Thomas was reduced to virtual nervous and physical prostration when he first began making his many trips by fast plane. It was not until he understood what was causing his difficulty — the confusing of his "inner clock" — that he adapted his schedules accordingly and was able to continue his career successfully and with a minimum of discomfort.

It was Dr. Brown's conclusion that evidence suggests the primary timing system for organisms to be the movements of Sun, Moon, and Earth. He goes on to suggest that nature side-stepped the variable and biologically potent forces such as light and temperature, in favor of more stable forces that would demand little or no adaptive response of a specific nature, and yet simultaneously would be so pervasive that no living thing would ever normally be deprived of their influence. Certainly, to again quote Dr. Brown, "Some of the evidence available is quite fantastic".

At this point it is quite logical that you should say — "Ah, but that is just one person. How about some other evidence?"

In 1945 and 1947, Dr. Henry S. Burr (Yale University Medical School) published reports concerning his observations in connection with TREE POTENTIALS. He found that there were strongly apparent cycles of growth, consisting of one month, four months and six months per year. In addition, there appeared to be a significant relationship to the phases of the Moon. While not identical, various graphs charted were analogous to the extent that the similarity can hardly be considered accidental.

In his works, Dr. Burr did not state categorically that the growth cycles were caused by the Moon, but did suggest strongly that electro-magnetic forces associated with the Moon's phases might conceivably be the cause.

In view of further work by other researchers since, this appears to be very plausible, to say the least.

It is becoming more and more evident that little-known electro-magnetic forces are at work in our Universe, and must be having some effects on living organisms. One has only to read reports relating to the concern for Astronauts when Solar flares occur to understand this. It has been observed and recorded that every 11½ years there are emissions of an electro-magnetic type from the planet Jupiter, which tend to coincide with the "solar flares" that are of such great concern.

Leonard J. Ravitz, Lecturer in Sociology at the Norfolk College of William and Mary, and Consultant in Neurology and Psychiatry in the Virginia Departments of Health and Education, published in 1962 a most informative report concerning periodic changes in the electro-magnetic field in health and disease. It is, I feel, most interesting that in the charts contained in this report he indicates the positions of the New and Full Moon, with these chart positions coinciding quite closely to various points of "ups and downs" in the condition of various patients.

Since the data involved in the above study are quite technical, let us turn to another report, prepared by Dr. Edson J. Andrews of Tallahassee, Fla., and based on his files. Here the subject is one that is readily recognizable — dealing as it does with bleeding following tonsillectomies.

In just over one thousand cases, Dr. Andrews found that

there was a greater tendency to post-operative hemorrhaging when the operations were performed at the time of the Full Moon. Endeavoring to be quite accurate, and wishing to check his figures, he obtained similar information from a colleague, Dr. Carl S. McLemore of Orlando, Fla. Here again the results of plotting on a chart revealed as Dr. Andrews says: "The astounding preponderance of hemorrhage at the full Moon and the relative absence at the new Moon are evident."

Not being content with this, Dr. Andrews adds that he had heard there were more babies born on the full Moon, but his friends who practiced obstetrics said this was not so. In 1956, 1957, and 1958, he plotted the births recorded at Tallahassee Memorial Hospital, and found that 401 babies were born within 2 days of the full Moon, 375 within 2 days of the new Moon, and 320 within 2 days of the 1st quarter.

He goes on to say: "It would seem then that we do have evidence that prolonged bleeding at the full Moon can occur and pretty good evidence that it is possible for human physiology to be so altered that it might explain periodic, prolonged bleeding. In the face of the evidence, however, it would seem that it might be well to investigate this possibility in more detail before we say 'just superstitition'." Meanwhile, because these data have been so conclusive and convincing to me, it is unthinkable in this day of scientific research to scoff at these discoveries.

So, we see again, that there is a rhythm caused by the Moon — a rhythm which when recognized and accepted, can be not only helpful but of great benefit to mankind.

But certainly we must recognize that the Moon is not the only heavenly body with a cycle that involves life. There is the Sun, as well as the planets and stars.

Experiments which we may safely assume to be carefully controlled, have shown that certain of the lower forms of animal life do respond (some insects hatch at full moon, etc.) to these latter bodies; and if they do so respond, is it so difficult to accept the fact that we humans also respond — even though we may not immediately recognize this fact?

In 1960 Dr. Max Renner of the Zoological Institute of the University of Munich published a report on his findings concerning the time-sense and astronomical orientation of the Honey-Bee.

Among other matters discussed, he mentions that bees "navigate" by combining Sun angle and Sun altitude, in all likelihood. Bees trained on the East Coast to fly northwest at 1 P.M. for feeding, were shipped to California, where (adhering to Eastern Standard Time) they searched for food at 10 A.M., but flew to the southwest. In other words, they kept the Sun in the left eye, so to speak!

Even as this was being written, an article in the ILLUS-TRATED LONDON NEWS (Nov. 22, 1969) came to my attention. Under discussion was the book THE MYSTERY OF ANIMAL MIGRATIONS by Matthieu Ricard, in which the author explores various experiments dealing with the "homing" instincts of several forms of animal life. In 1950, for example, Gustav Kramer disclosed the results of his experiments with Starlings, proving that these birds oriented themselves by the Sun. Shortly thereafter, other researchers had established that migrating birds of all species utilize celestial navigation; that is, they fly by the Sun during the day, and by "the stars" at night!

Frogs and toads can find their way to familiar breeding grounds unless the sky is overcast — in which case they will wander aimlessly!

Returning to the birds for a moment, the amazing aspect of their navigation is that they solve a problem without instruments, which will take a human as much as 30 minutes with azimuth circle, chronometer, and astronomical tables!

Then consider and marvel at the fact that fish do this same problem, when it is compounded by the refraction of light through water, so the apparent angle and height of the Sun as seen by the fish, is not double that seen by the bird, but varies according to an equation proposed by Rene Descartes. (For those with a mathematical turn of mind, this equation is: $\sin i = \sin r$.)

Truly, the Sun and the stars in their interminable cycles through the heavens are wondrous!

Earlier I mentioned that cycles have been and are being studied in relation to the stock market. In this connection, I would like to mention a book published in 1947 by Edward R. Dewey and Edwin F. Dakin, with the title CYCLES, THE SCIENCE OF PREDICTION.

Here the authors discuss their observations concerning among other matters, the "3½ Year Rhythm", the "9 Year Rhythm", the "18 Year Rhythm", and the "54 Year Rhythm", as they apply to various aspects of the national economy. From recent reports this work has not been allowed to fall by the wayside but is being pursued. Regrettably, due to the continuing unfortunate implications of "superstition" which all too often surround the science of prediction, many who practice it still refuse to acknowledge the fact openly.

In their book, however, the authors have used many charts and graphs which show clearly the various cycles; and when one acknowledges that a cycle is an orderly process it is apparent that prediction can be made with an extremely high probability of exactitude.

Now, you may ask, "how does this involve me personally?"

I mentioned in passing (p. 20) that the pre-natal epoch is 40 weeks. It has also recently been established through scientific tests that the period from conception to birth is 9 luni-solar months reflecting once again the 29.5 day cycle, the period from one full moon to the next or from one lunar phase to the same phase during the next luni-solar month. It has been established also that the true average menstrual cycle is 29.5 days.

- 337 -

It was found in one study that the sex urge among women who were chosen for survey through eliminating those on the pill or who had any abnormality relevant to sexual conditions that the most intense sexual urges were felt just before menstruation or most prolonged during the period just before ovulation.

It is amusing to reflect that although the lights were out in New York about 9 months before there was a rash of births in that area, the moon was shining all right. The night of the blackout was full moon.

Since the basic sexual and reproductive cycles are so closely associated with lunar cycles, this fact alone would have a great deal to do with the way we feel on any particular day.

We are capable as human beings of a wider range of thought response, and action than other creatures. It has been said many times that man has a voice. It has been recorded many times how difficult, sometimes impossible, to motivate a majority to action. As it is true that we have the ability to choose, it seems there is a powerful force in man which resists change, sometimes at all costs, even though apparently one stands to have everything to gain, nothing to lose. It is man's nature to respond to natural cycles and to adopt a rhythm of life which becomes very hard to change.

It is in understanding the natural rhythms of life, I believe, that we may be led to the right decisions when the need arises.

The detail given above has been presented to indicate how we are governed by cyclic patterns, and the rhythms developed thereby. We must remember at all times that the heavenly bodies are moving in an orderly fashion — that AT REGULARLY STATED TIMES THEY RETURN TO POSITIONS HELD EARLIER! If then, we accept the fact that these bodies had an effect on us originally, IT FOLLOWS THAT UPON THEIR RETURN TO CERTAIN POSITIONS THEY WILL TEND TO EXERT THE SAME EFFECT!

As an example of this, let me cite the mighty planet Saturn. A friend of mine who had little or no knowledge of this subject, was one day shown that when she was 29½, Saturn had returned to the place it held at her birth. This was also the year in which her first husband died unexpectedly. At age 59, she again suddenly became entangled in difficulties. The transit of Saturn takes 29½ years, remember. Had she been aware of this fact, it is possible the 2nd unfortunate event could have been avoided, or at the least mitigated.

This is not to say that each periodic return of Saturn brings misfortune! But, by being prepared for certain trends, one can take steps to assume control of possible situations. Remember always the adage: "The stars impel, but do not compel".

Jupiter's return can usually be expected to bring about an improvement in personal situations, particularly in the realm of finances; and a surge of energy normally accompanies the return of Mars.

I must point out and emphasize at this point, that from time to time much the same results may be expected as various aspects are formed by the planet under consideration and others. This can, of course, only be determined in advance, however, when one is familiar with the natal chart, as well as the movements that will take place in days to come.

It is my very sincere hope that more and more people will examine this subject with ever-increasing care — and above all, an open mind. As this greater understanding prevails, we will notice a stronger approach to the true meanings inherent in the Aquarian Age — the Brotherhood of Man — which we are now entering!

Your Own Sun Sign
and
"The Time When Your Luck Will Change"

Aries: The Time When Your Luck Will Change

Those who were born between March 20 and April 20, the first sign of the zodiac known as Aries, are "keyed" all their lives to the rhythm of the planet Mars, the ruler of this sign. Since Venus, the planet ruling close association with other people; the planet Mercury, considered to shape the trend of your thoughts; and Mars, the planet that sets things in motion, so to speak, all come into close aspect every 6 1/3 years — it is to be expected that much of the turbulence you will experience will rise when these three influences are in sharp focus. During "the peak" of the cyclic trend from these three combined influences, you are apt to act upon impulse and create your own world by following an objective you will feel an urgency to fulfill rather than take the path of cold reason. It is at such times that you may over-spend — as for instance, the Duke of Windsor not only gave up a throne and made a new life for himself, but he is said to have spent as much as $300 for flowers for the Duchess, and a fortune in jewels! This 6 1/3 year cycle often tends to quarrels and frequently accidents of temporary nature, especially while traveling or driving, fire or water losses, or theft. However, this 6 1/3 cycle is one that seems to bring "a destination point", directing the energies in such a manner as to force "a climax" involving associations which could have "hung on". When this occurs, it frequently drains "the life force" which if channeled in another direction would have led to "the top".

The 6 1/3 year cycles to watch for can best be found by counting from June 16, 1968 and on to the following 6 1/3 year period 1974 — and the following 6 1/3 — 1981.

Now to other cycles where road blocks can be hurdled and friendly hands will come forth to assist you, regardless of problems to be overcome — start with April 18, 1965 and on to 1971 — and the next 6 1/3 years to 1977. Count 6 1/3 years forward. These 6 1/3 year cycles will direct your feet into fields where "new ideas" will bring surprising openings!

While Jupiter will lend its protective influence every 12 years, the above cycles will give you the "up and down" trend so that you will see that no period of heavy burdensome conditions is lasting but will be replaced by one to which your natural energy is in harmony.

Other birthsigns may respond to certain cycles, particularly Jupiter's, in a similar manner to yours, but the years will not be alike nor the influences following.

Taurus: The Time When Your Luck Will Change

Those born between April 21 and May 22, in Taurus, one of "the fixed" zodiacal signs, are usually affected by slower or heavier cyclic patterns — being less likely to be uprooted by every breeze that blows, so to speak. The period where you can begin to pinpoint these cyclic influences, in my opinion, is the year 1968, as the fall of that year probably either severed ties you had for some time, took you away or removed someone who had held close contact with you. While earlier years could have shown high peaks, I feel this is a good one with which to start. 1968 undoubtedly brought some association with a distant place — travel, or a "means" of travel such as airplane, automobile or the like.

Beginning with the year 1968 and especially the months of August through most of December, you have only to project forward to the year 1975 to find the sensitive point (a 7½ year cycle) where once again "surging events" in relation to close ties will come into the foreground. This is an area of the zodiac where those born in this period always seem to find it necessary to touch the earth, so sooner or later they buy real estate in some field of activity, if only to own their home. There is also a smaller cycle however which is likely to affect the natives of the sign Taurus, leading their thoughts and conversations to lean toward selling or disposing of land or other possessions of monetary value, and this too is a 7½ year cycle starting with 1970. Simply add 7½ years to 1970 and you will have the next peak where overindulgences or other elements may become weighty problems — for a passing period. Since your success lies in working with money, or material possessions to make money, it is my judgment that the year of 1968 as a beginning point, and again 1975 will be those of accomplishment or where you will advance your position — in spite of any seeming walls to be climbed! A good birthsign!

Remember that while other birth periods may have a similar rhythm, the years and sensitive areas will be different in areas of interest.

Gemini: The Time When Your Luck Will Change

If you were born between May 23 and the 22nd of June, which is the sign Gemini, then there is great likelihood of your rearranging your furniture, your homelife or seeking a new area of interest every 3 1/6 years in the lesser paths of your life — while the mainstream that will affect the general course of your life, I am confident, you will find centered on a 19-year cyclic pattern. Marriage and other important events that stand out like neon signs almost always occur around the 19th, the 38th, the 57th year of a Gemini's life.

Regardless of the year of your birth, June 1971 will undoubtedly "touch off" a spark that will bring major changes into your life, especially in connection with your income or accumulated possessions. By adding 19 years to June 1971, you will find a future major destination point — in spite of the 3 1/6 year cyclic trend that will tend to create a smaller pattern in your personal affairs. Since your tendency is not to limit your interests to one monotonous path but to divide your interests into two separate areas, such as a vocation and an avocation — two different lovers you could marry at the same time, I believe that you will find the 3 1/6 year cycle one that will impress you far more than the longer 19-year cycle where the eclipse and nodes will be apt to mark "real climaxing points" but will seem quite far apart to you. What you "say", or write at that time, or THE PAPERS YOU WILL SIGN, will be of major importance. I feel that I should point out this element for I am certain they will be dominant factors. Someone born in November will probably come into the foreground as well. A most active birth period in which to be born whether you follow your 3 1/6 year cycle of smaller changes, or your 19-year major trend!

Other birthdate periods may appear quite similar to your own but in analyzing them closely you will find "the peak points" will contain quite different circumstances.

Cancer: The Time When Your Luck Will Change

If your birthdate falls between June 23 and July 21, then you were born under that most sensitive of all of the signs, Cancer — recently named "Moon Child". While your emotions will rise and fall every 14½ days, this will not be responsible for the major trends of your life, in my opinion. It has been my experience in dealing with the major cyclic patterns in the lives of those born in this sign of the zodiac that every 20 years marks "a turning point".

Since Cancer natives have their lives most deeply affected by their relatives or home conditions, a good starting year will be 1960-1961, when Jupiter and Saturn were both placed in the sign Capricorn, although this has of course, passed. Around that time a change was undoubtedly responsible for bringing new people into your life, then close to 10 years later an upheaval undoubtedly brought some sudden conclusion in relation to "a hidden" matter which had been "hanging" suspended for some time, but was brought out into the open. This period of around 1970, might prove to be "the bomb" that literally catapulted you into a new life. The next period of great magnitude will be late 1980 to 1981. While the same pattern may not repeat itself exactly, for instance where 1969 to 1970 undoubtedly involved you with "unorthodox people" and strange, foreign or unusual circumstances, 1980-1981 will more than likely be a major turning point where finances, and particularly "the source" from which you derive your money, will undergo "alterations" turning you in a different direction. In fact, it is very probable that you will feel a need in this area of your life to reach a decision that will mean IMPORTANT CHANGE. Quite often under this cycle "two paths" open before a Cancer native, one at a distance and the other close by. Usually the one "at a distance" is speculative but promises more while the one close by holds "security" — but has less glamour. It is rare to find a Cancer native or Moon Child who hasn't found "a secure nest" in their life time.

Your rhythm, in my experience, is attuned to a slower, long-range cyclic pattern, so although other birthsigns may seem to respond to cyclic peaks similar to your own, actually "the influences" at the time of your high or low points will be unalike!

Leo: The Time When Your Luck Will Change

If your birth came between July 22 and August 22, you were born in that glamorous "center of the stage personality", the sign known as Leo. It has been my experience that no Leo enters a room silently, unheard, or unseen, but that all eyes turn in their direction, so it follows that the life of someone born in this area of the zodiac is "keyed" to a "stepped-up rhythm". Since the Sun is the ruler of Leo, the basic cycle seems to respond to 4-year periods.

However, since Leos are always entangled in the lives of others, I feel that 1962 is a very good place in which to begin to find the basic, larger cyclic influence which in this instance seems to be 8 year periods. In fact, during that year you undoubtedly gave a lot of thought to your future security – possibly, sought legal or technical advice and this too probably involved another person. Following 1962, you are likely to have regained lost ground through "a windfall" and again where another person had a strong influence.

Now in 1970 another eight-year peak arises – with Jupiter and Saturn bringing into the foreground a similar cycle to 1962 emerging. It is most likely that what you experience in 1970 will not be quite an exact repetition – as you will find small differences. In 1970 the emphasis will be more on neighbors and those who are relatives or near enough in your affections to be termed "almost related". Adjustment or compromise seems to be indicated with your accepting something "less" while giving your "all". Re-arrangement, touching your place of residence, with marked lines tending toward a temporary period of "solitude", aloneness or "withdrawal" from close-by associations is one phase that is apt to stand out in this cyclic phase. You will be apt to sense hidden criticism so that unlike yourself, during other cycles, you will tend to draw into a shell temporarily. The "loss" of someone, who at one time was important to you, may, near the year of 1970, color your thoughts, although at the same time you will benefit or make strideful gains.

The following "uptrend" will be in 1974 with 1978 again demanding that you "curb" your natural outgoing impulses toward other people who will be responsible for a "web-like" set of conditions. An exciting, very full colorful four-year cyclic pattern with 8th - 12th - 16th - 20th years marking the intervening peak points. Yours is life rhythm filled with action!

Other birthsigns may seem "keyed" to cyclic patterns close to yours, but the events and reactions as well as circumstances and years will be of different range.

Virgo: The Time When Your Luck Will Change

The rhythm of those born in the wonderful birthsign of Virgo, it has been my experience, seems to revolve around Mercury, their ruling planet as well as Venus and Mars – and the eclipse which falls into close aspect every 6½ years – but with an emphasis in addition on every 13th year. While other birth periods, I have noted, are sensitive to this 6½ year rhythm, it is, in a quite different way from those who were born August 23 to September 23.

Virgo is the sign of "service", consequently it has appeared so often in my work that they have worked with something or someone for a 13-year period only to find around that time that a change is necessary. By adding a 6½ year period to that 13 years, it is amazing how you will arrive at the age when their lives took on "a climaxing point" that is to shape much of their future with a tendency toward rearranging their possessions. Almost always those born in this period will own property before they are through with this life's journey, and during these climaxing points will alter their holdings or will experience new plans in the positions they hold, or "walk out" on something. Someone you know well born in this sign and for whom I have always had great admiration is that talented actress, Ingrid Bergman. Her life followed this pattern. A gentleman born in this period whom I have known intimately has shifted his career. You, who are of the birthsign Virgo, tend to desire "perfection" in certain areas of your life I feel, so that constant "unfulfillment" wears away like a drop of water on a rock leading to an overwhelming urge toward fresh fields and a new start.

March of 1970 will give an impetus in the direction of changing close associates or associations – rearrangement where other business people will play a major role. You are apt to find yourself entangled in the affairs of others and at the same time "a sweeping away" of former close ties. Since this sign is usually interested in golf or other sports such as bowling, etc., there is considerable likelihood that new ties or new environment will color this area of your life as well. And to this the cyclic years I have pointed out, 1970 plus 6½ — 1976½ and so on, you will be able to obtain the shifting panorama of your life pattern with its well-earned success, I'm sure.

Libra: The Time When Your Luck Will Change

Those born between September 24 and October 23, the lively birth period known as Libra, I have found, respond to a seven-year cyclic pattern, as well as a smaller 3½ year rhythm. It has been my observation that the "peak points" of GREAT PROGRESS for those born in this period, seem to come from the 49th to 56th year of life and that prior to that time, there is an uncertainty concerning their marriage or the major course in life to follow especially near their 21st and 24½ years. While this sign frequently doesn't appear overly robust, they seem to have "an inner" strength which enables their body to renew or rebuild so that many Librans find their 63rd, their 70th and even 77th year of life "high points" because of surprising new developments. I would sum up the early years preceding the 21st birthdate for Librans as "expanding or growth", and the next seven or 28th year as requiring "effort" — while the following seven years or 35th is apt to be one of "pitfalls" threatening setbacks or sudden, unexpected situations which appear dangerous at the time, but seem to dissolve under the coming 3½ years!

Around your 42nd year is the time when explosive elements are apt "to flare" having to do with health concerns, as well as employment or your "source of income". The challenges you face around your 42nd year of life, I am convinced, will bring forth "new ideas" THAT WILL LIFT YOU OVER THE DIFFICULTIES which arise, enabling you to sail to "A CREATIVE HEIGHT" in your 49th year where opportunity will knock or "a windfall" will land squarely before you. Following the 49th year, I have noted "a changed Libran" almost always develops, whose attitude seems more prudent or one who is apt to dwell more on a peaceful, secure, homelife and companionship.

My only word of warning to those born in this sign is to exert that wonderful gift with which you were born, enabling you to see "both sides" of any matter before leaping into it. Doors that have hitherto been closed, I am certain, will open through the help of another person who will aid or support YOUR ADVANCED IDEAS, turning the difficult cycle you have jolted through, toward a smoother highway and a very happy late life!

Scorpio: The Time When Your Luck Will Change

Although those born in Scorpio, October 24th to November 22nd, are seemingly most deeply affected by Mars transiting sensitive areas of their birthcharts, I have noticed that there appears to be a longer range cycle which has strong bearing upon their lives every fifteenth year as well, and especially around the 45th year of life! Quite often the first influence I mentioned of Mars which is a four-year cycle brings an "uprooting" in the 16th year and again in the 20th - 24th and particularly 28th years. I know this appears to be confusing, but "the key" to this sign, it has been my experience, is "Ambition" and it is at these times that the natives of Scorpio seem called upon to give a great deal of "drive" while members of the opposite sex also appear to play a dominant role. The passions as well as the "inner longings" always incline to be so intense as to cause those born in this sign to feel almost uncontrollable desires. Frequently I have looked at a birthchart before reading the letter accompanying the request for a forecast and noticed one of the Mars cycles to be a major influence at that moment, which I felt would bring an overwhelming urge in a given direction with an intense longing at the same time "to end" an entanglement in which they found themselves. Almost without exception after turning then to the client's letter, I found that to be the very state of their situation from which they desired to extricate themselves.

During 1970, almost all "Scorpio-born subjects" will find it necessary to follow the wishes, dictates, or rules laid down by others and when this period moves on, the extraordinary intensity of those born in this sign, will come more into the limelight through their courage, actions and personal efforts. Notice, around the 15th year, 30th year, and as I said before, 45th year as being most outstanding, while the 60th too should be quite remarkable as you will have Mars and the 15th year cycles converging! A most exciting combination! A splendid, and I might add, a most courageous sign in which to be born!

Sagittarius: The Time When Your Luck Will Change

Jupiter, considered to be the most beneficent of all of the planets is the ruling force, it seems, in the life of every Sagittarian (born between November 23 and December 21) even though they may have strong planets in another sign which will lend a somewhat changeful cyclic influence to that individual's life. As Jupiter's cycle occurs every "twelve years" it follows that at the age of six years, 12 years, 18 and 24, and so on are sensitive points.

In 1971, Jupiter crosses the sign Sagittarius and as the eclipse pattern then will be in strong aspect, I doubt that any Sagittarian will be able to escape "a major turning point" regardless of the general 6 and 12 year cyclic pattern. Even so, later, when the 6 or 12 year cycle occurs according to the year of your birth, something will be "highlighted" that started in the year of 1971 — if the eclipse and Jupiter influences of 1971 do not coincide with that 6 and 12 year rhythm of your birth year. Sagittarians are inclined, I have found, to get into "tight holes" so to speak, yet being extremely fortunate, "a hand of protection" always seems to bring them through át the last minute. Sooner or later the Sagittarian is placed in a position of authority or where they "tell" others what to do.

I feel that the planet Uranus has a strong influence, as well, in the life of a Sagittarian because you who were born in this zodiacal sign are so inventive. In your life, as a native of this sign, when a particular object has a "price tag" that is too exorbitant, you will invent "a means" of putting together "a makeshift" I am confident, that costs far less but will answer the purpose! This Uranian cycle may remain in the background, but its rhythm is of "a seven year" pattern. Since the nearest Jupiter's cycle and this Uranian influence come to "a meeting", in a cyclic pattern, are the 35th and 36th years of life — it has been my experience that these are the years when "excess" tendencies need to be guarded against at that time, otherwise, "misdirected elements" could prove explosive! While the individual's birthchart may increase or lessen these vibrations it is truly amazing how the major trends in the life of any Sagittarian will take on a responsiveness to these two planets, especially in "buying or selling real estate", in altering their home life, in entanglements or striking "a windfall" at the last minute which will turn the tides of fortune in their direction!

This is one of my favorite signs, although its natives live a little on the dangerous side, I know all their faults and still I consider it one of "the luckiest" because of the security that almost always come to them through the efforts or help of another person! A truly magnificent birth period!

- 350 -

Capricorn: The Time When Your Luck Will Change

Capricorn is always associated with the serious elements of life, particularly an inner feeling of standing "alone", having to work "hard" in order to achieve, and "fear" of being without security in late years of life. All of these characteristics have the quality of Saturn, the ruler of Capricorn. It requires 29½ years for Saturn to make a complete revolution and RETURN TO THE EXACT POSITION IT HELD AT YOUR BIRTH! However, there are intermediate points where it seems to bring those born in this sign to "a cross roads", demanding that "decisions be made" as to their future security which literally "holds in balance" the secureness so important to a Capricornian's "inner" peace of mind.

Over the years I have noticed that every 14 3/4 to 15th year of life the native of this sign is pushed into a corner where only great effort, and by this I mean actual "elbow grease", will lift the strain "money-wise" or will open a closed door. I said there are small cycles that move "within" the larger ones and in the Capricornian's life pattern it has come to my attention that the planet Mars every 7½ and every 15 years will add "fuel to a flaming situation" in which these early January folk find themselves (actually, the birth period is December 22 to January 20th inclusive.) At these peak points a "financial situation" almost invariably leads to "a change" in the home pattern, especially since an older person frequently has a great deal to do with their life, although foremost it is usually career or money matters. AT THE   7½ YEAR INTERVALS AND THE 29½ to 30TH YEAR, AND PARTICULARLY NEAR THE 59TH YEAR, THE CAPRICORNIAN WILL HOLD "A RENDEZVOUS" WITH DESTINY!

In 1972, Jupiter will transit this sign and the eclipse will occur in Capricorn, as well, so I predict that it will be an important time for each of you born in this zodiacal sign, as well as for President Nixon, for it will be "a sensitive point" in his birthchart (as he is a Capricornian) one that is bound to bring his name lasting limelight that will distinguish him from all other presidents. Whether you are a business man or woman, or whatever your status, if you were born with strong planets in your own sign, or only the Sun in Capricorn and all the other planets scattered around the zodiac, this will be a momentous period for you! Dramatic decisions will color this time so that whatever road your life follows after 1972, it will bring prominent mention of your name, in some degree or manner!

Aquarius: The Time When Your Luck Will Change

Your birth period, the sign Aquarius, (January 21st to February 19th, inclusive) is one that seems to be sensitive to sharp rises and falls in your rhythm pattern. Some of the other signs of the zodiac have only slight curves upward or downward. But, the life of the Aquarian, in my experience, tends to follow "an explosive change" from former paths they have followed during a cyclic pattern. The transit of Uranus across any sign is seven years — so that, as an Aquarian, you will respond to every 7th - 14th - 21st - 28th - 35th and so on. The seven-year cycle can be the same as another birthsign, EXCEPT THAT THEY WILL BEGIN AND FALL IN VERY DIFFERENT YEARS. Aquarians began a momentous new pattern in February of 1962 with six planets in their own sign!

In 1969 "a turning" was undoubtedly in evidence that will be seen later, as time moves on, but the most noticeable one will occur in 1976 — for both the eclipse of the Sun and the Moon will add to the vibrations from the planet Uranus with Saturn and Jupiter in close aspect! This leads me to the conclusion that your life will take on "an urgent attitude", one that will seem to demand sweeping decisions and "a cutting off" from the past with a clean start in a new direction like a breath of fresh spring air! It was under such aspects that President Roosevelt made such sweeping changes, giving our country new life and a different path. In looking back, the pattern becomes clearer, enabling us to arrive at quite accurate conclusions as to the shape of things to come. Aquarius – your birth period, is "in tune" with activities offering aid to "the poor and underprivileged". I feel certain the lines, generally speaking, your life will follow, will touch fields directed toward "benefit for other people", and "groups or gatherings" will play a major part in important discussions as well as your own activities. You won't stand still, of this I am certain, but will "move on" to a new, lofty peak area in your life! Watch your seven-year cycles by adding seven to the years I have outlined above! An exciting sign in which to be born!

Pisces: The Time When Your Luck Will Change

Pisces, symbolized by the two fishes, one swimming upstream and the other down, starts February 20th and closes March 19th (approximately, although the year of birth may alter this by a day). The ruling planet is Neptune with Jupiter as secondary in importance. Neptune moves slowly so the life of a Piscean appears to be touched most strongly in middle age by this ponderous planetary influence, usually at the age of 45, particularly. The rhythm "set" by this planet seems to be one of 15-year periods – with the age of 90 frequently being reached by those born in this sign – even though there is "a delicacy" about the natives of this sign at certain intervals in their lives. A seeming "cross" rhythm occurs from the planet Jupiter which often lends an "out-of-step" trend, I have noticed. For example, every 12 years this planet sets in motion experiences having religious connotations that are intensified, as is also a peculiar 6th sense or "intuitive" faculty. I cannot tell you the number of times I have heard natives of this sign relate "a dream or hunch" only to see it fulfilled with a surprising degree of accuracy. Count back to the year 1962 and I am certain you will see that year was "a starting point" that led to your having had since then a continuous stream of different people walking "in and out" of your life, while you personally lived under a confining element! The "truth" has come into the foreground as to whom to trust, for someone or possibly several have fallen short of the faith you placed in them during the time following 1962. From the "turnover" in associates, possible loss of marriage partner or in another way that has marked this cycle, I feel certain ONE person has stood out because of his or her loyalty, although a few others have displayed good wishes on your behalf with a more or less lukewarm attitude.

You will be closing this cycle very shortly with 1973 slowly beginning a whole new "outline" that will clearly be seen in 1974, for your life will show an opening to a new arrangement encompassing family ties and probably change in location. While other zodiacal signs also respond to Jupiter's 7-year rhyrhm, as well, the natives of Sagittarius for instance, the years when those born in other signs will be affected will not be the same as yours! Unless unusual planetary configurations in the individual's personal chart at birth alter the natural trend, in spite of physical difficulties, these kindly Pisceans are promised "a long life and security" as life moves on! A wonderful birth period!

The Most Startling Cycle of All!

Put your hand in mine while we walk down a narrow street, poorly lighted, on a dark, suspenseful night with an eerie instinctive sense that we are apt to be attacked from some foreboding doorway or place of hiding. The streets where even the bright lights flicker, show few pedestrians and inside where those seeking companionship gather, the number had dwindled because fear of attack from an assailant kept many home, no matter how lonely it might be there. As we pause to lean against a wall for a moment our ears catch the voices of a small group preparing to wend their separate ways homeward, expressing conclusions to earlier discussions which lie uppermost in their hearts, as each one views them — the burden of increased taxes, the slavery, high interest rates, shortage of money — the need for a means to care for their families that they might provide food and shelter and as a final summation — the hunger of the soul felt by each one for "a faith" — a new religion, something to lift suffering humanity out of the dregs into which it has fallen. There is no peace in the world, for leaders of nations wrangle endlessly about "peace" — but peace is not forthcoming!

THIS WAS THE WORLD INTO WHICH CHRIST WAS BORN SOME 2,000 YEARS AGO! The "common people" were subjugated to the whims of powerful rulers — their meager goods could be seized in payment of taxes, and what difference if they starved? They were subject to enforced servitude which could be brought about through any number of specious reasons.

Security? The "man on the street" could hardly conceive of the meaning of the world.

Under such conditions it was only natural that the people longed for a leader — a strong champion who would lead them upward, away from the depressing and depressive circumstances under which they existed — one can hardly say "lived".

And such a leader appeared — one who offered much to those who would believe and follow.

Let us be honest. Man has come to the brink, the very edge of the pit through his insatiable desires.

Must the final step be taken, though? I think not. If I thought otherwise, I would not be writing to you at this time. Why do I feel that mankind will see the light, so to speak, and draw back without taking the final step?

In the heavens we gaze on, there are two mighty planets exuding power which man can turn to his benefit if he so desires.

Saturn, the Teacher, the Disciplinarian, has all too often

been termed "The Great Malefic". This is so very unfortunate, since the rewards of obedience can be of inestimable value. Conversely, the results of disobedience can be heavy. MAN HAS ONLY "TO CHOOSE" which way he will follow — the result is quite literally up to him.

Jupiter is associated with "the higher mind" — the mind that expresses itself in "abstract" thought; religion, philosophy, and the like. What is extremely vital to mankind is that on ABOUT every 25th conjunction of Jupiter and Saturn A GREAT RELIGIOUS OR PHILOSOPHICAL LEADER IS BORN!

You will note I said "about every 25th conjunction" or to put it another way, ABOUT EVERY 500 YEARS! It must be borne in mind that very infrequently will any planetary aspect result in immediate effects; and when we are considering such truly ponderous bodies as Saturn and Jupiter, the effects may be set in motion some time before or after the actual conjunction.

What proof have we of this? Let us examine the pages of recorded history and see what we find.

Many scholars claim that Zoroaster was the first truly great religious leader, and while there is some debate as to the exact year of his birth, it seems to have been decided that it was either about 1000 B.C., or approximately 600 B.C. — a span of 400 years; well within the effective time of the Saturn-Jupiter conjunctions.

If we accept the date of 1000 B.C. for the birth of Zoroaster, it intrigues the imagination that at the approximate time of a Saturn-Jupiter conjunction this religious teacher was born! If we accept the date of approximately 600 B.C., we are struck by the fact that this time period was the time of a great quartet of religious and philosophical leaders — for Buddha was born around 500 B.C., Confucius in 551 B.C., and Lao-Tse about 600 B.C. Coincidence? Personally, I find that very hard to accept and believe! Here we have two great religions and two important schools of philosophy, all preaching the betterment of mankind through his own development of the better side of his nature — his love for his fellowman — his understanding of the problems of others and his willingness to help.

For a comparatively recent event in history, the exact date of birth for Jesus has been strangely difficult to pinpoint. The latest evidence appears to point to 6 B.C. according to our present calendar — once again the 500 year cycle! Jesus extended the teachings of Zoroaster and Buddha in the concept of religion for "all" men, and at the same time added the indefinable "something" that makes Christianity unique in so many ways. The philosophy of Confucius and Lao-Tse is also present in His teachings.

Once again the mighty planets moved around and around the Zodiac 25 times, and about 567 A.D. another religious leader was born — Mohammed! Is there anyone who does not know the effects of Mohammedanism on the civilized world?

In 1779, William Cowper wrote — "God moves in a mysterious way His wonders to perform . . ." I mention this because the cycle was broken in 1095 A.D., but only by the substitution of an event (or several similar ones, actually) for a "personality". It was in this year that the great religious crusades were begun; continuing until 1291 A.D.

It is well known that these crusades accomplished little if anything of significant success; and is it so difficult to believe that because of this failure on the part of Man, the next cycle saw the birth of two strong persons who did much to reshape religious thought? I refer to Martin Luther (1483) and John Calvin (1509). It was, of course, largely due to their efforts that the religious Reformation took place. In this connection we must not overlook the following: 1517, Luther nailed his 95 theses to a church door in Wittenberg; 1519, Zwingli introduced the Reformation in Switzerland; 1520, Luther burned the papal bull and canon law; 1534, the Act of Supremacy made the King the head of the Church of England; 1536, Calvin published INSTITUTES OF CHRISTIAN

- 357 -

RELIGION; and in 1549 "the first Book of Common Prayer" (in the vernacular) for the Church of England was issued! Truly a momentous and active period resulting from that 500 year conjunction of Jupiter and Saturn!

What can we anticipate at the next major (or 500-year) conjunction of Saturn and Jupiter; which will occur in the year 2000 A.D., in June? This will in my opinion, usher in the definitive stage of the Age of Aquarius; the period when Man will turn to his brother; when we will experience a great spiritual re-awakening; when "HUMANISM" WILL SURGE UP AND UP!

I believe we are now experiencing the millenium. We are in a period of high taxes just as the world was at the time of Jesus' birth. We are and have been since 1914 in a state of almost continual war. Spiritual needs have been going "downhill" rapidly. This will be changed, I am convinced, at the next 500-year Saturn-Jupiter conjunction!

It is my conviction that the world will witness the return of a great religious leader who will elevate Mankind to the true spiritual plane on this earth. I do not believe the earth will be destroyed physically, but rather that Man will be so changed in his approach to his existence that he will not be recognized if judged by today's standards.

We hear much these days about "God is dead". Let me say to you, "GOD IS DEAD ONLY TO THOSE WHO DENY THE UNIVERSAL INTELLIGENCE"! In the full fruition of the Aquarian Age which is even now evolving, we will know that "A Divine Intelligence" is very much alive, and I feel very deeply that we will be more than happy to acknowledge this fact and heed the Exhortation of Paul to the Philippians: 2:4 — "Look not every man on his own things, but every man also on the things of others."

Yes, my friend: " . . . ye shall hear of wars, and rumors of wars . . . "; but remember, always, this from the constitution of the United Nations Educations, Scientific and Cultural Organization: "Since wars begin in the minds of men, it is in the

- 358 -

minds of men that the defenses of peace must be constructed".

The minds of men have the capabilities for peace — the coming Age will direct those capabilities in the proper channels — of this I am morally certain!

It is this coming glorious Aquarian Age to which mankind is blinded because of the painful stumblings today as he travels straight as an arrow to the end of that master 500-year cycle which has marked all other 500-year endings! You are an important part of, as well as a witness to one of the major destination points historically for humankind that will lead to a truly better place for "all" — the Age of Aquarius!

And now farewell — remember the road that lies ahead for you is only "a step away" from a sunny tomorrow!

This has been a labor of love—no road too steep—no threatening cloud too frightening!

MARGUERITE CARTER

See guard with machine gun at distance — as I walked on the silent streets to the museum in East Berlin in search of valuable historical records.

Knowest thou beloved, that the
good THY hopes embrace, is close
akin to that which lies within
the heart of all mankind? That
every joy and pleasant scene thy
thought can trace and which thou
holdest in thy seeking mind, is
dear to every race of men, who
also seek to find the shining,
joyous face of happiness within
their lives?

Then knowest thou, the will
of Him who sent us here!
With all thy heart, seek every
joy that thou canst ever learn
of happiness; nor dwell in any
of thy days, upon the fear
that thou offendest thus
some secret, hidden turn
of words which are not clear,
in unforgiving law, or stern,
unyielding judge and drear
restraint, which sever every
joy like burnished knives!

Instead of these beloved, in
the viewing of thy thought,
encompass all that thou wouldst
have, of every pleasant thing,
and KNOWEST that thou HAST each
good thy heart hath sought and,
seeking, willest thou as well,
that every human heart shouldst
ring with joy, each pleasure of
a dream brought forth to LIVE—
and thus Thy thought shall bring
to THEE That good for which thy
deepest yearning strives!
                              ALAN CARTER

After having sold several thousand copies of "The Time When Your Luck Will Change" and because a tremendous interest was shown in my personal experiences by the complimentary letters received, I considered relating a part of my life which I have kept a closely guarded secret. Very dear friends, workers who have been engaged in a confidential capacity, even particular members of my family, were unaware of the startling "experiences" I have known. UNDER NO CIRCUMSTANCES WOULD I EVER COMMERCIALIZE THIS AREA OF MY LIFE! But now as I am no longer young and the present trends in the world appear to be those of confusion and being "out of touch" with "Something" far more real than the materialistic world which is miring us down, I have decided to break what has been a hard and fast rule in my life — that of never discussing "isms" — fortune telling and so on with which I am in disagreement completely.

In the early 30's, I wrote a horoscope feature for leading newspapers and magazines which appeared in the U.S.A., Canada and England. The feature was appearing in Canada's two leading magazines, (Chatelaine, which has now been discontinued) and MacLeans. I went there to supervise answering the mail as it ran to several thousand replies, so I had an assistant and approximately 30 girls working under me. I left Indiana to go to Canada alone to work, as my husband could not be accepted as a worker there due to regulations.

* * * * *

(The following is a copy in the confidential files of a major European University where they are doing research in this field and was witnessed by two people who were present.)

We "shook hands" when I kissed her goodbye (my husband's mother whom I loved deeply) upon being assured she would be all right until I returned (although she had been in ill health for a long time) I truly believed her as her handgrip was so strong she almost paralyzed my hand and I was young and strong. I arrived in Toronto where "the Magazine" had their attorney "LAND" me legally with many technical papers to be signed and sworn to — among them an agreement that I would not drive a car (automobile) while there. As my husband wasn't there and I hadn't driven in years, I had no reason not to readily agree. In a short time after my feature had started however, my husband came to Toronto with our son, deciding to outfit a canoe to go into the northern wild country which meant passing through a series of canal locks. His idea was to write a feature article or story about their adventures. His folks seemed all right at home (his father was a well-known doctor, the medical director of one of the largest Insurance companies here). My son and husband outfitted a canoe for every wild adventure and left Toronto. They would send me notes from little towns along the way. All seemed well and serene — as my husband's father, being a physician, would warn us of any sudden turn of events, we felt.

One morning, I went to the magazine office where I worked in a glass enclosure and could watch through the glass all of the procedures that were taking place in carrying out the details of handling the mail, when about 9 a.m., I became so restless I couldn't sit in my desk chair. I got up and walked the floor, I had no idea as to what was wrong with me. .Some "STRANGE OVERPOWERING FORCE" simply seemed to push aside my normal attempt at self-control. Because of my work, I have always tried to remain very level-headed in my judgments, NOT permitting myself to engage in anything which might in any way be construed as unorthodox and never partaking in any "isms" so to speak, although I had studied Theosophy when about 16 years of age and lived up to its rigid requirements for two years. By 10 a.m., I was overwhelmed by this strange force and just as though another person spoke, I called my assistant into my office and told her I was leaving the office to try to stop my husband and son — for her not to worry, but to keep the work going out as I would be back. I was as "startled" at what I said as though I was hearing someone else ORDER me to do this.

After signing an agreement not to drive our car and having

been warned it could mean either a heavy fine or jail sentence by the magazine attorneys and officials of the Canadian government, who had taken me through the steps of "landing," I went like someone in an hypnotic state straight to my hotel, got into our car, which my husband had parked there when he left on his trip, and started to drive to wherever he might be. Remember, I hadn't driven in years and never had any desire to.

I had to drive to various "locks" where men were stationed, to inquire if my husband and son had passed through there in a canoe. Finally, it was getting late so I knew I would have to stay in some small village overnight, although I had no luggage with me. I went into "a lock" office rather late where the man questioned me closely when I asked that he telephone ahead and stop my son and husband. Without hesitation when he said I'd have to have a very good reason, it would have to be an emergency, I said, "my husband's mother is dying". The man said in that case, he would telephone ahead and stop them and I walked out of that place with the guiltiest feeling I've ever known for I was either the world's biggest liar or I had lost my reason. I turned it over and over in my mind as I drove down the lonely country road to pick up my folks, wondering if indeed I was insane — possibly my work had resulted in mental imbalance, I concluded. About 11, or near noon the next day, I reached where my husband and son had already put up their canoe and supplies and started back to Toronto for they too felt something was wrong. My husband's first words were that he knew I'd had some kind of word. But I assured him I HADN'T, which made me feel that my mind actually was slipping, as he kept telling me he knew that I had. To make a long story short, we drove straight through without stopping to the old home place in Mooresville, Indiana from Canada. As we drove up in front of the house, we all looked to see if a wreath was on the door — but there wasn't any sign of anything amiss. As we drove down the long lane, I felt certain I had become a serious mental case. When we entered the house, Dr. McConnell was there and he put his arms around us to say how pleased he was that we had come. We both glanced into my mother-in-law's bedroom at the same time. The bed was all made up but she wasn't there so we asked where she was. My husband's father said, "she's gone" and we both said, "where, shopping"? He said, "didn't you get my telegram or letter"? We both said, "No" we hadn't had any word! Then Dr. McConnell told us she had died suddenly and was to be buried the following morning! IF we hadn't driven straight through, we wouldn't have made it.

Dr. McConnell returned with my husband, my son and me to my work in Canada and THERE UNOPENED ON MY DESK LAY BOTH HIS TELEGRAM AND LETTER WHICH I HAD NEVER RECEIVED!

* * * * *

This is "one" of many *actual* happenings — not conjecture but a true description of something that has had a deep influence upon my personal life — I do know it has not merely been extra sensory perception alone. There is another "dimension" in addition to this world of "physical senses" in which we live — a world "apart" which is far more meaningful in making our lives one of true fulfillment! Within each person's heart lies a still silent voice telling them of "something" beyond the very material "sludge" which is swallowing mankind, literally. Nothing could ever supplant the tremendous "Faith" these experiences have given me. If in some way I can encourage you to follow the words of Bailey — "Walk boldly and wisely in that Light thou hast; there is a hand will help thee on" — then I will have fulfilled my destiny, as your friend! There is a place for you no one else can fill!